Van Leeuwen

ARTISAN ICE CREAM

LAURA O'NEILL, BEN VAN LEEUWEN, *and* PETE VAN LEEUWEN

with OLGA MASSOV

PHOTOGRAPHS BY SIDNEY BENSIMON

ecco

An Imprint of HarperCollinsPublishers

Cover design by Sara Wood
Cover and title page illustration of Van Leeuwen truck by Taylor Vaught and Greg Yagolnitzer
Interior design by Suet Yee Chong
All photographs by Sydney Bensimon, except for page xii by Jeffrey Furticella and page xx by Joanna Trimble

Library of Congress Cataloging-in-Publication Data has been applied for.

ISBN 978-0-06-232958-5

15 16 17 18 19   OV/QGT   10 9 8 7 6 5 4 3 2 1

in memory of our dear friend
david hampton—we love and miss you

CONTENTS

OUR STORY

Since our first pair of buttery yellow trucks, lovingly dubbed the Eagle and the Bobcat, hit the streets of New York in 2008, Van Leeuwen Artisan Ice Cream has become a symbol for the revitalization of the American ice cream truck, a return to traditional ice cream making, and the celebration of responsibly sourced natural ingredients from the finest small producers in the world. A lot of hard work and many cheerful days—and nights—of trial and error have gotten us to where we are today, but it all began with the simple idea of bringing ice cream back to the basics. Real ingredients, rich, classic flavors—and little more.

When we set out in our ice cream truck for the first time in June 2008, headed to Battery Park in Lower Manhattan, we had the dream of selling ice cream—but not just any ice cream. The ice cream we wanted to sell could be made with basic pantry ingredients, without any stabilizers, thickeners, or emulsifiers added to enhance the ice cream's texture and mouthfeel. We were hoping to build a sustainable, environmentally conscious business that would allow us to sell our ice cream for a living, establish meaningful relationships with amazing purveyors, and run a socially conscious company where we paid people fair wages and could offer them benefits.

We were so grateful and delighted by such a warm reception from the community as well as the media. On that very first day, we were approached by a Whole Foods buyer about getting our ice cream into their New

York stores! The coverage we received from the *New York Times, New York* magazine, Gothamist, and other local press was also generous and kind.

We knew our ice cream was different—that our dedication to quality, simplicity, and taste was distinct—and we knew that ice cream is the evergreen popular treat. We had no idea that the reaction would be as immediate and as positive as it was. Our business has grown rapidly, and today includes trucks and stores in both New York City and Los Angeles, sales to tristate-area grocery stores, and plans to expand to other markets.

It turns out our quest for an old-fashioned ice cream coincided with a cultural shift: people returning to their kitchens to put up their own preserves and pickles, make cheese and bread, and churn their own small-batch ice cream. When we started thinking about writing a book, we wanted to share our knowledge with like-minded readers—the ones who eschew additives in their ice cream (and other food) and want to make it the way their grandmother might have.

We want this to be a fresh chance to get back to the basics, and to get you, our readers, back in the kitchen, armed with the techniques, recipes, principles, and stories that have sculpted our flavors. Most of all, we want you to make and savor delicious ice cream for years to come, and to understand ice cream making well enough to create your own favorite flavors.

AN IDEA BORN

Van Leeuwen Artisan Ice Cream made its auspicious start as the result of an ad-inspired whim of a summer job: "Make $1k a week running your own business!"

Home for the summer from his first year of college, Ben Van Leeuwen answered the call and, before long, was piloting a Good Humor truck through the streets of Riverside, Connecticut, with his brother Pete.

They found the work fun and loved interacting with people, but over the next few summers, as they returned to the trucks, they began to question the very product they were serving. Like most of the ice cream you can find outside of upscale restaurants, especially ice cream from trucks, it was packed with artificial ingredients. Ever read the back of the ice cream carton? Among the usual ice cream ingredients, you will find emulsifiers, fillers, and stabilizers like xanthan gum, a thickener engineered to boost body, texture, and shelf life. It was a few years before I'd meet up with Ben and Pete, and together, we'd hatch our plan to bring quality ice cream to the masses first with trucks and then with bona fide brick-and-mortar shops.

Ice cream makers, in the absence of rich, quality ingredients like egg yolks and smaller amounts of heavy cream, pack their ice cream with stabilizers to make it *resemble* the kind of ice cream your grandmother might have made. It lowers costs and increases the profit margin for the producer but, as a result, the consumers are dealt an inferior product. What you're eating, essentially, isn't your grandmother's ice cream but a confectionary product strategically engineered to lower costs and boost profit. Certainly, better ice cream can be made with just the basics found in your pantry and refrigerator!

Ben and Pete were food lovers from childhood and grew up in a household that emphasized whole foods and cooking at home. While their parents didn't fetishize food, there were always hearty, comforting meals in the house: Transylvanian goulash with tender pork braised with homemade sauerkraut and paprika; cream and turkey crepes; pan-fried flounder; chicken cacciatore; split pea soup with ham; and lentil soup generously studded with carrots. The dishes were lovingly prepared by their mother, who had picked up good home cooking from her own mother, who, in turn, had learned to cook from her aunt, who had emigrated from Eastern Europe to Portland, Oregon, and worked as a private chef for wealthy families in town.

Food was such a strong presence in their childhood experiences that the first recorded word to have rolled off Pete's tongue was "cookie," delivered in the form of a howl, as he lunged from his mother's arms toward the treat he wanted.

Childhood dishes stayed with Ben and made a powerful imprint on his palate and how he perceived food. He never took to soda or the saccharine-sweet ice cream sold off trucks. The habits he formed as a child rose to the surface while he was driving his Good Humor truck, and as he handed out ice cream that he himself didn't enjoy, he started to envision a better version of it.

Why not, he began to wonder, *make ice cream the old-fashioned way?* And what better way to get it to the people than to load it up on a truck and bring it to them?

For my part, I grew up in Melbourne, Australia, on the other side of the globe, in a house with a vegan mother and sister. For most of my childhood and teenage years, I ate a mostly vegetarian diet. There was always lots of good, real food in the house: bread from the local bakery, meat from our butcher (that my father and brother looked forward to eating),

in-season vegetables from our greengrocer, and lots and lots of fruit. I remember preferring a savory breakfast to a sweet one—I never had much of a sweet tooth—eating things like Vegemite, tomato, or avocado on toast. That said, I definitely had my share of Slurpees on hot days after school. Meat appeared infrequently in our home—Dad was only allowed to cook it outside on the grill—but vegetable soups, curries, salads, and pasta were ever present.

In the winter of 2006, I went on vacation to visit my brother in London, and one night, while at a live music bar in Camden, I met Ben, who was spending a semester of his senior year in London. I'd been feeling restless about my job and direction in life—I had a feeling I was ready for a change, but I couldn't put my finger on what change that would be.

Ben and I struck up a conversation and realized we had a great deal in common. We saw each other for a few days before I returned to Australia, and then Ben came to visit me there during his spring break, and then again later in the year. On his second visit, Ben suggested that I move to New York (and find that change I'd been seeking), and I thought to myself, *Why not? What do I have to lose?*

Back at home, I was at a crossroads: I had been working in event production for three years, and while I didn't hate my job, I wasn't exactly leaping out of bed in the morning. I had never been to New York, but something about making that leap felt right to me.

In the Australian summer of 2006, a few months before I moved to the United States, Ben called me with an idea: "I think we should start our own ice cream truck business when you get here." He had told me about his and Pete's Good Humor truck experience and that he had been thinking about going into business to make better ice cream.

Ben was aware that while New York didn't face a shortage of ice cream trucks, none were serving anything that was as simple as what came from a home pantry. The ice cream truck idea sounded a little crazy to me, but given the fact that I had no solid work plans upon arrival, I was excited by the prospect of a totally new venture.

And that is how Van Leeuwen Artisan Ice Cream was born: Ben, Pete, and me plunging, headfirst, into the world of small-batch ice cream making. With Ben fresh out of college, and me fresh off the boat, we moved into Pete's apartment in Greenpoint, brimming with hope that we were going to create something amazing. It helped that we didn't overanalyze the situation and the obstacles ahead, or else we might have gotten too scared to start our ice cream endeavor.

In hindsight, taking such a leap was both a crazy and prudent move on our part—great risks require great leaps, and if we had suddenly gotten too risk averse and practical . . . who knows? We might have never tried to get the business off the ground, or we might not have listened to our gut. None of us had formal culinary training, but we had all been keen home cooks for many years and were driven to make this work.

The idea was simple: Let's serve delicious, real ice cream out of beautiful trucks, and let's get back to a time when ice cream was made with whole ingredients, not filled with additives. Of course, we had to learn a lot more to bring this idea to reality, and we needed funding! The truck model was perfect for us; it eliminated much of the overhead faced by a start-up brick-and-mortar place, and offered more flexibility for trial and error. While the ice cream truck wasn't a new idea, it was one that was in dire need of reinvention.

One afternoon, Ben and I sat down and began to put together a scrappy document that, in time, grew to become our business plan. We outlined America's obsession with ice cream, the void in the city of something truly great, our ideals of quality, and ideas for design and marketing. We even noted that, as an affordable luxury *and* a comfort food, ice cream is recession-proof. And by the time we launched, right as the 2008 recession started to hit, we got to prove that point.

We sent our business plan to everyone who might have the means to invest: family, friends, college professors, and so on. Our goal was to raise about a hundred thousand dollars to cover retrofitting the trucks and the first production run. Surprisingly, the wealthy folks we knew weren't the ones who got on board; most of our investments trickled in a few thousand dollars at a time from friends who were excited about our plans and believed in our idea. We ended up raising around seventy thousand dollars and then took out a line of credit for another twenty-five thousand. The idea was that we could start with what we had while the three of us held down a gaggle of jobs to support ourselves.

At the same time we were fund-raising, we were experimenting with ice cream in our home kitchen. We'd make batches of ice cream, and then invite our friends over to get feedback on the results. We'd feed them ten batches of the same flavor, solicit feedback and comments on every sample, and zero in on what worked and what didn't. While the idea of eating ice cream sounds appealing, taste-testing ten batches at a time was arduous.

Pretty early in our research we learned that almost all ice creams sold in supermarkets had what are known as stabilizers. Stabilizers, both natural and artificial, help the ice cream have a creamy mouthfeel without actually being high in egg yolks or butterfat. In many cases, adding stabilizers is a way to lower costs and boost profits.

In a move that seemed downright anti-profit, we decided to make *our* ice cream the old-fashioned way. If it didn't come from our pantry, it didn't belong in our ice cream. We wanted our ice cream to be dead simple: fresh whole milk, heavy cream, egg yolks, and cane sugar (but not too much).

And the best part of all was that we were succeeding. The ice cream we were making in our small-batch home ice cream maker was rich, creamy, and delicious—no stabilizers needed!

GREENPOINT

During the summer of 2008, you couldn't go two blocks in Brooklyn without hearing that staple of the American summer soundtrack: the siren song of passing ice cream trucks. The new wave of the food truck movement, which wouldn't sweep the country for a few more years, was in its early stages. A handful of brave souls were starting to put out high-

quality food from trucks, but where ice cream was concerned, the streets still belonged to Mister Softee and Good Humor.

We had a steep hill to climb and a lot to learn about starting a business. We had to learn how to make the ice cream itself; find ways to scale the amounts; procure and furnish our trucks; and raise enough money to do all of those things, and then some! We were driven, sharing diverse skill sets and a vision that seemed just simple enough to work. Once our business plan was hammered out, we began to navigate the labyrinthine system of money and permits, all while juggling multiple jobs to pay rent. For a while I was working at an art gallery in Portchester, at a small Brooklyn record label, and at a film festival. Pete worked as an art handler and also as a brand manager for a vodka company, while still finding the time to play in two bands. And, for a little while, Ben had a desk job and then worked as a server at Michelin-starred Dressler, a sadly now shuttered Williamsburg, Brooklyn, restaurant.

When we had any spare time, we'd pile into the kitchen to experiment; with each new batch and flavor, we had a feeling we were onto something special. We quickly learned that, when it came to making great, wholesome ice cream, simplicity was king. It all be-gan with perfect custard, which consisted of nothing more than farm-fresh, hormone-free milk and cream, egg yolks, and cane sugar. In order to achieve the right consistency the traditional way, we had to make sure we were achieving an ultra-high butterfat custard—generally around 22 percent—adjusted to the contours of each recipe. This made for a rich, sturdy base, the perfect canvas for exploring flavors, which allowed us to avoid thickeners and emulsifiers. Ben, being a spreadsheet lover, created spreadsheets with built-in formulas for ingredient amounts and fat percentages.

At the same time, we scaled way back on the sugar content to let the individual flavors really pop. We learned that most producers were loading their ice cream with sweeteners to create a sticky, generic flavor that overwhelmed the palate. We, however, were after ice cream where you could actually taste the

flavor and that would taste as it should. Pistachio ice cream would taste of pistachios, chocolate of chocolate, and so on.

We also noticed that the more of sweet flavor you ate, the more it intensified on your palate. Nina Planck once wrote, quoting her mother, "If you taste sugar on the first bite, it will be cloying by the last." If you start eating ice cream and it tastes noticeably sweet on the first bite, by the time you are done, what had started out as pleasant will most likely have become overwhelmingly sweet, and that thickness and stickiness will linger unpleasantly on your palate long after you've finished eating.

We researched extensively and obsessively, asking a community of friends, chefs, and food lovers in Brooklyn for advice on ingredients; trying all sorts of nuts, vanilla, coffee, and chocolate—and we started digging up some fascinating stuff. We wanted the flavor ingredients to match the quality of our base, so we searched high and low to find quality producers that shared our ideals. Wherever we could, we engaged with our local community for the best possible ingredients, but we also wanted to source the best ingredients we'd tasted in our travels worldwide. In the end, we sourced the best we could find—in some cases the ingredients were local and in others, global.

We found astonishingly good pistachios that grow near the slopes of Mount Etna in Bronte, Sicily (see page 159), which are harvested only once every two years, so the trees can save up their energy and deliver a remarkable harvest each time. We've tried a lot of pistachios and these are, by far, the best we've found. They are also certified by the Slow Food Institute of Italy.

We discovered exquisite chocolate from France (see page 154) made by chocolatier Michel Cluizel. The company sources beans from eight plantations around the world and makes fine chocolate without any soy lecithin or processing of the beans with alkali.

We also found exceptional local, as well as global, ingredients: tart red currants from the Hudson Valley (see page 198) and chocolate chips for our Mint Chip Ice Cream (page 33) made by the wonderful folks at Askinosie in Missouri.

As our arsenal of ingredients expanded, we grew more excited about the idea of using our ice cream to celebrate the best small producers and most dynamic ingredients in the world. We wanted to tell the stories of the fascinating flavors we were finding, and to educate our patrons about fine ingredients and the value of responsible sourcing.

Our goal and our point of difference were becoming clear. We were making simple, delicious ice cream, with no shortcuts or odd-sounding ingredients. Ice cream that celebrated ingredients perfected by nature, not modern chemistry.

THE FINAL STRETCH

We experimented day and night in our tiny kitchen, and emerged with some surprising flavors. Our initial attempt to come up with a Dark 'n' Stormy ice cream proved unsatisfactory, since working with alcohol in ice cream can be a tricky thing. But we discovered that just the ginger alone made for an incredible flavor that shined, and that's how the Ginger Ice Cream (page 111) was born—the result of a happy accident. As we found new, exciting flavors to share, and continued to tweak our ice cream base, we still had a few more important hurdles to overcome.

First and foremost, we needed somewhere to produce our ice cream on a larger scale, to serve more customers; and second, we needed trucks from which to sell it.

As we tried to find a producer, we were met with a surprising amount of resistance: Nobody, it seemed, wanted to make ice cream *our* way. It was "too impractical," we were told, "too inefficient." But we persisted, and after some searching, we ended up finding a dairy in upstate New York (about six hours from Brooklyn) that was making ice cream for a few brands. We went to them, our recipes in hand, and asked, "How can we make these ice cream flavors on a large scale and get them to New York to sell?"

They took one look at our recipe and said, "Well, first you'll need some stabilizers, milk powder, and so on."

"But why?" we insisted. "We've been making these recipes at home and they are amazing, no stabilizers or fillers needed."

No on had an answer for us, except, apparently, that's what everyone was doing. Unsatisfied with that answer, we insisted on using only the ingredients we used in our home batch testing. The way we saw it, if we could make ice cream this good at home, why couldn't we make it for everyone? We worked together with the dairy to adapt the recipes for their equipment but still without using any stabilizers. And the results were amazing!

For the first two and a half years, all our ice cream was made upstate using our recipes, local dairy supplies, and the special flavors we would source and ship in.

Fortunately, our commitment to using only the best, natural ingredients paid off. Before too long, we were splitting our time be-

tween a small dairy in upstate New York and Greenpoint, Brooklyn. One day we'd hand-grate a bushel of nutmeg, the next we'd try to figure out how to steep fifty-pound bags of Earl Grey tea. (The solution, as we learned from our friend and local brewer Dan Suarez, was to use giant bags designed for hops!)

The rest of our time was spent in a littered yard under a bridge in Queens, where a guy named Patrick had agreed to retrofit a pair of decommissioned postal trucks we'd found on eBay. Patrick's was a pretty bare-bones operation: no contracts, no e-mails, and no design. Basically, he custom-cut holes in the truck and figured out how to fit the stuff, like freezers and such, inside. We wanted the trucks to have an old-time elegance and a classic look that would continue to look fresh as time went on. With experience in event production, I led the charge on the design front. I asked Patrick to put in large, open windows perfect for letting in lots of breeze and sunshine—and found our buttery yellow paint color in a vintage General Motors catalog. To create our now signature Victorian-influenced botanical illustrations for each of our flavors we worked with a local artist, Elara Tanguy. Finally, we threw on some chrome bumpers, and the Eagle and the Bobcat—two beautiful, creamy-yellow, airy trucks—conveyed the whimsical, nostalgic fun of eating ice cream!

By the spring of 2008, we were ready to test the waters. While waiting for our permits to clear in New York, we ran the trucks out in Connecticut, where Ben and Pete had grown up, for a month. That practice run turned out to be a great way to iron out the kinks: to figure out scooping temperatures, decide on equitable pricing, and realize we needed things like counters underneath our windows.

Before we knew it, summer had arrived,

our permits came through, and it was finally time to take our ice cream to the streets. We kicked things off by throwing a big tasting party for all the friends who'd helped us along the way. We got everyone to vote for their favorite varieties, and narrowed the list down to ten flavors: vanilla, chocolate, mint chip, gianduja, pistachio, hazelnut, strawberry, currants and cream, ginger, and espresso. We wanted to do the classic flavors really well and to celebrate singular, quality ingredients.

Our very first day out in a truck was June 21, 2008, in Battery Park—there was a street fair. By some strange twist of fate, our coauthor, Olga, happened to be there, purely by chance. She spotted the yellow truck and immediately made a beeline for some ginger ice cream. She says she distinctly remembers that moment because she had never heard of our ice cream, and immediately fell in love with its taste. Years before we ever sat down to talk about

working on a book together, she had become a Van Leeuwen ice cream devotee, stopping by our Bergen Street location at least twice a week.

A few days later, we set out for SoHo, on the corner of Prince and Greene Streets (now our iconic spot), exhausted and excited to start our ice cream journey. We thought it might be a calm way to test the waters—we didn't expect to see customers line up to taste our ice cream.

That first summer it was just the three of us, plus our friend Dan and two girls, Kristin and Sophie, whom we hired to help scoop on the weekends. Some days, we'd have the trucks out from ten a.m. to one a.m.; it was grueling and demanding, but we were receiving such an enthusiastic response and we were happy and proud to see our idea take root. We worked for months on end without taking a single day off. We were tired, but we were so happy. Because we were so busy,

summer just flew by and before we knew it, we were heading into fall.

By the end of that first summer, we had added a third truck, the Rattlesnake, and were gearing up for a nice long winter break. In this next generation of trucks, we wanted to add something that would allow us to be out and about all year round. To buttress weaker ice cream sales in the colder months, we introduced coffee and pastries.

Because we didn't want these to seem like an afterthought, we were deeply committed to making quality, delicious baked goods. Everything had to meet the Van Leeuwen standards—every detail mattered. To make coffee, we purchased two beautiful Mirage Veloce espresso machines from the Netherlands—if you have ever seen these machines (or made coffee with them), you know they are works of art in every sense of the word. We trained our baristas to make high-quality espresso drinks with microfoam milk; we used the same quality ingredients in our pastries as we did in our ice cream. While our coffee business in the winter didn't do as well as the ice cream business did in the summer, it was enough to keep us afloat and keep some of our team members employed during the winter months.

In February 2010, we opened our first tiny brick-and-mortar storefront where it had all begun—in Greenpoint, Brooklyn. We loved the truck business, but we were ready for expansion. The trucks were not without challenges. A storefront, for example, couldn't break down, or get a flat tire. And we were looking forward to offering our customers a *space* to experience, not just ice cream.

In the following year, we added three more trucks: Kangaroo, Panda, and Turtle, the latter one arriving after we secured a permit to sell at Central Park's Tavern on the Green. We

also added two more storefronts: one in Brooklyn's Boerum Hill and one in the East Village.

One of the challenges in making our ice cream upstate was that we were limited to making only certain flavors. The minimum runs were quite large and the equipment was sparse. We couldn't roast bananas, for example, or swirl caramel, and these were the types of things we really wanted to have more control over.

So, in 2012, to simplify and streamline our expanding operation, we decided to move our production down to Brooklyn and build our very own little ice cream kitchen. We found an old, shuttered Polish restaurant in Greenpoint and it became the official Van Leeuwen headquarters: home to our ice cream production, bakery, and the very first Van Leeuwen office! We hired our amazingly talented head of pro-

duction, Jane Nguyen, and Alvaro Flores, an indispensable team member whom we trained from the ground up. From that point on, all our ice cream, including the prepackaged pints that are sold in the tristate area, has been made at our headquarters.

Having an actual office felt exhilarating—we had spent the past four years working off our couches. A physical office allowed us to hire a full-time employee: Kristin Vita, the very first person we hired back in 2008 to work weekends, had always said that if we ever grew big enough, she'd love to quit her day job and come on full-time in an office role.

These days we are streamlining our operations and exhaustively developing new flavors and products. We now have two trucks in Los Angeles, and have signed leases for two Van Leeuwen stores there: one in the Arts Dis-

offer more flavors, and continue to source the best possible ingredients.

In early 2014, we introduced seven vegan ice cream flavors: Mint Chip (page 150), Pistachio (page 158), Coffee (page 161), Chocolate (page 152), Peanut Butter and Chocolate Chip (page 147), Salted Caramel (page 148), and Roasted Banana (page 157). We had been tinkering with the vegan flavors for some time, and after many months of testing, we finally settled on a formula that we were proud to share. We found that making our own cashew milk made all the difference to the final product, and, once again, we avoided using thickeners. And in the late 2014, we signed a lease for a new Van Leeuwen location to open in the West Village sometime in 2015.

By the time you hold this book in your hand, there may be other developments taking place that we haven't even planned yet. But, no matter the flavors or the locations, you can always count on the very things that propelled Van Leeuwen ice cream into existence. Everything is still made in our headquarters. Our commitment to quality ingredients and delicious ice cream, to our customers, and to our local and international purveyors—whether they provide us with chocolate, pistachios, red currants, or our unique vanilla extract—remains as steadfast as it was when we first started out on those muggy SoHo streets in our buttercup yellow truck. Our business might have grown, but our approach and our commitment to ice cream remain the same.

trict and one in Culver City. Pete has moved to LA to head up our West Coast operation. We are also running a Balinese restaurant, Selamat Pagi (which means "good morning"), in the front space of our headquarters in Greenpoint. Balinese might sound random coming from an Aussie and two Americans, but Ben and I traveled to Bali several times while visiting my family in Australia (it's a far less expensive trip from there!) and fell in love with its cuisine.

Despite the fact that we are going on our eighth year, we still buzz with the vibrant energy we had at the very beginning, and our approach is still that of a scrappy start-up. We don't rest on our laurels and don't take anything for granted. And we keep on pushing forward, trying to make better ice cream,

We hope you love cooking from this book as much as we loved putting it together. We want this to become the kind of stained, dog-eared book that shows years of use and love. We sincerely hope that this becomes your go-to companion for making ice cream, and a timeless reference for years to come.

laura, ben, and pete

for Van Leeuwen
stomers Only.
Thank you!

INTRODUCTION

A BRIEF HISTORY OF ICE CREAM

Early writings tell of ice dessert as far back as the second century BC, but it's hard to pinpoint its exact "inventor." We know that Alexander the Great was fond of snow and ice flavored with honey and nectar; the Bible mentions King Solomon consuming iced drinks; and Emperor Nero would send servants into the mountains to fetch snow, which was then flavored with fresh fruit juices.

While salt was used in the Arab world in making ice cream as far back as the thirteenth century, the dessert didn't reach Europe until Marco Polo visited China in the mid-1200s and brought back a recipe for what seems to be sherbet. Though it's not clear how ice cream spread throughout Europe, some evidence suggests that Catherine de Medici introduced it to France in the 1500s when she married Henry II of France. England seems to have come upon ice cream around the same time, but according to Harold McGee—the legendary food writer, who happens to be an expert on the chemistry, technique, and history of food—it wasn't until 1672 that the term *ice cream* was first used, in a document from the court of Charles II. In the late 1700s, the French developed a rich egg-based custard and also discovered that frequent stirring of the custard resulted in a less icy texture.

Ice cream and its variants were restricted

to royalty and nobility until about 1660s, but once the Sicilian chef Procopio introduced a recipe blending milk, cream, butter, and eggs at Café Procope in Paris, ice cream became available to the general, though moneyed, public. In time, ice cream became less expensive, but because of the time and effort it took to produce a single batch, it remained a rare treat.

In the United States, ice cream remained special and exclusive, reserved for the special few, until 1843, when Nancy Johnson of Philadelphia patented a freezer that contained a large bucket for a salt/water mix, a separate cylinder for the ice cream mix, and a mixing blade that allowed the user to manually churn the base, which in time turned it into a frozen dessert.

In the twentieth century, ice cream became a lot more popular and accessible. Soda shops, soda fountains, and ice cream parlors popped up seemingly everywhere. During Prohibition, these cafés served as meeting and hangout places in lieu of bars and pubs. Once cheap refrigeration took off, so did ice cream. Ice cream manufacturers used a number of tactics to distinguish themselves to consumers, and one such tactic was offering not just affordable ice cream, but a variety of flavors to tempt the palate. Baskin Robbins, for example, became known for its thirty-one flavors (one for every day of the month).

With a few more industrial developments, ice cream soon became fairly commonplace and a fixture in home freezers. As ice cream became an industrial product, manufacturers figured out ways to make larger and smoother batches in far less time than they had been able to with manual cranking. The smooth texture became another hallmark, and in order to enhance it, companies replaced traditional ingredients with gelatin and concentrated milk, along with a number of stabilizers intended to extend ice cream's shelf life for storage in unpredictable home freezers. Competition over selling the most ice cream led to price wars, which, in turn, led to the increased use of additives, powdered milk, stabilizers, and artificial flavors and colors. Because manufacturers still had to make a profit on the product, despite dropping costs for the consumer, many of these low-quality ingredients became commonplace. Most of this ice cream was made in the Philadelphia style (without egg yolks), as it helped to keep down the costs. Egg yolks, a relatively expensive ingredient used in French custard (our preferred method), became prominent as super-premium ice creams (like Häagen-Dazs) increased in popularity.

A quick word on gelato, with which ice cream is sometimes confused. Gelato simply means "ice cream" in Italian. Many think it's a completely different product and, because it has a European name (and origins), is of better quality. Italy, as well as the rest of the world, has no shortage of quality gelati, but just as with ice cream, gelato may be laden with stabilizers and artificial colors and flavors. Gelato, traditionally, had a similar composition to ice cream—rich with egg yolks, cream, and milk—but these days can range from a custard base to one that is eggless and has more milk than cream. Historically, Italian gelati were typically made with more eggs and cream than almost any other region's ice cream. It wasn't until after World War II, in the face of both financial woes and rising advancements in food technology, that low fat and eggless became the status quo for gelato. Since then, gelato has become known as both eggless and low fat, when in reality those are relatively new characteristics for Italy's version of ice cream.

HOW TO MAKE GREAT CUSTARD EACH AND EVERY TIME

This isn't a recipe for a custard—rather, treat it as a way to understand the important players in French custard and what happens during the cooking process. As you go through the recipes in this book, you will see that amounts of each ingredient will vary from slightly to quite a bit—this is because, depending on the flavor of your ice cream, there's no "set" formula. However, if you understand what happens while you make the custard, then the recipe will be much easier to read—and use!

1. Pour the cream and milk into a double boiler or a heatproof bowl set over a saucepan of gently simmering water (the bottom of the bowl should not touch the water). The water bath, which produces gentler and more evenly distributed heat than you'd get with the saucepan directly over the heat source, is there to ensure you do not overcook your custard—it will also give you the silkiest, smoothest custard ever. Whisk in some sugar (the recipe will tell you how much) and salt, and stir until they have dissolved. Warm the mixture until you see steam rising from the top.

2. Meanwhile, prepare an ice bath in a large bowl and set another bowl over it. Set aside.

3. Set a kitchen towel under a medium bowl—this will prevent the bowl from slipping around. In this bowl, whisk together the egg yolks with the remaining sugar until uniform.

4. Now, you will temper the egg yolks—this part can be intimidating, but trust us, you will get the hang of it in no time. While whisking, add a small splash of the hot dairy mixture to the yolks. Continue to add the dairy mixture, whisking it in bit by bit, until you've added about half. Add the yolk mixture to the remaining dairy mixture in the double boiler, or in the bowl of the water bath. Set the heat to medium or medium-low (you'll need to monitor it to see how your stove works best), and cook the custard, stirring continuously with a wooden spoon, until steam begins to rise from the surface and the custard thickens enough to coat the back of the spoon. While cooking your custard, be sure to scrape the bottom of the saucepan or bowl—and do not let your custard come even close to a boil! To test the custard, you can use any heatproof utensil with a straight edge, but we like a wooden spoon the best—it's a little better at showing the custard coating the spoon. Hold the spoon horizontally and run your finger through the custard. If the trail from your finger stays separated, the custard is ready to be cooled. You can also use a thermometer and take your custard off the heat when it reaches between 170°F (77°C) and 175°F (79°C).

5. Strain the custard into the bowl sitting over the prepared ice bath and stir for 3 to 5 minutes, or until the custard has

cooled. Transfer the custard to a quart-size container, cover, and refrigerate for at least 4 hours or, preferably, overnight. This step is important—overnight rest en-sures a thicker base, which in turn will give you a smoother, creamier ice cream. It allows the sugar to fully hydrate and to be incorporate into the custard.

notes You may need to chill the bowl of your ice cream machine in advance—if your canister requires pre-freezing, place it in the freezer about 12 hours before you start the base. After your ice cream base has had an overnight rest in the refrigerator, the ice cream maker bowl will be ready for use.

When custard is cooked, evaporation will always occur. Depending on your pot, the BTUs of your stove, the weather (seasons, humidity), and slightly over- or undercooking, evaporation levels can vary drastically.

When evaporation occurs, your water content is reducing in the overall mix. Since milk fat, milk solids, egg yolks, and sugar will not evaporate, their content, as a percentage of the mix, will increase.

For example, if you start with 1 quart of mix, and 10 percent evaporates during cooking, your liquid amount will go down, but because your overall fat, sugar, and eggs will remain the same, they, as a percentage, will increase.

Thus, it is possible that, owing to too much evaporation, you will end up with a mix that is too sweet (too much sugar) and/or too rich (too much fat and/or egg yolks).

When we work on our recipes, we develop all of them to account for evaporation. We developed high-fat, solid, and egg recipes that can withstand some variance; their stability allows us to easily correct an overevaporated batch of custard to get perfect ice cream texture each and every time.

So, how do we do this? We add back a little milk! Because milk is mostly water (87 percent), adding it will increase overall volume and decrease the fat and sugar percentages in the custard. Start with a tablespoon and taste; usually one or two, for the batch size tested for this book, will do the trick.

WHAT IS EMULSION?

When we talk to audiences about ice cream, the word *emulsion* comes up pretty quickly as someone in the audience always/often asks, "What's an emulsion? How do you define it?"

So let's get the definition out of the way because it will help in discussing (on a geeky level) what ice cream is and why it works the way it does.

An emulsion is a homogeneous solution that has separate parts that appear uniform and smoothly joined together. Put another way, emulsions comprise liquid droplets that are mixed (or merged) with another liquid's droplets.

The best-known example of an emulsion is vinaigrette, in which fat particles (oil) are mixed with water particles (vinegar). If you emulsify your salad dressing and then let it sit on your countertop for a bit, the oil and the vinegar will likely separate. The separation is a natural occurrence and happens because emulsions tend to coalesce, or gather in like parts, if you will—not dissimilar to how, in high school, you tended to hang out with the kids who were most like you. This process of coalescence makes emulsions "unstable" in the culinary sense; they will, when given a rest, ultimately break apart. Ice cream, if you think about it, is a kind of emulsion that has been chilled, churned, and transformed from a bona fide liquid state to a somewhat solid one.

In ice cream custard, the milk proteins act as emulsifiers and help stabilize the oil-in-water (dairy fat and water) emulsions by preventing fat droplets from coalescing.

When emulsifiers are added to ice cream, they actually *reduce* this stability, meaning the fat globules will be more likely to *partially* coalesce when whipped in the ice cream machine. Partial coalescence, when it comes to ice cream, is exactly what we want; we want the milk fat globules from the cream to cluster and clump together. This improves ice cream texture by preventing the bubbles, whipped in by the ice cream machine, from breaking down, which helps the ice cream to maintain a creamy mouthfeel.

GUMS

Gums are mostly derived naturally: carrageenan comes from seaweed, guar gum from guar beans, and xanthan gum is a largely indigestible polysaccharide produced by the bacterium called *Xanthomonas campestris*. Gums are used to give a smoother texture and a fuller body to the ice cream. They are particularly useful in ice creams that don't use egg yolks. We rarely use any of these in our ice creams and when we do, we prefer to use agar agar or carob bean gum.

POWDERED MILK

Powdered milk is an inexpensive way to bulk up milk solids in your ice cream, which will make ice cream taste thicker and fuller. Especially for some large-scale producers, using some powdered milk is an effective way to emulate the evaporation that occurs during the cooking of custard on a stovetop. Evaporation is essential, as it condenses milk, increasing the overall milk solids, which makes for a chewier, creamier ice cream.

EGG YOLKS

Stabilizers in and of themselves aren't bad, but we feel that when you have good ingredients at home—milk, cream, egg yolks, sugar—you don't need additional stabilizers to achieve smooth, luscious ice cream. Egg yolks, full of naturally occurring lecithin, are already fantastic emulsifiers and will give your ice cream body and lusciousness with no need for powders or gums. If lecithin, or another emulsifier, is *not* added to an ice cream mix, the fat particles will resist partial coalescing. In plain English, this means that the ice cream will not have the same smooth texture as an ice cream containing egg yolks (or another emulsifier). But—and there's always a "but," isn't there?—if *too* much emulsifier is added, too much fat is *de*-emulsified and the fat droplets become so large that you can taste them. In other words, the ice cream will taste like someone just added butter to it, an occurrence aptly known as "buttering."

WHY YOU SHOULD ALWAYS TRY TO AGE YOUR CUSTARD

There's a slew of reasons why aging your custard is a good idea. Mainly, this will deliver a creamier ice cream in the end. A colder base churns better and smoother; overnight rest tends to thicken the custard, which also helps to produce a creamier ice cream. Aging also helps the lecithin from egg yolks to better attach to the fat droplets, which, as we previously mentioned, helps with partial coalescence resulting—you guessed it—in smoother ice cream and ice cream that has a higher resistance to meltdown; and aging properly allows for the sugar molecules to hydrate and to be incorporated into the custard. And, finally, cooling the mix to just under 40°F (below 4°C) makes the fat inside the droplets begin to crystallize, which also helps with partial coalescence and smoother ice cream.

WHAT IS ARTISAN AND WHY DO WE USE IT IN OUR NAME?

We're well aware of how overused the words *artisan* and *artisanal* are these days. Dunkin' Donuts has its artisan bagels, Panera Bread has its artisan loaves. It's become an on-trend word, rather than something that has much meaning.

To us, the word *artisan* means focusing on quality rather than efficiency. It means creating something out of a passion for creation as opposed to a passion to succeed, be recognized, or make money. Artisanal food is food made with great attention to detail in the sourcing of ingredients as well as in the process itself. It involves a constant evolution, a constant process of learning and improving, never being complacent. It's holding quality, rather than profit, as a true benchmark of excellence.

A NOTE ON YIELD

You will note that in our recipes, the yield for ice cream and sorbets always says "about" with a measurement following it. Why couldn't we be more precise?

Ice cream base, custard or otherwise, when frozen in a machine, will expand by a certain amount as air is incorporated into it. For home machines, depending on what machine you are using, that amount can vary anywhere from 20 to about 30 percent, while for commercially produced ice cream that amount can be more than 100 percent! The amount of volume exceeding that of the base/custard is called "overrun." The overrun will depend on your ice cream flavor, how fast it is churned, how much air it incorporates (thicker bases may stay more compact than thinner ones), as well as how much of the base evaporates during the cooking process. The latter bit can be affected by just about anything: from the size and width of the bowl containing the base, to the intensity of the heat from your stove, to how much humidity is in the air, to the phases of the moon. We kid about that last part, but ice cream yields, if you want to get incredibly precise, are all affected by a multitude of elements. So, in some cases you will get a bit less than a quart, while in others, it might be a bit over (not that anyone has ever complained about excess ice cream).

INGREDIENTS

ALCOHOL—Alcohol helps keep ice cream texture soft and provides flavor (as in our Apple Crumble with Calvados and Crème Fraîche, page 69). We recommend using alcohol you would want to drink—i.e., it should be good enough to be consumed on its own.

CHOCOLATE—Throughout the book, we use various types of chocolate: unsweetened, dark, milk, and white, as well as unsweetened cocoa powder (Dutch process or natural), pure cocoa butter, and cocoa nibs. For the most part, we're devoted to Michel Cluizel chocolate (see Pete's Ingredient Spotlight—Chocolate, on page 154) for reasons we'll get into later. However, as long as you use your favorite quality chocolate, the one that tastes good to *you*, then you're guaranteed to get quality results. Our favorite chocolate chips, which we use in our Mint Chip Ice Cream (page 33), come from a great Missouri company, Askinosie.

COCONUT CHIPS—Unless we call for unsweetened coconut, we prefer our coconut to be unsweetened.

COCONUT MILK—Use high-quality whole (not light) coconut milk—we like the Native Forest brand, since it doesn't contain emulsifiers. Thai and other Asian stores often carry good coconut milk. Please note that coconut milk is not the same as Coco Lopez, which is a sweetened concoction.

COFFEE—One of the things that has been important to us from the very beginning at Van Leeuwen Artisan Ice Cream is to serve good coffee. We tested out different roasters and finally settled on Toby's Estate, an Australian coffee roaster with a roastery nearby in Williamsburg. However, when it came to getting the most true coffee flavor for our coffee ice cream, freeze-dried coffee worked so much better that, much to our surprise, we wound up going with that. So long as it's a quality coffee brand, you should be in good shape.

CRÈME FRAÎCHE—Higher in fat than sour cream but also pleasantly tangy, crème fraîche can be used interchangeably with sour cream except when you want to heat it (probably not applicable in this book, but still)—sour cream tends to break when heated and crème fraîche does not.

EGGS—All the recipes in this book have been tested using large, organic eggs. The better quality your eggs, the better quality your ice cream.

FRUIT—Whether stone or citrus, fruit is always best when it's ripe and at the peak of its season. Some fruit works great picked during its season and frozen. For this reason, we can serve our Currants and Cream Ice Cream (page 90) year-round. We prefer local, organic, unsprayed fruit, and try to use it as much as possible. Please keep in mind that where the fruit was grown, the climate during its growing season, and when it was picked (after rain or during a dry spell) will affect its sugar content and moisture level. Because of these variables, among others, your fruit ice creams and sorbets will vary slightly from batch to batch.

HEAVY CREAM—A funny thing: Most heavy cream contains some kind of an emulsifier (usually carrageenan gum) so it will help to give you smoother ice cream. However, we recommend that you seek out heavy cream without any additives, which we think tastes so much better.

HONEY—Some research supports the theory that local honey—harvested as close as possible to where you live—holds the greatest nutritional benefit and may help you build immunity to seasonal allergies, as well as help with digestion. Raw, unpasteurized honey is full of enzymes and compounds that make it a nutritional powerhouse and not just a sweetener for your yogurt and tea. Pasteurization, however, destroys much of those beneficial enzymes, which is why natural food proponents emphasize raw honey over its pasteurized cousin. Pregnant and nursing women should not consume unpasteurized honey, and children under one year of age should not be fed honey of any sort.

MILK—We make all our ice cream with whole, organic milk and recommend you do the same. There's virtually no difference between whole and low-fat milk, fat percentage-wise—about 3 percent versus 2 percent—but it will make a nice difference in your ice cream. Low-fat or skim milk may result in icy or grainy ice cream. If you're one of the lucky few to get your milk directly from a small dairy farmer, then you may get extra-fatty (and nutritious) milk with about 4 percent fat.

NUTS—Nuts are terrific when they're fresh and pretty terrible when they're stale. Because of their high oil content, nuts have a tendency to go rancid rather quickly; you can slow down their spoilage by keeping them in a cool, dark place, such as a refrigerator or freezer.

NUT BUTTERS—In choosing your peanut or almond butter, seek out the kinds that have only one ingredient: the nut in question. Anything more and you will be messing with the ice cream consistency. For ice cream, we prefer the smooth variety to the chunky kind.

SALT—Unless we specify it, the recipes in this book were tested using Diamond Crystal kosher salt, which has a clean taste that is perfect for highlighting the flavors in ice cream. In ice cream such as Salted Caramel (page 127), we like briny, flaky sea salt; Maldon is our preferred brand and is widely available. Or, if you can get your hands on it, Murray River pink flaky salt from Australia is pretty amazing.

SOUR CREAM—Sour cream will add a pleasantly tangy taste to your ice cream. Seek out brands with as few ingredients as possible; some brands pack their sour cream with unnecessary additives.

SPICES, EXTRACTS, OILS—Throughout this book we use spices and extracts: like cardamom (see pages 115, 139), cinnamon, vanilla (see page 34), and mint extract (see pages 33, 150), just to name a few. We go into detail on some of these ingredients but, generally speaking, always use the best-quality spices and extracts you can find. You are almost always guaranteed to find fresher and better quality spices from a specialty company.

SUGAR—In most recipes, we use organic, granulated sugar. Sugar helps with flavor and also texture. Not enough and the ice cream will be hard and icy; too much and the ice cream won't properly freeze (and it'll taste jaw-achingly sweet, too). We also like to use palm sugar as well as dark/light sugar. A quick note about palm sugar: It's not the same as palm oil. These are two very different ingredients.

TEA—Adding tea is a great way to infuse your ice cream with flavor—and one of the easiest. Find a quality tea manufacturer, preferably of loose tea leaves, that you like, and take good care of your tea. Store it in a well-sealed, clean container free of any other scents (tea is excellent at absorbing other odors), and keep it in a dark, dry, cool place.

YOGURT—Because yogurt is already lower in fat than most dairy products, we recommend using full-fat yogurt for a better result.

EQUIPMENT

BAKING DISH—If you plan on making granitas, a ceramic baking dish (anything that will be nonreactive, basically) is a good thing to own. For our recipes, you'll need one between 8 and 12 inches long with 2-inch-high sides.

BAKING SHEETS—You'll need a couple sturdy, thick baking sheets that won't warp, in both half-sheet (18 x 13-inch) and quarter-sheet (9 x 13-inch) sizes. These will come in handy, and not just for making cookies (see pages 187, 192) and crumble (see page 69). You will find yourself using them in many other instances, including roasting vegetables.

BLENDER—We wish we could combine blender and immersion blender into one category, but in order to successfully (read: just like in our stores) execute our ice creams, they're both necessary. For the traditional blender, we use a Vitamix and stand behind it 100 percent. Its hefty price seems excessive and cost-prohibitive to many. And yet we implore you to save for one. You may never need to buy another blender again—these things not only do not break, but the quality of blending (not to mention all the other things it can do) is just unparalleled by any other machine. We think that buying one blender in your lifetime is a pretty sound (and cost-effective) investment.

CHEESECLOTH—Handy for spice sachets for infusions and, of course, indispensable in making ricotta (see page 97).

DIGITAL SCALE—We can't stress enough the importance of a digital scale; it is particularly useful (indispensable, even!) in our vegan recipes. If you're still on the fence about getting one, we guarantee you that once you do, you'll start using it a lot more than your measuring cups and spoons. Compact, cheap, far more precise than measuring by volume—and leaves you with fewer dishes to clean.

ICE CREAM MACHINE—There are several options on the market. Ice and rock salt machines require hand-cranking (an excellent workout but also one that requires you to spend a lot of hands-on time making ice cream). Self-refrigerating machines, which we prefer and used to test recipes for this book, are great for regular home ice cream makers because they

allow you to make your ice cream without much advance planning or if you have limited freezer space. If you're a frequent ice cream maker, that convenience will, in time, pay for itself. These machines are more expensive than the machines with bowls you pre-freeze, but again, it depends on how often you make or plan to make ice cream. The machines that come with bowls that need to be pre-frozen work well for most home cooks. Their affordability and relatively compact size (especially when compared with self-refrigerating machines) win over many home cooks. Whatever machine you go with, make sure you research and read the reviews to find the best-quality model that fits your budget.

ICE CREAM SCOOPS—Our favorite ice cream scoop is made by Zeroll, a solid scoop that is filled with antifreeze. As with other solid scoops, don't wash them in the dishwasher or they'll get ruined. There are also spring-loaded scoops, but we don't like them nearly as much.

IMMERSION BLENDER—Compact, easy-to-clean, and inexpensive, the immersion blender is a pro at emulsifying ingredients (as in our vegan ice creams, pages 145 to 161).

KNIVES—Are you surprised to find knife recommendations in an ice cream book? It might seem strange, but you do need knives to chop and peel ingredients, so here's our basic knife set recommendation: paring, chef's, and serrated bread knife. Paring knives should not cost a lot of money—restaurant supply stores sell them for $5 to $8. Chef's knives, on the other hand, are a whole other matter. Buy a good one with a blade between 8 and 10 inches that weighs nicely in your hand and has some heft—you will use it for just about everything. Because it'll be your most frequently used knife for general chopping, this is a knife worth spending some money on. A serrated bread knife is the best knife for chopping chocolate. It's also great for cutting tomatoes and, well, slicing bread. A good one is not terribly pricey, and should last you a lifetime.

MEASURING CUPS AND SPOONS—Be sure to have both liquid and dry measuring cups as well as a set of measuring spoons. Liquid measuring cups come in clear glass or plastic and sport a spout for easier pouring. Dry measuring cups and measuring spoons are most often made of plastic or stainless steel and often come as a set.

SAUCEPANS, SKILLETS, AND POTS—You should own a few heavy-bottomed pots and pans; they will come in handy in everything from making caramel (see page 142) to toasting nuts (see page 157). Stainless steel and enameled iron (not aluminum) are best as they are nonreactive and are excellent at conducting and evenly distributing heat.

SPATULAS—Heatproof silicone spatulas are great for stirring custard and getting every bit of it out of the bowl. We like having a few on hand, in a few different sizes. The ones with wooden handles last longer if you hand-wash them.

STAINLESS-STEEL AND GLASS BOWLS—It's always good to have a few in different sizes on hand. Kitchen supply stores will sell them to you for a song—no need to go to a special culinary store for fancy ones. If you don't like the bowls wobbling on your counter space, place a towel underneath the bowl.

STRAINERS—Fine or medium mesh will be useful for straining your custards as well as fruit purees that might contain seeds. Get sturdy ones that will stand up to pressure.

THERMOMETER—A good instant-read thermometer is useful in making candy, monitoring the temperature of custard, and even checking whether meat is done (not that you need it in this book). Thermapen is the king of culinary thermometers and is worth every penny despite the hefty price tag.

WHISKS—Have a few sturdy ones on hand for whipping cream, stirring egg yolks, and so on. Tiny ones are handy for stirring spices together; the flat ones are useful for getting into those rounded edges of the pot.

WOODEN SPOONS—A workhorse of just about every kitchen, home or professional. We like wooden spoons for stirring our custard. When we're not using a thermometer, it's the most reliable way to check whether custard is done.

ZESTERS—Nothing beats a Microplane zester, and if you don't own one yet, run, don't walk, to the nearest cookware store to get one. The most basic ones will let you get beautiful, finely grated citrus zest and shaved chocolate. You can even use it in your savory cooking (e.g., for grating cheese over pasta). They won't break the bank and they'll last forever.

GOAT CHEESE WITH BLACKBERRY-
RED CURRANT COMPOTE ICE CREAM,
PAGE 88

one

ICE CREAM

You could say that here at Van Leeuwen, we love ice cream. It's our life—from dawn to dusk—and it is love of ice cream that prompted us to start our company in the first place. We wanted to make the kind of ice cream our grandmothers made back in the day, without any odd additives, and with ingredients readily available in our cupboards.

Anyone who knows our ice cream first-hand knows that we're unabashed fans of the French (yolk-based) custard. We love the smooth body and mouthfeel of creamy ice cream, and base our ice creams on this formula while varying the number of yolks and the amounts of fat and sugar, depending on the specific flavor.

We're also known for ice cream that tastes less sweet compared with others. We've purposefully scaled back on sugar, because we know that when we eat something sweet, each subsequent bite tastes sweeter and sweeter. That first sweet bite might be pleasant but is likely to taste way too sweet by the end.

Having said all that, the ice creams in this book are *slightly* sweeter and richer than the ice creams in our shop. This is because when we scaled our recipes down for smaller-batch testing, in some cases we wound up with fractions of egg yolks. Instead, we chose to scale some ingredients up or down, depending on each individual flavor.

We also wanted to showcase the best ingredients we could find. We scoured the globe to find pistachio paste from Sicily's Mount Etna, single-plantation chocolate from Michel Cluizel, and palm sugar from an inspiring, ecologically responsible farm in Indonesia, just to name a few. And we're constantly tasting new ingredients to find the best in class.

Some of the recipes here have been created for the book and have since been featured in our stores and as limited-edition pints. Others are mainstays and patron favorites. These are some of our favorite flavors, and we are excited to share them with you. Once you get the hang of these—and get comfortable with making custard (see page 4 for detailed instructions)—we hope you have fun experimenting in the kitchen and making your own favorite flavors. When it comes to ice cream, the sky is the limit.

CHOCOLATE ICE CREAM

We are unabashed, die-hard chocolate lovers, so you might think that we love all chocolate ice cream. Not so. We are, in fact, so picky that it took us some time (and eating lots of chocolate) to create a chocolate ice cream we are happy with.

    With your first spoonful, you'll immediately realize this ice cream is a different beast altogether. This is a deep, rich chocolate ice cream, the most chocolatey chocolate ice cream we've ever had, as if you took a dark chocolate candy bar and made ice cream out of it. We use unsweetened 99% cacao Michel Cluizel chocolate and unsweetened cocoa powder, which both deliver an intense chocolate taste. We keep the sugar to a minimum: enough to make the ice cream pleasantly sweet, but not nearly enough to make it cloying.

MAKES ABOUT 1 QUART

SPECIAL EQUIPMENT
Immersion blender

1½ cups heavy cream

1½ cups plus 2 tablespoons whole milk

¾ cup plus 2 tablespoons (175 grams) sugar

½ teaspoon (2 grams) kosher salt

6 large egg yolks

2 ounces (56 grams) unsweetened chocolate discs (99% cacao), preferably Michel Cluizel (see Sources, page 218)

¼ cup (28 grams) unsweetened cocoa powder

1. Pour the cream and milk into a double boiler or a heatproof bowl set over a saucepan of simmering water (the bottom of the bowl should not touch the water). Whisk in ¼ cup (50 grams) of the sugar and the salt and stir until both have dissolved. Warm the mixture until you see steam rising from the top.

2. Meanwhile, prepare an ice bath in a large bowl and set another bowl over it. Set aside.

3. In a medium bowl, with a kitchen towel underneath it to prevent slipping, whisk together the egg yolks with the remaining ½ cup plus 2 tablespoons (125 grams) sugar until uniform. While whisking, add a splash of the hot dairy mixture to the yolks. Continue to add the dairy mixture, whisking it in bit by bit, until you've added about half. Add the yolk mixture to the remaining dairy mixture in the double boiler. Set the heat under the double boiler to medium and cook the custard, stirring continuously with a wooden spoon and reducing the heat to medium-low as necessary, until steam begins to rise from the surface and the custard thickens enough to coat the back of the spoon. Hold the spoon horizontally and run your finger through the custard. If the trail left by your finger stays separated, the custard is ready to be cooled. Remove the custard from the heat and stir in the chocolate and cocoa powder until the chocolate has melted completely and, using an immersion blender, buzz the custard until it is uniform.

4. Strain the custard into the bowl sitting over the prepared ice bath and stir for 3 to 5 minutes, or until the custard has cooled. Transfer the custard to a quart-size container, cover, and refrigerate for at least 4 hours or, preferably, overnight. When properly chilled and hydrated, the custard will be thick, like pudding.

5. Pour the chilled custard into an ice cream maker and freeze according to the manufacturer's instructions. Place the container

in which you refrigerated the custard in the freezer so you can use it to store the finished ice cream. Churn the ice cream until the texture resembles "soft serve." Transfer the ice cream to the chilled storage container and freeze until hardened to your desired consistency. Alternatively, you can serve it immediately—it will be the consistency of gelato. The ice cream will keep, frozen, for up to 7 days.

SPICY CHOCOLATE ICE CREAM

We first tried spicy chocolate in Bali, and the combination of spices and chocolate blew us away. This wasn't just chocolate spiked with some chiles; instead, it was rich with cinnamon and black peppercorns with a gentle, warm heat that tickled the back of our throats.

If you can find them, fire-cured vanilla beans, popular in Indonesia, lend beautifully to this flavor. Typically fire-curing is seen as inferior to sun-curing but for some flavors it delivers a wonderful smoky note.

This ice cream will work with a range of different spicy peppers, but our favorite, hands down, is the chile d'arbol. Still, every palate and taste is different, so by all means, use the chiles you have on hand, and play around with different ones to see which chile or combination of chiles appeals the most to you. Maybe it's a smoky chipotle or an assertive Thai chile that will become your favorite go-to.

MAKES ABOUT 1 QUART

6 whole black peppercorns

4 chiles d'arbol, seeded and crushed

1 teaspoon ground cinnamon

½ smoked or regular vanilla bean, split lengthwise and seeds scraped out

1 cup heavy cream

2½ cups whole milk

¾ cup (150 grams) sugar

½ teaspoon (2 grams) kosher salt

6 large egg yolks

3 ounces (85 grams) unsweetened chocolate discs (99% cacao), preferably Michel Cluizel (see Sources, page 218)

1. With a mortar and pestle or in a spice grinder, finely grind the peppercorns, chiles d'arbol, cinnamon, and vanilla bean seeds and pod. Set aside.

2. Pour the cream and milk into a double boiler or a heatproof bowl set over a saucepan of simmering water (the bottom of the bowl should not touch the water). Whisk in ½ cup (100 grams) of the sugar, the ground spice mix, and the salt and stir until the sugar and salt have dissolved. Warm the mixture until you see steam rising from the top. Remove from the heat, cover, and let the mixture steep for 15 minutes. Transfer to a blender and blend until fully pureed. Strain the mixture back into the double boiler (if using a Vitamix, there is no need to strain).

3. Meanwhile, prepare an ice bath in a large bowl and set another bowl over it. Set aside.

4. In a medium bowl, with a kitchen towel underneath it to prevent slipping, whisk together the egg yolks with the remaining ¼ cup (50 grams) sugar until uniform. While whisking, add a splash of the hot dairy mixture to the yolks. Continue to add the dairy mixture, whisking it in bit by bit, until you've added about half. Add the yolk mixture to the remaining dairy mixture in the double boiler. Set the heat under the double boiler to medium and cook the custard, stirring continuously with a wooden spoon and reducing the heat to medium-low as necessary, until steam begins to rise from the surface and the custard thickens enough to coat the back of the spoon. Hold the spoon horizontally and run your finger through the custard. If the trail left by your finger stays separated, the custard is ready to be cooled. Remove the custard from the heat and stir in the chocolate until it has melted completely and the custard is uniform.

5. Strain the custard into the bowl sitting over the prepared ice bath and stir for 3 to 5 minutes, or until the custard has cooled. Trans-

fer the custard to a quart-size container, cover, and refrigerate for at least 4 hours or, preferably, overnight.

6. Pour the chilled custard into an ice cream maker and freeze according to the manufacturer's instructions. Place the container in which you refrigerated the custard in the freezer so you can use it to store the finished ice cream. Churn the ice cream until the texture resembles "soft serve." Transfer the ice cream to the chilled storage container and freeze until hardened to your desired consistency. Alternatively, you can serve it immediately—it will be the consistency of gelato. The ice cream will keep, frozen, for up to 7 days.

GIANDUJA

This might be the hardest flavor for our customers to pronounce—we even spell it out phonetically: jon-doo-yuh! Despite that, it's still one of our most popular flavors.

Gianduja is a confectionary product from the town of Turin in Piedmont, Italy, invented during Napoleon's regency. It's a pairing of hazelnuts and chocolate, a beloved combination all over the world, but nowhere as much as in Italy where the flavor was born as a way to stretch the chocolate a bit further by combining it with hazelnuts. The name *gianduja* is derived from the name of one of the characters of the commedia dell'arte, who wears the mask of an honest peasant from the Piedmontese countryside, a bon vivant with a certain inclination for wine, food, and beautiful girls.

Gianduja, the ingredient (not the character), was, essentially, Nutella before there ever was Nutella—a high-quality version of it, so to speak. We love not only the flavor but also the story behind it, the historical significance of gianduja and its role in Italian folklore.

To make our gianduja ice cream, we use a mix of pure hazelnut pastes from Sicily and Piedmont, combining different terroir flavors. The hazelnuts from Sicily, grown on volcanic soil, are smokier, with a higher mineral taste, while the hazelnuts from Piedmont are sweeter and milder. Together, they create a more complex and balanced taste than each cultivar on its own. (And the factory in Piedmont that processes our hazelnuts actually uses the nutshells to create energy to run the factory—something we absolutely love!)

We combine this hazelnut paste with our Michel Cluizel 99% Infini Noir dark chocolate for a rich, smooth, unparalleled flavor. In our mind, it redefines hazelnut chocolate and elevates it to a whole new level.

GIANDUJA ICE CREAM

Gianduja, a classic and wildly popular Italian flavor, combines chocolate and hazelnuts to form an irresistible confection (see page 21). The name *gianduja* originated with one of the characters from the commedia dell'arte, a peasant from the Piedmont region of Italy, Turin specifically. The name of the flavor is a nod to its geographic origin. We like to think of gianduja as Nutella that tastes ten times better because it uses the best ingredients available. As you can probably guess, the marriage of chocolate and hazelnuts naturally extends to ice cream and other desserts, and has an ardent and devoted following.

MAKES ABOUT 1 QUART

1½ cups heavy cream

1¼ cups whole milk

¾ cup (150 grams) sugar

½ teaspoon (2 grams) kosher salt

6 large egg yolks

¼ cup (50 grams) hazelnut paste (see Sources, page 21)

¼ cup (30 grams) unsweetened cocoa powder

½ ounce (16 grams) unsweetened chocolate (99% cacao), preferably Michel Cluizel (see Sources, page 218)

1. Pour the cream and milk into a double boiler or a heatproof bowl set over a saucepan of gently simmering water (the bottom of the bowl should not touch the water). Whisk in ½ cup (100 grams) of the sugar and the salt and stir until they have dissolved. Warm the mixture until you see steam rising from the top.

2. Meanwhile, prepare an ice bath in a large bowl and set another bowl over it. Set aside.

3. In a medium bowl, with a kitchen towel underneath it to prevent slipping, whisk together the egg yolks with the remaining ¼ cup (50 grams) sugar until uniform. While whisking, add a splash of the hot dairy mixture to the yolks. Continue to add the dairy mixture, whisking it in bit by bit, until you've added about half. Add the yolk mixture to the remaining dairy mixture in the double boiler. Set the heat under the double boiler to medium and cook the custard, stirring continuously with a wooden spoon and reducing the heat to medium-low as necessary, until steam begins to rise from the surface and the custard thickens enough to coat the back of the spoon. Hold the spoon horizontally and run your finger through the custard. If the trail left by your finger stays separated, the custard is ready to be cooled. Whisk in the hazelnut paste, cocoa powder, and chocolate until the paste and chocolate have melted completely and, using an immersion blender, buzz the mixture until the custard is uniform.

4. Strain the custard into the bowl sitting over the prepared ice bath and stir for 3 to 5 minutes, or until the custard has cooled. Transfer the custard to a quart-size container, cover, and refrigerate for at least 4 hours or, preferably, overnight.

5. Pour the chilled custard into an ice cream maker and freeze according to the manufacturer's instructions. Place the container in which you refrigerated the custard in the freezer so you can use it to store the finished ice cream. Churn the ice cream until the texture resembles "soft serve." Transfer the ice cream to the chilled storage container and freeze until hardened to your desired consistency. Alternatively, you can serve it immediately—it will be the consistency of gelato. The ice cream will keep, frozen, for up to 7 days.

MILK CHOCOLATE ICE CREAM

Good milk chocolate ice cream requires good milk chocolate—period. And believe us, we've tasted enough bad milk chocolate to understand why so many chocolate purists look down on dark chocolate's milk sibling. Despite widespread belief, good milk chocolate exists; we recommend that you go out and purchase a few good bars, and have a tasting (now this is the kind of research we can readily get behind). For our milk chocolate ice cream, we love Michel Cluizel's 45% milk chocolate—it delivers such a dreamy milk chocolate ice cream that we, chocolate purists ourselves, can't get enough of it. In our stores and trucks, we recommend topping this ice cream with some salted Marcona almonds, which offset the sweetness of the custard. When paired, these two combine to taste just like a European milk chocolate bar.

MAKES ABOUT 1 QUART

SPECIAL EQUIPMENT
Immersion blender

1½ cups heavy cream

1½ cups whole milk

½ cup plus 2 tablespoons (125 grams) sugar

½ teaspoon (2 grams) kosher salt

6 large egg yolks

105 grams (about 4 ounces) milk chocolate (45% cacao), preferably Michel Cluizel (see Sources, page 218)

Crushed salted Marcona almonds, for topping (optional)

1. Pour the cream and milk into a double boiler or a heatproof bowl set over a saucepan of gently simmering water (the bottom of the bowl should not touch the water). Whisk in ½ cup (100 grams) of the sugar and the salt and stir until they have dissolved. Warm the mixture until you see steam rising from the top.

2. Meanwhile, prepare an ice bath in a large bowl. Set aside.

3. In a medium bowl, with a kitchen towel underneath it to prevent slipping, whisk together the egg yolks with the remaining 2 tablespoons (25 grams) sugar until uniform. While whisking, add a splash of the hot dairy mixture to the yolks. Continue to add the dairy mixture, whisking it in bit by bit, until you've added about half. Add the yolk mixture to the remaining dairy mixture in the double boiler. Set the heat under the double boiler to medium and cook the custard, stirring continuously with a wooden spoon and reducing the heat to medium-low as necessary, until steam begins to rise from the surface and the custard thickens enough to coat the back of the spoon. Hold the spoon horizontally and run your finger through the custard. If the trail left by your finger stays separated, the custard is ready to be cooled.

4. Strain the custard into a bowl and stir in the milk chocolate until fully melted and incorporated. Using an immersion blender, buzz the custard until emulsified. Place the bowl over the prepared ice bath and stir for 3 to 5 minutes, or until the custard has cooled. Transfer the custard to a quart-size container, cover, and refrigerate for at least 4 hours or, preferably, overnight.

5. Pour the chilled custard into an ice cream maker and freeze according to the manufacturer's instructions. Place the container in which you refrigerated the custard in the freezer so you can use it to store the finished ice cream. Churn the ice cream until the texture resembles "soft serve." Transfer the ice cream to the chilled storage container and freeze until hardened to your desired consistency. Alternatively, you can serve it immediately, topped with Marcona almonds—it will be the consistency of gelato. The ice cream will keep, frozen, for up to 7 days.

MOCHA ALMOND FUDGE ICE CREAM

When Pete was a child, his favorite ice cream was Baskin-Robbins's Jamocha Almond Fudge, and while reminiscing one summer afternoon, we thought it might be a fun recipe to re-create in the Van Leeuwen kitchen. Mocha ice cream is essentially a cross between chocolate and coffee, combining the best of both. A swirl of Hot Fudge Sauce (page 183) and some sliced almonds give this ice cream incredible richness and texture.

MAKES ABOUT 1 QUART

2 cups heavy cream

1 cup whole milk

¾ cup (150 grams) granulated sugar

20 grams unsweetened chocolate (99% cacao), preferably Michel Cluizel (see Sources, page 218)

¼ cup (20 grams) freeze-dried coffee

¼ cup (25 grams) natural unsweetened cocoa powder

½ teaspoon (2 grams) kosher salt

6 large egg yolks

¼ cup (32 grams) slivered almonds

¼ cup Hot Fudge Sauce (page 183), plus more to taste

1. Pour the cream and milk into a double boiler or a heatproof bowl set over a saucepan of gently simmering water (the bottom of the bowl should not touch the water). Whisk in ½ cup (100 grams) of the sugar, the chocolate, coffee, cocoa powder, and salt and stir until the sugar has dissolved. Warm the mixture until you see steam rising from the top.

2. Meanwhile, prepare an ice bath in a large bowl and set another bowl over it. Set aside.

3. In a medium bowl, with a kitchen towel underneath it to prevent slipping, whisk together the egg yolks with the remaining ¼ cup (50 grams) sugar until uniform. While whisking, add a splash of the hot dairy mixture to the yolks. Continue to add the dairy mixture, whisking it in bit by bit, until you've added about half. Add the yolk mixture to the remaining dairy mixture in the double boiler. Set the heat under the double boiler to medium and cook the custard, stirring continuously with a wooden spoon and reducing the heat to medium-low as necessary, until steam begins to rise from the surface and the custard thickens enough to coat the back of the spoon. Hold the spoon horizontally and run your finger through the custard. If the trail left by your finger stays separated, the custard is ready to be cooled.

4. Strain the custard into the bowl sitting over the prepared ice bath and stir for 3 to 5 minutes, or until the custard has cooled. Transfer the custard to a quart-size container, cover, and refrigerate for at least 4 hours or, preferably, overnight.

5. Pour the chilled custard into an ice cream maker and freeze according to the manufacturer's instructions. Place the container in which you refrigerated the custard in the freezer so you can use it to store the finished ice cream. Churn the ice cream until the texture resembles "soft serve." Using a spatula, fold in the almonds and chocolate fudge. Transfer the ice cream to the chilled storage container and freeze until hardened to your desired consistency. Alternatively, you can serve it immediately—it will be the consistency of gelato. The ice cream will keep, frozen, for up to 7 days.

ROCKY ROAD ICE CREAM

One of the stories of how Rocky Road ice cream got its name has to do with the stock market crash of 1929; that the name was concocted in order to give the country "something to smile about" during the Great Depression. Other stories claim it was just a reinterpretation of the classic candy bar's name. Whatever the real story is, few ice cream lovers can resist the allure of chocolate ice cream, homemade marshmallow, and sliced almonds. While it's more common to use candied nuts, we found them to be a bit too sweet when combined with ice cream, and decided plain sliced almonds worked much better. And for a bit more crunch and flavor, we added cocoa nibs.

MAKES ABOUT 1 QUART

SPECIAL EQUIPMENT

Stand mixer, candy thermometer, immersion blender

FOR THE MARSHMALLOW CREAM

¾ cup (150 grams) sugar

½ cup (180 grams) Lyle's Golden Syrup (see Sources, page 218)

¼ teaspoon (1 gram) kosher salt

2 large egg whites, at room temperature

¼ teaspoon cream of tartar

1½ teaspoons pure vanilla extract

FOR THE ROCKY ROAD ICE CREAM

1½ cups heavy cream

1½ cups whole milk

½ cup plus 2 tablespoons (125 grams) granulated sugar

1 teaspoon (4 grams) kosher salt

(continued on next page)

1. To make the marshmallow cream, in a medium, heavy-bottomed saucepan, stir together the sugar, golden syrup, salt, and ¼ cup water until combined. Clip a candy thermometer to the pan and bring the mixture to a boil over high heat, stirring occasionally, until it reaches 240°F on a candy thermometer.

2. Meanwhile, place the egg whites and cream of tartar in the bowl of a stand mixer fitted with the whisk attachment. Starting with the mixer on low and gradually increasing to medium-high speed, whip the egg whites until they hold soft peaks. (Be sure to have those whipped before the syrup is done.)

3. Once the syrup has reached 240°F, remove it from the heat. With the mixer on low speed, slowly add 2 tablespoons of the syrup to the egg whites to temper them. Raise the mixer speed to medium and carefully drizzle in the remaining syrup, making sure that the syrup flows along and down the inside of the bowl (this will help cool the syrup before it reaches the egg whites). Raise the mixer speed to high and whip until the marshmallow cream is stiff and glossy, 4 to 5 minutes. Add the vanilla and whip for a minute more. Use immediately, or cover and refrigerate for up to 2 weeks. This will make about 8 cups.

4. To make the Rocky Road ice cream, pour the cream and milk into a double boiler or a heatproof bowl set over a saucepan of gently simmering water (the bottom of the bowl should not touch the water). Whisk in ½ cup (100 grams) of the sugar and the salt and stir until they have dissolved. Warm the mixture until you see steam rising from the top.

5. Meanwhile, prepare an ice bath in a large bowl. Set aside.

6. In a medium bowl, with a kitchen towel underneath it to prevent slipping, whisk together the egg yolks with the remaining 2 tablespoons (25 grams) sugar until uniform. While whisking, add a splash of the hot dairy mixture to the yolks. Continue to add the dairy mixture, whisking it in bit by bit, until you've added about half. Add the yolk mixture to the remaining dairy mixture in the double boiler. Set the heat under the double boiler to medium and

(continued)

6 large egg yolks

¾ cup (60 grams)
    unsweetened natural
    cocoa powder, preferably
    Michel Cluizel (see
    Sources, page 218)

1 ounce (30 grams)
    unsweetened dark
    chocolate (99% cacao),
    preferably Michel Cluizel
    (see Sources, page 218)

¼ cup Homemade
    Marshmallow Cream
    (recipe above)

2 tablespoons (12 grams)
    sliced almonds

2 tablespoons (20 grams)
    cocoa nibs

cook the custard, stirring continuously with a wooden spoon and reducing the heat to medium-low as necessary, until steam begins to rise from the surface and the custard thickens enough to coat the back of the spoon. Hold the spoon horizontally and run your finger through the custard. If the trail left by your finger stays separated, the custard is ready to be cooled.

7. Strain the custard into a bowl and stir in the cocoa powder and chocolate until the chocolate has melted completely and the mixture is uniform. Using an immersion blender, buzz the custard until emulsified. Place the bowl over the prepared ice bath and stir for 3 to 5 minutes, or until the custard has cooled. Transfer the custard to a quart-size container, cover, and refrigerate for at least 4 hours or, preferably, overnight.

8. Pour the chilled custard into an ice cream maker and freeze according to the manufacturer's instructions. Place the container in which you refrigerated the custard in the freezer so you can use it to store the finished ice cream. Churn the ice cream until the texture resembles "soft serve." Using a spatula, fold in the marshmallow cream, almonds, and cocoa nibs until combined. Transfer the ice cream to the chilled storage container and freeze until hardened to your desired consistency. Alternatively, you can serve it immediately—it will be the consistency of gelato. The ice cream will keep, frozen, for up to 7 days.

ben's note Spread leftover marshmallow cream over a sheet pan dusted with a mixture of equal parts cornstarch and powdered sugar. Dust the top of the marshmallow spread with the same mixture and allow to air-dry for several hours. Cut into small squares to enjoy marshmallows in your cocoa.

WHITE CHOCOLATE WITH ALMOND-COCOA NIB BRITTLE

Technically, white chocolate is not really chocolate, as it does not contain any cocoa solids. Overwhelmingly, most white chocolate is a low-grade, poor-quality confection that tastes sickly sweet and waxy, but when you find high-quality white chocolate, you realize how delicious it is! Unfortunately, white chocolate has gotten a bad rap over the years, because most of it is now manufactured with hydrogenated or other low-grade fats. When properly made—with cocoa butter, sugar, and milk solids—it is absolutely delicious.

With this ice cream, we wanted to officially kick off the white chocolate redemption. We make a cocoa-butter-based custard and throw in some Almond-Cocoa Nib Brittle toward the end of churning. We're pretty sure this ice cream just might make you see white chocolate in a whole new light.

MAKES ABOUT 1 QUART

SPECIAL EQUIPMENT
Immersion blender

FOR THE ALMOND-COCOA NIB BRITTLE
Very cold butter, for the baking sheet

1 cup (200 grams) sugar

4 tablespoons (½ stick/ 56 grams) unsalted butter

3 tablespoons (60 grams) brown rice syrup

¼ teaspoon baking soda

¾ teaspoon (3 grams) kosher salt

¾ cup (75 grams) sliced almonds

6 tablespoons (30 grams) cocoa nibs

1 teaspoon finely ground Sichuan peppercorns

(continued on next page)

1. To make the almond–cocoa nib brittle, lightly butter the bottom of a 9 × 13-inch rimmed baking sheet. Line the baking sheet with parchment paper trimmed to fit and very lightly butter the paper as well.

2. In a medium, heavy-bottomed saucepan, combine the sugar, butter, and brown rice syrup with ¼ cup water; stir everything together so all the sugar is wet. Cook the mixture over high heat until it turns dark amber, 8 to 10 minutes. Remove from the heat and add the baking soda, followed by the salt. The caramel will rise and bubble.

3. Using a wooden spoon, fold in the almonds, cocoa nibs, and pepper. Pour the mixture over the prepared baking sheet and use the back of the spoon to spread it to a thickness of about ¼ inch thick. Let cool completely.

4. Take a piece of the cooled, hardened brittle and place it in a plastic bag. Using a mallet, break the brittle into little pieces; you will need about ⅓ cup (34 grams) of broken brittle for the ice cream. Reserve the rest for snacking. The brittle will keep in an airtight container at room temperature for up to 2 weeks.

5. To make the white chocolate ice cream, pour the cream and milk into a double boiler or a heatproof bowl set over a saucepan of gently simmering water (the bottom of the bowl should not touch the water). Whisk in ½ cup (100 grams) of the sugar and the salt and stir until they have dissolved. Warm the mixture until you see steam rising from the top.

6. Meanwhile, prepare an ice bath in a large bowl. Set aside.

7. In a medium bowl, with a kitchen towel underneath it to prevent slipping, whisk together the egg yolks with the remaining 2 tablespoons (25 grams) sugar until uniform. While whisking, add a splash of the hot dairy mixture to the yolks. Continue to add the dairy mixture, whisking it in bit by bit, until you've added about half. Add the yolk mixture to the remaining dairy mixture in the

(continued)

**FOR THE WHITE
CHOCOLATE ICE CREAM**

1 cup heavy cream

1½ cups whole milk

½ cup plus 2 tablespoons
(125 grams) sugar

1 teaspoon (4 grams) kosher
salt

6 large egg yolks

½ cup (100 grams) cocoa
butter, melted

1 teaspoon pure vanilla
extract

double boiler. Set the heat under the double boiler to medium and cook the custard, stirring continuously with a wooden spoon and reducing the heat to medium-low as necessary, until steam begins to rise from the surface and the custard thickens enough to coat the back of the spoon. Hold the spoon horizontally and run your finger through the custard. If the trail left by your finger stays separated, the custard is ready to be cooled.

8. Strain the custard into a bowl and stir in the cocoa butter and vanilla. Using an immersion blender, buzz the liquid until emulsified. Set the bowl over the prepared ice bath and stir for 3 to 5 minutes, or until the custard has cooled. Transfer the custard to a quart-size container, cover, and refrigerate for at least 4 hours or, preferably, overnight.

9. Pour the chilled custard into an ice cream maker and freeze according to the manufacturer's instructions. Place the container in which you refrigerated the custard in the freezer so you can use it to store the finished ice cream. Churn the ice cream until the texture resembles "soft serve." Using a spatula, fold in the reserved ⅓ cup (34 grams) brittle until combined. Transfer the ice cream to the chilled storage container and freeze until hardened to your desired consistency. Alternatively, you can serve it immediately—it will be the consistency of gelato. The ice cream will keep, frozen, for up to 7 days.

MINT CHIP ICE CREAM

We don't really understand why most mint chip ice cream comes in this odd shade of green that doesn't look like *any* plant, never mind mint. Our mint chip ice cream is a creamy white speckled with chocolate chips and is one of our best sellers. It's incredibly easy to make and is most certainly a crowd-pleaser. We recommend showing some restraint with the mint extract—after all, you can always add more—lest your ice cream wind up tasting like toothpaste.

MAKES ABOUT 1 QUART

2 cups heavy cream

1 cup whole milk

½ cup plus 2 tablespoons (125 grams) sugar

¼ teaspoon (1 gram) kosher salt

6 large egg yolks

1½ teaspoons mint extract

½ cup (60 grams) dark chocolate chips (72% cacao)

ben's note You can also make fresh mint ice cream by blending fresh mint leaves into your cooled custard. You will wind up with a different taste from the ice cream here, but it's also quite wonderful.

1. Pour the cream and milk into a double boiler or a heatproof bowl set over a saucepan of simmering water (the bottom of the bowl should not touch the water). Whisk in ½ cup (100 grams) of the sugar and the salt and stir until they have dissolved. Warm the mixture until you see steam rising from the top.

2. Meanwhile, prepare an ice bath in a large bowl and set another bowl over it. Set aside.

3. In a medium bowl, with a kitchen towel underneath it to prevent slipping, whisk together the egg yolks with the remaining 2 tablespoons (25 grams) sugar until uniform. While whisking, add a splash of the hot dairy mixture to the yolks. Continue to add the dairy mixture, whisking it in bit by bit, until you've added about half. Add the yolk mixture to the remaining dairy mixture in the double boiler. Set the heat under the double boiler to medium and cook the custard, stirring continuously with a wooden spoon and reducing the heat to medium-low as necessary, until steam begins to rise from the surface and the custard thickens enough to coat the back of the spoon. Hold the spoon horizontally and run your finger through the custard. If the trail left by your finger stays separated, the custard is ready to be cooled.

4. Strain the custard into the bowl sitting over the prepared ice bath and stir for 3 to 5 minutes, or until the custard has cooled. Transfer the custard to a quart-size container, cover, and refrigerate for at least 4 hours or, preferably, overnight.

5. Add the mint extract to the chilled custard. Pour the custard into an ice cream maker and freeze according to the manufacturer's instructions. Place the container in which you refrigerated the custard in the freezer so you can use it to store the finished ice cream. Churn the ice cream until the texture resembles "soft serve." In the last minute of churning, fold in the chocolate chips and churn until incorporated. Transfer the ice cream to the chilled storage container and freeze until hardened to your desired consistency. Alternatively, you can serve it immediately—it will be the consistency of gelato. The ice cream will keep, frozen, for up to 7 days.

···

VANILLA

Let's get one thing out of the way: There's nothing plain about vanilla. Quality vanilla is elegant, complex, and multilayered. If you take care to source quality vanilla beans for your ice cream, it will turn out anything but "plain"—it will be superlative!

When it comes to vanilla, European cuisine can be grateful to the Spanish conquistadores who, in 1520, observed Emperor Montezuma drinking a beverage containing, among other things, ground black vanilla pods. Impressed, the Spaniards took vanilla back home. European cooking—dessert in particular—was never the same.

The vanilla plant is an orchid of the genus *Vanilla*, originating primarily from Mexican flat-leaved Vanilla species. Because of its origins, the vanilla plant thrives in a hot, humid, tropical environment. Presently, there are three major species of vanilla grown globally, all of which derive from a species originally found in Mesoamerica, including parts of modern-day Mexico. The various subspecies are grown on Madagascar, Réunion, and other tropical areas along the Indian Ocean; in the South Pacific; in the West Indies; and in Central and South America. The majority of the world's vanilla is known as Bourbon vanilla (after the former name of Réunion, Île Bourbon) or Madagascar vanilla, which

is produced in Madagascar and neighboring islands in the southwestern Indian Ocean and in Indonesia.

Until the nineteenth century, the country responsible for producing most of the world's vanilla was Mexico. It wasn't until the early 1800s, when the French shipped vanilla to the islands of Réunion and Mauritius, that vanilla cultivation began there. In time, cultivation spread to the island of Madagascar, and by the late 1800s, the region was producing about 80 percent of the world's vanilla crop. Today, most of the world's Bourbon vanilla is grown in Indonesia.

Because of the differences in terroir, vanilla's flavor characteristics depend on geography. Tahitian vanilla is a bit more floral, delicate, less in-your-face; Bourbon vanilla has that classic taste we all conjure up when we think of vanilla. And in Bali, vanilla beans are smoked, which imparts a unique flavor to the beans.

Next to saffron, vanilla is the second most expensive spice in the world. Growing vanilla pods is extremely labor intensive, and the crop and production can be affected by weather events, such as cyclones, as well as political instability. To this day, the plants must be manually pollinated using the same method that was developed by Edmond Albius in 1841. The hand-pollination must be carried out early in the morning on the day on which the flower opens. An expert can pollinate anywhere from 1,000 to 1,500 blossoms a day.

Once fertilized, the pods are left to mature for four to nine months, and are picked just as their color starts to change from green to yellow. The longer the bean, the more desirable it is.

After harvest, the beans are slated for fermentation and curing. First, the beans are sweated: The pods are spread out under the sun until hot, and then rolled in blankets to "sweat" until the following morning. This process is repeated many times over, until the pods become pliable and deep brown in color. Next, the beans are dried in the sun or in heated rooms. All in all, the curing and drying process can take up to five or six months.

Of course, we'd be remiss if we didn't mention all those products that are flavored with imitation vanilla or artificially manufactured vanillin, both flavors lacking the richness and complexity of real vanilla flavor. Isolating vanillin and trying to reproduce it artificially began in the late 1850s, and by the turn of the twentieth century, imitation vanilla was all the rage.

You can count on us never using imitation vanilla—only the real deal.

When we started making vanilla ice cream in large production batches, we didn't have the capabilities to split vanilla beans by hand and scrape out the beans. We didn't have the production capacity to process whole vanilla beans, so we were purchasing extract from a pastry chef we found in Vancouver. The Bourbon and Tahitian beans are aged for three months in oak barrels in vodka and then the beans are ground to a paste to achieve maximum flavor.

Eventually, we found Mr. Recipe, real name Aaron Isaacson, a one-man spice emporium who supplies chefs in New York (and beyond) with enormous, plump vanilla beans along with other spices of exceptional quality. Or, to be more accurate, Mr. Recipe found Laura at Whole Foods. Not one to mince words, he got right to the point: "I've got vanilla that's better than what you're using. In fact, I've got the best vanilla anyone can get their hands on!" Of course, we were skeptical: Here was this eccentric-looking guy with a waxed, upturned mustache, who randomly had the hookup on the best vanilla? As it turned out, Isaacson was dead serious; somehow, he not only gets his hands on exceptional product but also has the most incredible spice grinders that have burrs so sharp, they don't tear the bean—they grind it clean. It is his vanilla powder that we now use along with the original, spectacular extract—and our vanilla ice cream has never been better!

VANILLA ICE CREAM

Vanilla ice cream seems perfectly straightforward and easy, and in many ways it's one of the most unfussy flavors in this book. But to get it *truly* right, you need quality vanilla beans. To make our ice cream in large batches, we buy vanilla in bulk and wholesale—something that makes no sense for the home cook; so for the purpose of the book, we tested this recipe with some plump Madagascar vanilla beans we picked up at our local grocery store. When looking for a quality bean, make sure the beans look moist and "fat"—this means they are fresh and flavorful.

MAKES ABOUT 1 QUART

2 cups heavy cream

1 cup whole milk

½ cup plus 2 tablespoons (125 grams) sugar

1 plump vanilla bean, split lengthwise and seeds scraped out

¼ teaspoon (1 gram) kosher salt

8 large egg yolks

If you have a Vitamix, puree the vanilla bean pod directly with the dairy mixture after it has steeped; process until the pod has been completely incorporated. It will make your ice cream even more flavorful.

1. Pour the cream and milk into a double boiler or a heatproof bowl set over a saucepan of gently simmering water (the bottom of the bowl should not touch the water). Whisk in ½ cup (100 grams) of the sugar, the vanilla seeds and pod, and the salt and stir until the sugar and salt have dissolved. Warm the mixture until you see steam rising from the top. Remove from the heat, cover, and let the mixture steep for 15 minutes. Remove the vanilla bean pod (see Ben's Note on what to do with it) or, if you have a Vitamix, see the sidebar.

2. Meanwhile, prepare an ice bath in a large bowl and set another bowl over it. Set aside.

3. In a medium bowl, with a kitchen towel underneath it to prevent slipping, whisk together the egg yolks with the remaining 2 tablespoons (25 grams) sugar until uniform. While whisking, add a splash of the hot dairy mixture to the yolks. Continue to add the dairy mixture, whisking it in bit by bit, until you've added about half. Add the yolk mixture to the remaining dairy mixture in the double boiler. Set the heat under the double boiler to medium and cook the custard, stirring continuously with a wooden spoon and reducing the heat to medium-low as necessary, until steam begins to rise from the surface and the custard thickens enough to coat the back of the spoon. Hold the spoon horizontally and run your finger through the custard. If the trail left by your finger stays separated, the custard is ready to be cooled.

4. Strain the custard into the bowl sitting over the prepared ice bath and stir for 3 to 5 minutes, or until the custard has cooled. Transfer the custard to a quart-size container, cover, and refrigerate for at least 4 hours or, preferably, overnight.

5. Pour the chilled custard into an ice cream maker and freeze according to the manufacturer's instructions. Place the container in which you refrigerated the custard in the freezer so you can use it to store the finished ice cream. Churn the ice cream until the texture resembles "soft serve." Transfer the ice cream to the chilled storage container and freeze until hardened to your

desired consistency. Alternatively, you can serve it immediately—it will be the consistency of gelato. The ice cream will keep, frozen, for up to 7 days.

> **ben's note** *Don't toss that vanilla bean. Rinse it, dry it, and then throw it in your sugar jar. Within a day, you'll have the most fragrant vanilla sugar, which will enhance everything. Vanilla beans are expensive, so use them to their utmost potential!*

A FUN WAY TO HIGHLIGHT VANILLA ICE CREAM:
PEACH MELBA WITH RIESLING POACHED PEACHES AND RASPBERRY COULIS

Peach Melba is a classic dessert, invented in the early 1890s at the Savoy hotel in London to honor Dame Nellie Melba, famous Australian soprano. Its typical presentation includes vanilla ice cream, peaches, and raspberry sauce. In some instances, we've seen it served alongside wafers or cookies, but those elements weren't part of the original dessert.

SERVES 4

2 medium peaches

⅔ cup dry Riesling

¼ cup (50 grams) sugar

½ plump vanilla bean, split lengthwise and seeds scraped out

1 pint fresh raspberries

Vanilla Ice Cream (page 37)

1. Bring a large pot of water to a boil; prepare an ice bath in a large bowl and set aside. Make an "x" incision on top of each peach. Blanch the peaches in the boiling water for 30 seconds, then use a slotted spoon to immediately transfer them to the prepared ice bath and let cool. When cool, use a paring knife to peel and quarter the peaches. Set aside.
2. In a medium saucepan, combine the Riesling, sugar, and vanilla bean seeds and pod and cook over medium heat, stirring, until the sugar has dissolved and the mixture is simmering. Add the quartered peaches, reduce the heat to low, cover, and poach until the peaches are softer, about 10 minutes. Using a slotted spoon, transfer the peaches to a plate. Raise the heat to medium-high and bring the wine-sugar syrup to a lively simmer. Cook until the syrup has reduced by about half, 5 to 7 minutes. Remove from the heat and let cool.
3. In a blender, combine the raspberries with the reduced syrup and blend until smooth. Strain the coulis through a fine-mesh strainer into a bowl, pressing on the solids; set aside.
4. Scoop the vanilla ice cream into chilled bowls and top with the poached peaches and raspberry coulis.

— CHOCOLATE CHIP COOKIE DOUGH ICE CREAM —

The best part of making cookies as a kid was sneaking bits and pieces of the dough when Mom wasn't looking. Of course, there's also the iconic Ben & Jerry's Chocolate Chip Cookie Dough ice cream, which was all the rage in the United States when Ben and Pete were little. No matter where you stood on ice cream flavors (Vanilla or chocolate? Strawberry or black raspberry?), the cookie dough flavor was a favorite in everyone's book. So this recipe is an homage to what we think is one of the best ice cream flavors ever created, guaranteed to bring out the kid in you.

MAKES ABOUT 1 QUART

2 cups heavy cream

1 cup whole milk

½ cup plus 2 tablespoons (125 grams) sugar

½ large plump vanilla bean, split lengthwise and seeds scraped out

¼ teaspoon (1 gram) kosher salt

8 large egg yolks

1 cup cookie dough from Chocolate Chip Cookies (page 187)

1. Pour the cream and milk into a double boiler or a heatproof bowl set over a saucepan of gently simmering water (the bottom of the bowl should not touch the water). Whisk in ½ cup (100 grams) of the sugar, the vanilla bean seeds and pod, and the salt and stir until the sugar and salt have dissolved. Warm the mixture until you see steam rising from the top. Remove from the heat, cover, and let the mixture steep for 15 minutes. Carefully remove the vanilla pod.

2. Meanwhile, prepare an ice bath in a large bowl and set another bowl over it. Set aside.

3. In a medium bowl, with a kitchen towel underneath it to prevent slipping, whisk together the egg yolks with the remaining 2 tablespoons (25 grams) sugar until uniform. While whisking, add a splash of the hot dairy mixture to the yolks. Continue to add the dairy mixture, whisking it in bit by bit, until you've added about half. Add the yolk mixture to the remaining dairy mixture in the double boiler. Set the heat under the double boiler to medium and cook the custard, stirring continuously with a wooden spoon and reducing the heat to medium-low as necessary, until steam begins to rise from the surface and the custard thickens enough to coat the back of the spoon. Hold the spoon horizontally and run your finger through the custard. If the trail left by your finger stays separated, the custard is ready to be cooled.

4. Strain the custard into the bowl sitting over the prepared ice bath and stir for 3 to 5 minutes, or until the custard has cooled. Transfer the custard to a quart-size container, cover, and refrigerate for at least 4 hours or, preferably, overnight.

5. Pour the chilled custard into an ice cream maker and freeze according to the manufacturer's instructions. Place the container in which you refrigerated the custard in the freezer so you can use it to store the finished ice cream. Churn the ice cream until the texture resembles "soft serve." Break or chop the cookie dough into small pieces and use a spatula to fold it into the ice cream by hand until incorporated. Transfer the ice cream to the chilled storage container and freeze until hardened to your desired consistency. Alternatively, you can serve it immediately—it will be the consistency of gelato. The ice cream will keep, frozen, for up to 7 days.

ESPRESSO ICE CREAM

There are lots of ways to make coffee-flavored ice cream, but this is by far our favorite. We've discovered that using a quality freeze-dried coffee (it exists!) produces the most crowd-pleasing flavor that is most true to the taste of coffee. We also add a touch of heritage kettle-boiled palm sugar and a hint of unsweetened chocolate to round out the flavor.

MAKES ABOUT 1 QUART

2 cups heavy cream

1 cup whole milk

½ cup plus 2 tablespoons (125 grams) granulated sugar

3 tablespoons plus 1 teaspoon (16 grams) freeze-dried coffee

8 teaspoons (16 grams) unrefined palm sugar

4 grams 99% unsweetened chocolate, preferably Michel Cluizel (see Sources, page 218)

1½ teaspoons (4 grams) unsweetened cocoa powder

¼ teaspoon (1 gram) kosher salt

6 large egg yolks

1. Pour the cream and milk into a double boiler or a heatproof bowl set over a saucepan of gently simmering water (the bottom of the bowl should not touch the water). Whisk in ½ cup (100 grams) of the granulated sugar, the coffee, palm sugar, chocolate, cocoa powder, and salt, and stir until the sugars and salt have dissolved. Warm the mixture until you see steam rising from the top.

2. Meanwhile, prepare an ice bath in a large bowl and set another bowl over it. Set aside.

3. In a medium bowl, with a kitchen towel underneath it to prevent slipping, whisk together the egg yolks with the remaining 2 tablespoons (25 grams) granulated sugar until uniform. While whisking, add a splash of the hot dairy mixture to the yolks. Continue to add the dairy mixture, whisking it in bit by bit, until you've added about half. Add the yolk mixture to the remaining dairy mixture in the double boiler. Set the heat under the double boiler to medium and cook the custard, stirring continuously with a wooden spoon and reducing the heat to medium-low as necessary, until steam begins to rise from the surface and the custard thickens enough to coat the back of the spoon. Hold the spoon horizontally and run your finger through the custard. If the trail left by your finger stays separated, the custard is ready to be cooled.

4. Strain the custard into the bowl sitting over the prepared ice bath and stir for 3 to 5 minutes, or until the custard has cooled. Transfer the custard to a quart-size container, cover, and refrigerate for at least 4 hours or, preferably, overnight.

5. Pour the custard into an ice cream maker and freeze according to the manufacturer's instructions. Place the container in which you refrigerated the custard in the freezer so you can use it to store the finished ice cream. Churn the ice cream until the texture resembles "soft serve." Transfer the ice cream to the chilled storage container and freeze until hardened to your desired consistency. Alternatively, you can serve it immediately—it will be the consistency of gelato. The ice cream will keep, frozen, for up to 7 days.

T E A

You can tell that tea is one of our favorite ingredients because we have several ice cream flavors in the book infused with it. Tea is an excellent flavoring agent: flavorful, elegant, sophisticated.

One of the oldest beverages we drink, tea is only second to water in popularity! There's such a wealth of history behind tea's prevalence and cultural influences, we could write pages and pages about it. But we don't want to put you to sleep!

It is commonly believed that tea drinking originated in southern China where the country borders Myanmar (formerly Burma). From there, it quickly spread throughout China and was introduced to the Portuguese through trade. In the seventeenth century, tea gained a following in England, and it was the English who eventually introduced tea to India, where it quickly became popular.

The teas most commonly found on the market are white, green, oolong, and black, with many other less popular varieties in existence. An evergreen plant, most of the world's tea is grown in Asia; however, some teas are grown as far north as Cornwall in the United Kingdom. Tea leaves are extremely sensitive to moisture and odors and easily absorb their flavor, which means you must store tea in a cool, dark place in a well-sealed container.

Recently, tea has been enjoying a resurgence as a health beverage. It's been credited with helping to lower blood pressure and decreasing the risk of certain cancers thanks to compounds called catechins, present in all tea leaves and found in the highest concentration in white and green varieties.

Some high-end tea is packaged in premade bags (muslin, silk, and the like), but most bagged tea is of lower quality; the manufacturer likely uses tea fannings, or "dust" produced from the sorting of higher quality tea. Generally speaking, you can guarantee better quality tea if you buy it loose, and as an additional benefit, loose tea leaves also allow you to control how much tea to use.

We love quality tea and sell it in our shops as well as using it in our ice cream, which we think is an excellent conduit of flavor. From Earl Grey Tea Ice Cream (page 47), one of our all-time best sellers and a classic, to Masala Chai with Black Peppercorns (page 139), to Genmaicha with Honey (page 50), tea adds a delicate, elegant flavor to our recipes.

In our search for a tea company we liked across the board, we found a tea company that deals in organic and fair-trade-certified teas, the Wisconsin-based Rishi. Once we tried their Earl Grey tea, flavored with real bergamot oil (not bergamot flavoring as is, sadly, all too common!), we were hooked. If you take a look at (and a whiff of) loose Rishi tea, you will immediately notice its large leaves and elegant fragrance. It's a bit more expensive than the competition, but once you brew yourself a cup, or make some ice cream that includes their tea, you'll agree with us—that incredible taste is worth a few extra dollars.

EARL GREY TEA ICE CREAM

When we added Earl Grey ice cream to our trucks' offerings in 2009, New Yorkers went mad for it. Not surprisingly—black tea, combined with bergamot oil, cuts through the summer heat about as well as anything. We use a high-quality loose tea from our favorite tea brand, Rishi (see page 45), which uses pure Italian bergamot citrus oil (and not bergamot flavoring), to make the most intensely fragrant Earl Grey tea ice cream.

   Making Earl Grey flavor in bulk proved to be quite a challenge. We needed to find bags large enough to steep such big quantities of tea, and durable enough so that the bags would keep together when we were done steeping. Tea absorbs a lot of liquid, and those bags grow heavy. A friend of Ben's who was working at Brooklyn's Sixpoint Brewery at the time gave us giant mesh steeping bags the brewery used for hops—and they made the whole large-batch operation a cinch. Of course, at home, things are much simpler; you can use good tea in tea bags or loose tea that you place in a separate tea bag, and you can even let the tea leaves float in the dairy mixture and strain them out later. The key is to find tea you love—it will make a real impact on the quality of your ice cream.

MAKES ABOUT 1 QUART

2 cups heavy cream

1 cup whole milk

¾ cup (150 grams) sugar

6 tablespoons (30 grams) loose Earl Grey tea

½ teaspoon (2 grams) kosher salt

6 large egg yolks

1. Pour the cream and milk into a double boiler or a heatproof bowl set over a saucepan of gently simmering water (the bottom of the bowl should not touch the water). Whisk in ½ cup (100 grams) of the sugar, the tea, and the salt and stir until the sugar and salt have dissolved. Warm the mixture until you see steam rising from the top. Remove from the heat and strain the mixture into a bowl, pressing on the tea leaves to extract as much infused liquid as possible. Discard the tea leaves and return the infused dairy mixture to the double boiler.

2. Meanwhile, prepare an ice bath in a large bowl and set another bowl over it. Set aside.

3. In a medium bowl, with a kitchen towel underneath it to prevent slipping, whisk together the egg yolks with the remaining ¼ cup (50 grams) sugar until uniform. While whisking, add a splash of the hot dairy mixture to the yolks. Continue to add the dairy mixture, whisking it in bit by bit, until you've added about half. Add the yolk mixture to the remaining dairy mixture in the double boiler. Set the heat under the double boiler to medium and cook the custard, stirring continuously with a wooden spoon and reducing the heat to medium-low as necessary, until steam begins to rise from the surface and the custard thickens enough to coat the back of the spoon. Hold the spoon horizontally and run your finger through the custard. If the trail left by your finger stays separated, the custard is ready to be cooled.

4. Strain the custard into the bowl sitting over the prepared ice bath and stir for 3 to 5 minutes, or until the custard has cooled. Transfer the custard to a quart-size container, cover, and refrigerate for at least 4 hours or, preferably, overnight.

5. Pour the chilled custard into an ice cream maker and freeze according to the manufacturer's instructions. Place the container in which you refrigerated the custard in the freezer so you can use it to store the finished ice cream. Churn the ice cream until the texture resembles "soft serve." Transfer the ice cream to the chilled storage container and freeze until hardened to your desired consistency. Alternatively, you can serve it immediately—it will be the consistency of gelato. The ice cream will keep, frozen, for up to 7 days.

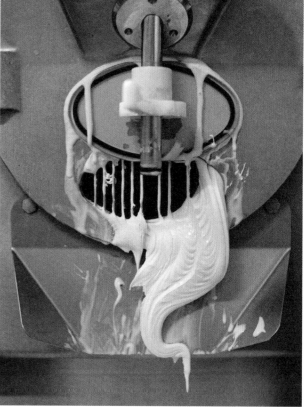

CHAMOMILE-HONEY ICE CREAM

This is one of our go-tos when the temperatures and humidity climb into the stratosphere and we need to cool off. While playing around with various tea-infused ice creams, we were quite surprised by what a refreshing flavor chamomile turned out to be—perfect for the hottest days of summer. Highlighted by a bit of mild local honey, a spoonful of this ice cream conjures up summer's warm, golden light and a gentle breeze. I've never been a fan of chamomile tea, so it came as a surprise to find out how much I loved this flavor—herbaceous and refreshing, it's everything you want summer ice cream to be.

MAKES ABOUT 1 QUART

2 cups heavy cream

2 cups whole milk

1½ tablespoons (27 grams) mild honey

⅓ cup (60 grams) loose chamomile flowers

¼ teaspoon (1 gram) kosher salt

6 large egg yolks

½ cup (100 grams) sugar

ben's note Seek out loose chamomile flowers in health food, tea, or spice shops, rather than buying premanufactured chamomile tea bags. You will see that in the bags, the contents look more like wood dust and are far less fragrant than loose dried chamomile buds. If you look for the latter, your ice cream will be truly stunning and memorable!

1. Pour the cream and milk into a double boiler or a heatproof bowl set over a saucepan of gently simmering water (the bottom of the bowl should not touch the water). Whisk in the honey, chamomile flowers, and salt and stir until the honey and salt have dissolved. Warm the mixture until you see steam rising from the top. Remove from the heat, cover, and let the mixture steep for 5 minutes. Strain the mixture through a fine-mesh strainer into a bowl; discard the chamomile in the strainer. Return the dairy mixture to the double boiler.

2. Meanwhile, prepare an ice bath in a large bowl and set another bowl over it. Set aside.

3. In a medium bowl, with a kitchen towel underneath it to prevent slipping, whisk together the egg yolks and sugar until uniform. While whisking, add a splash of the hot dairy mixture to the yolks. Continue to add the dairy mixture, whisking it in bit by bit, until you've added about half. Add the yolk mixture to the remaining dairy mixture in the double boiler. Set the heat under the double boiler to medium and cook the custard, stirring continuously with a wooden spoon and reducing the heat to medium-low as necessary, until steam begins to rise from the surface and the custard thickens enough to coat the back of the spoon. Hold the spoon horizontally and run your finger through the custard. If the trail left by your finger stays separated, the custard is ready to be cooled.

4. Strain the custard into the bowl sitting over the prepared ice bath and stir for 3 to 5 minutes, or until the custard has cooled. Transfer the custard to a quart-size container, cover, and refrigerate for at least 4 hours or, preferably, overnight.

5. Pour the chilled custard into an ice cream maker and freeze according to the manufacturer's instructions. Place the container in which you refrigerated the custard in the freezer so you can use it to store the finished ice cream. Churn the ice cream until the texture resembles "soft serve." Transfer the ice cream to the chilled storage container and freeze until hardened to your desired consistency. Alternatively, you can serve it immediately—it will be the consistency of gelato. The ice cream will keep, frozen, for up to 7 days.

GENMAICHA WITH HONEY ICE CREAM

We've had plenty of matcha ice cream before—popular in Japanese restaurants and made with the powdered, bright green tea of that name—but we decided to make ours with *genmaicha*, green tea combined with toasted brown rice for a deeper flavor, because we were so fascinated with the amazing taste of this tea.

Genmaicha, historically, was consumed by poorer Japanese—the rice served as filler and reduced the price of the tea, which used to be very expensive. These days, *genmaicha* is not relegated to the lower classes but is, in fact, considered upscale. The toasted brown rice adds an earthy flavor to the tea, which we thought would translate particularly nicely to the ice cream base. For our tea, we turned to our favorite supplier, Rishi. We add a touch of honey, rather than plain sugar, to highlight the grassy notes in the tea.

Tea-infused ice creams are some of the easiest (and most rewarding) flavors to make in this book, but the trick is to get the best ingredients available to you. Try to find good-quality *genmaicha* for truly spectacular results!

MAKES ABOUT 1 QUART

½ cup (45 grams) *genmaicha*

2 cups heavy cream

1 cup whole milk

½ cup plus 2 tablespoons (180 grams) mild honey

¼ teaspoon (1 gram) kosher salt

8 large egg yolks

1. Using a mortar and pestle or in a spice grinder, finely grind 2 tablespoons (11 grams) of the *genmaicha*. Set aside.

2. Pour the cream and milk into a double boiler or a heatproof bowl set over a saucepan of gently simmering water (the bottom of the bowl should not touch the water). Whisk in the honey, the remaining 6 tablespoons (34 grams) *genmaicha*, and the salt and stir until the honey and salt have dissolved. Warm the mixture until you see steam rising from the top.

3. Meanwhile, prepare an ice bath in a large bowl and set another bowl over it. Set aside.

4. In a medium bowl, with a kitchen towel underneath it to prevent slipping, whisk together the egg yolks until uniform. While whisking, add a splash of the hot dairy mixture to the yolks. Continue to add the dairy mixture, whisking it in bit by bit, until you've added about half. Add the yolk mixture to the remaining dairy mixture in the double boiler. Set the heat under the double boiler to medium and cook the custard, stirring continuously with a wooden spoon and reducing the heat to medium-low as necessary, until steam begins to rise from the surface and the custard thickens enough to coat the back of the spoon. Hold the spoon horizontally and run your finger through the custard. If the trail left by your finger stays separated, the custard is ready to be cooled.

5. Strain the custard into the bowl sitting over the prepared ice bath, pressing on the solids in the strainer; discard the tea leaves in the strainer. Add the reserved finely ground *genmaicha* and stir for 3 to 5 minutes, or until the custard has cooled. Transfer the custard to a quart-size container, cover, and refrigerate for at least 4 hours or, preferably, overnight.

6. Pour the chilled custard into an ice cream maker and freeze according to the manufacturer's instructions. Place the container in which you refrigerated the custard in the freezer so you can use it to store the finished ice cream. Churn the ice cream until the texture resembles "soft serve." Transfer the ice cream to the chilled storage container and freeze until hardened to your desired consistency. Alternatively, you can serve it immediately—it will be the consistency of gelato. The ice cream will keep, frozen, for up to 7 days.

ben's note Your yield here will be somewhat lower, because the tea leaves will absorb some of the liquid.

BLACK SESAME ICE CREAM

We started making black sesame ice cream after we opened Selamat Pagi, our Balinese restaurant. We were looking to make more Asian flavors, and our Selamat Pagi chef at the time, Sophia Loch, suggested black sesame. It sounded like the perfect way to end a meal. Besides the flavor itself, inky black ice cream makes for a dramatic presentation.

To make this ice cream, we grind sesame seeds with sugar and sesame oil, and incorporate it into ice cream at the very end. While black sesame ice cream echoes Japanese traditions, the flavors perfectly complement Balinese ingredients, and our patrons really love the taste. You can also opt to swirl the sesame paste into the ice cream for a marbled effect—it will look, and taste, beautiful.

MAKES ABOUT 1 QUART

FOR THE BLACK SESAME PASTE

3 tablespoons (21 grams) black sesame seeds

1 tablespoon toasted sesame oil

1 tablespoon (12 grams) sugar

Pinch of kosher salt

FOR THE ICE CREAM BASE

2 cups heavy cream

1 cup whole milk

½ cup plus 2 tablespoons (125 grams) sugar

¼ teaspoon (1 gram) kosher salt

6 large egg yolks

1. To make the black sesame paste, in a dry skillet, toast the sesame seeds over medium-low heat until fragrant, about 2 minutes. Immediately transfer the seeds to a mortar and pestle, and pound them until they form a sticky paste, almost the consistency of grout. Add the sesame oil, sugar, and salt, and incorporate until smooth (see Ben's Note). Set aside.

2. To make the ice cream base, pour the cream and milk into a double boiler or a heatproof bowl set over a saucepan of gently simmering water (the bottom of the bowl should not touch the water). Whisk in ½ cup (100 grams) of the sugar and the salt and stir until they have dissolved. Warm the mixture until you see steam rising from the top.

3. Meanwhile, prepare an ice bath in a large bowl and set another bowl over it. Set aside.

4. In a medium bowl, with a kitchen towel underneath it to prevent slipping, whisk together the egg yolks with the remaining 2 tablespoons (25 grams) sugar until uniform. While whisking, add a splash of the hot dairy mixture to the yolks. Continue to add the dairy mixture, whisking it in bit by bit, until you've added about half. Add the yolk mixture to the remaining dairy mixture in the double boiler. Set the heat under the double boiler to medium and cook the custard, stirring continuously with a wooden spoon and reducing the heat to medium-low as necessary, until steam begins to rise from the surface and the custard thickens enough to coat the back of the spoon. Hold the spoon horizontally and run your finger through the custard. If the trail left by your finger stays separated, the custard is ready to be cooled.

5. Strain the custard into the bowl sitting over the prepared ice bath and stir for 3 to 5 minutes, or until the custard has cooled. To get a richly colored, inky black ice cream, stir in the black sesame paste until fully incorporated. (If you'd rather have the ice cream show a black sesame swirl, hold off for now.) If your sesame paste

is a bit chunky and you'd prefer a finer texture, transfer the custard to a blender and puree until smooth. Transfer the custard to a quart-size container, cover, and refrigerate for at least 4 hours or, preferably, overnight.

6. Pour the chilled custard into an ice cream maker and freeze according to the manufacturer's instructions. Place the container in which you refrigerated the custard in the freezer so you can use it to store the finished ice cream. Churn the ice cream until the texture resembles "soft serve." To give the ice cream a black sesame swirl, rather than having uniformly colored ice cream, add the sesame paste in the last 30 seconds of churning. Transfer the ice cream to the chilled storage container and freeze until hardened to your desired consistency. Alternatively, you can serve it immediately—it will be the consistency of gelato. The ice cream will keep, frozen, for up to 7 days.

ben's note You can also grind the toasted black sesame seeds with the sesame oil in a food processor. Including kosher salt results in a finer grind, as the abrasiveness of the salt helps wear down the individual sesame seeds.

STICKY BLACK RICE ICE CREAM

When Ben and I were in Bali, we fell so hard for the island's native sweet, sticky black rice, we'd indulge in it twice a day. It was the most amazing treat: In some cases, the rice was cooked in coconut milk, while in others, a glorious, sweet syrup was poured over the rice tableside. The black rice we use is also called "purple rice" or "forbidden rice." According to some legends, the rice was thought to be so nutritious it was considered worthy enough only, and reserved, for royalty.

    When we got back to the States, we couldn't stop thinking about that incredible flavor. We thought the black rice would lend itself beautifully to ice cream, and began serving it at Selamat Pagi—it was an instant hit. It's a tricky flavor to nail down because of the starch, so we were happy to have a chance to further perfect the recipe for this book.

MAKES ABOUT 1 QUART

FOR THE STICKY BLACK RICE

½ cup (68 grams) sticky black rice, also known as forbidden rice

Pinch of kosher salt

1 cup (212 grams) coconut milk, preferably organic and without stabilizers

1 cup plus 2 tablespoons (135 grams) palm sugar (see Sources, page 218)

FOR THE ICE CREAM BASE

2 cups heavy cream

1 cup whole milk

1 cup (200 grams) sugar

¼ teaspoon (1 gram) kosher salt

6 large egg yolks

1. To make the sticky black rice, in a medium saucepan, combine the rice, salt, and 2 cups water and bring to a boil over medium-high heat. Stir in the coconut milk and sugar, reduce the heat to low, cover, and cook until the water is mostly absorbed and the rice is soft and gooey; this can take anywhere from 1 hour to 1 hour and 30 minutes. You are looking for a loose rice pudding consistency. Measure out ¾ cup of the cooked rice for the ice cream and set aside (see Ben's Notes for what to do with the remaining rice).

2. To make the coconut ice cream base, pour the cream and milk into a double boiler or a heatproof bowl set over a saucepan of simmering water (the bottom of the bowl should not touch the water). Whisk in ¾ cup (150 grams) of the sugar and the salt and stir until both have dissolved. Warm the mixture until you see steam rising from the top.

3. Meanwhile, prepare an ice bath in a large bowl and set another bowl over it. Set aside.

4. In a medium bowl, with a kitchen towel underneath it to prevent slipping, whisk together the egg yolks with the remaining ¼ cup (50 grams) sugar until uniform. While whisking, add a splash of the hot dairy mixture to the yolks. Continue to add the dairy mixture, whisking it in bit by bit, until you've added about half. Add the yolk mixture to the remaining dairy mixture in the double boiler. Set the heat under the double boiler to medium and cook the custard, stirring continuously with a wooden spoon and reducing the heat to medium-low as necessary, until steam begins to rise from the surface and the custard thickens enough to coat the back of the spoon. Hold the spoon horizontally and run your finger through the custard. If the trail left by your finger stays separated, the custard is ready to be cooled.

5. Strain the custard into the bowl sitting over the prepared ice bath and stir for 3 to 5 minutes, or until the custard has cooled. Stir in the reserved ¾ cup sticky black rice. Transfer the custard to a quart-size container, cover, and refrigerate for at least 4 hours or, preferably, overnight.

6. Pour the chilled custard into an ice cream maker and freeze according to the manufacturer's instructions. Place the container in which you refrigerated the custard in the freezer so you can use it to store the finished ice cream. Churn the ice cream until the texture resembles "soft serve." Transfer the ice cream to the chilled storage container and freeze until hardened to your desired consistency. Alternatively, you can serve it immediately—it will be the consistency of gelato. The ice cream will keep, frozen, for up to 7 days.

ben's notes While black rice might not be easily available at regular grocery stores, we've found that health food stores, as well as Whole Foods, tend to have it in stock. Black rice—not to be confused with wild rice, which is also black in color, but isn't even technically a rice—has a unique, earthy-sweet flavor all its own. It's worth seeking out and worth having in your pantry.

You'll have more sticky rice than needed for this ice cream, but that's a good thing. We love to take the remaining rice and serve it warm with coconut milk sweetened with palm sugar, and topped with sliced mango and coconut flakes—it makes an amazing Bali-style breakfast!

CREMA DI RISO ICE CREAM

Years ago, I got to live in Italy with an Italian family for six months. There was a *gelateria* by the train station in town, and I quickly learned that *gelaterias* near train stations or monuments were just giant tourist traps serving subpar gelato—a disappointing lesson, since I fancied all gelato in Italy to be a thing of beauty. Like everywhere else, Italy has good food worth seeking out and bad food where the establishments don't rely on repeat service since tourist traffic is so high.

To rectify the sad gelato situation, Giulio, the son of my host family, took me on his bike to this place hidden deep in the suburbs of Rome; it was a *gelateria*, but one without a display case (a very good sign!)—only silver tins. I remember getting a scoop of *crema di riso* simply because it sounded so unusual. It was lovely: Rice pudding, as interpreted in gelato, was just incredible. And since then, I've been deeply in love with the flavor.

When we started testing *crema di riso* ice cream, we loved the results we were getting—they were perfectly reminiscent of my memories of Italy. We were also pretty smitten with *kheer*, an Indian dessert made with rice, milk, and spices, and we thought that combining the idea of *crema di riso* with the flavors of *kheer* might work pretty well. You might wonder how an ice cream studded with rice would be a good idea, but we urge you to give it a try; we're pretty confident that this might become one of your all-time favorite flavors.

MAKES ABOUT 1 QUART

1 cup (210 grams) jasmine rice

1½ cups whole milk

¾ cup (150 grams) sugar

1 dried bay leaf

½ teaspoon ground cardamom

½ plump vanilla bean, split lengthwise and seeds scraped out

¼ teaspoon freshly grated nutmeg

Kosher salt

2 cups heavy cream

8 large egg yolks

1. Place the rice in a saucepan and add enough water to cover. Bring the water to a boil over high heat, then reduce the heat to low and simmer the rice until softened, 6 to 7 minutes. Drain the rice and return it to the pan. Add 1 cup of the milk, ½ cup (100 grams) of the sugar, the bay leaf, cardamom, vanilla bean pod and seeds, nutmeg, and a pinch of salt. Bring to a simmer over medium heat, then reduce the heat to low and simmer, uncovered, until the rice is fully cooked and the milk has mostly been absorbed, about 25 minutes. Remove from the heat and set aside to cool completely. Transfer to an airtight container and refrigerate until ready to use.

2. Pour the heavy cream and the remaining ½ cup milk into a double boiler or a heatproof bowl set over a saucepan of gently simmering water (the bottom of the bowl should not touch the water). Add a pinch of salt and stir until it has dissolved. Warm the mixture until you see steam rising from the top.

3. Meanwhile, prepare an ice bath in a large bowl and set another bowl over it. Set aside.

4. In a medium bowl, with a kitchen towel underneath it to prevent slipping, whisk together the egg yolks with the remaining ¼ cup (50 grams) sugar until uniform. While whisking, add a splash of the hot dairy mixture to the yolks. Continue to add the dairy mixture, whisking it in bit by bit, until you've added about half. Add the yolk mixture to the remaining dairy mixture in the double boiler. Set the heat under the double boiler to medium and cook the custard, stirring continuously with a wooden spoon and

reducing the heat to medium-low as necessary, until steam begins to rise from the surface and the custard thickens enough to coat the back of the spoon. Hold the spoon horizontally and run your finger through the custard. If the trail left by your finger stays separated, the custard is ready to be cooled.

5. Strain the custard into the bowl sitting over the prepared ice bath and stir for 3 to 5 minutes, or until the custard has cooled. Fold in the cooked rice, and transfer the custard to a quart-size container, cover, and refrigerate for at least 4 hours or, preferably, overnight.

6. Pour the chilled custard into an ice cream maker and freeze according to the manufacturer's instructions. Place the container in which you refrigerated the custard in the freezer so you can use it to store the finished ice cream. Churn the ice cream until the texture resembles "soft serve." Transfer the ice cream to the chilled storage container and freeze until hardened to your desired consistency. Alternatively, you can serve it immediately—it will be the consistency of gelato. The ice cream will keep, frozen, for up to 7 days.

ben's note When parcooking your rice, cook it in water as we recommend, rather than in milk. Something about milk proteins toughens the rice, making it take much, much longer to cook. We learned this the hard way, of course, and wanted to save you some frustration (and time!).

STRAWBERRY ICE CREAM

Our strawberry ice cream tastes like ice cream with strawberries, as opposed to strawberry ice cream, if that makes sense. It doesn't have that overly sweet milk-shake taste, and we're enormously proud of that. To get our strawberry ice cream just right, we went through a lot of trial and error. *A lot.* In fact, this was one of our hardest flavors to nail down. We wanted our ice cream to be rich yet redolent of strawberries for that unmistakable classic summer flavor. At the same time, we didn't want the strawberry to taste candylike or to be masked by butterfat, which can be an easy trap to fall into.

In the end, because strawberries are so high in water content, we upped the fat but calibrated it so that the strawberries still shone through. We wound up using almost no milk—mostly cream—to get the right texture, bite, and flavor. To get more consistent results, we make a compote out of strawberries, which allows us to control the total water content in the ice cream, and allows us to further highlight the berry flavors. Seek out the best in-season local strawberries you can find; typically these tend to be smaller berries with a concentrated sweet taste.

MAKES ABOUT 1 QUART

SPECIAL EQUIPMENT
Immersion blender

FOR THE ICE CREAM BASE
2 cups heavy cream

½ cup whole milk

¾ cup (150 grams) sugar

¼ teaspoon (1 gram) kosher salt

6 large egg yolks

FOR THE STRAWBERRY COMPOTE
10 ounces (284 grams) fresh or frozen strawberries, hulled and diced

¼ cup (50 grams) sugar

1 tablespoon fresh lemon juice

1. To make the ice cream base, pour the cream and milk into a double boiler or a heatproof bowl set over a saucepan of gently simmering water (the bottom of the bowl should not touch the water). Whisk in ½ cup (100 grams) of the sugar and the salt and stir until both have dissolved. Warm the mixture until you see steam rising from the top.

2. Meanwhile, prepare an ice bath in a large bowl and set another bowl over it.

3. In a medium bowl, with a kitchen towel underneath it to prevent slipping, whisk together the egg yolks with the remaining ¼ cup (50 grams) sugar until uniform. While whisking, add a splash of the hot dairy mixture to the yolks. Continue to add the dairy mixture, whisking it in bit by bit, until you've added about half. Add the yolk mixture to the remaining dairy mixture in the double boiler. Set the heat under the double boiler to medium and cook the custard, stirring continuously with a wooden spoon and reducing the heat to medium-low as necessary, until steam begins to rise from the surface and the custard thickens enough to coat the back of the spoon. Hold the spoon horizontally and run your finger through the custard. If the trail left by your finger stays separated, the custard is ready to be cooled.

4. Strain the custard into the bowl sitting over the prepared ice bath and stir for 3 to 5 minutes, or until the custard has cooled. Transfer the custard to a quart-size container, cover, and refrigerate for at least 4 hours or, preferably, overnight.

5. To make the strawberry compote, while the custard cools, in a nonreactive bowl, combine the strawberries, sugar, and lemon juice and let stand for at least 2 hours. If necessary, cover and refrigerate the compote until ready to use. Using a potato masher, mash the strawberries until the compote is chunky.

6. Combine the chilled custard with 1½ cups of the strawberry compote and, using an immersion blender, buzz the mixture until well mixed. Pour the custard into an ice cream maker and freeze according to the manufacturer's instructions. Place the container in which you refrigerated the custard in the freezer so you can use it to store the finished ice cream. Churn the ice cream until the texture resembles "soft serve." Transfer the ice cream to the chilled storage container and freeze until hardened to your desired consistency. Alternatively, you can serve it immediately—it will be the consistency of gelato. The ice cream will keep, frozen, for up to 7 days.

BLUEBERRY ICE CREAM

To make this ice cream, perfected by Jane Nguyen, our production coordinator, we pushed the boundaries of butterfat, creating a super-high-fat base in order to compensate for blueberries' water content. We make a blueberry compote and then swirl it throughout the base for a gorgeous uniform color. Cooking the blueberries helps get rid of some water, which ensures that the ice cream won't be icy. When frozen, water crystallizes, which can form pockets of ice within ice cream (never a good sign). If you want to get really geeky about it, here's something to think about: Prime time for berry picking is after a few dry days; after it rains, berries tend to take on a lot of water, which can dilute their flavor. Out of season, frozen tiny wild Maine blueberries are a great choice, as they are readily available nationally and year-round, but they might require slightly longer cooking time, as frozen berries contain moisture from ice crystals.

MAKES ABOUT 1 QUART

FOR THE BLUEBERRY COMPOTE

1 pint blueberries

¼ cup (50 grams) sugar

2 tablespoons fresh lemon juice

½ teaspoon finely grated lemon zest

FOR THE ICE CREAM BASE

2½ cups heavy cream

½ cup whole milk

¾ cup plus 2 tablespoons (175 grams) sugar

¼ teaspoon (1 gram) kosher salt

8 large egg yolks

1. To make the blueberry compote, combine the blueberries, sugar, lemon juice, lemon zest, and ⅔ cup water in a saucepan. Heat over medium-low heat until jamlike and syrupy, about 10 minutes. Remove from the heat and set aside to cool.

2. To make the blueberry ice cream, pour the cream and milk into a double boiler or a heatproof bowl set over a saucepan of gently simmering water (the bottom of the bowl should not touch the water). Whisk in ½ cup (100 grams) of the sugar and the salt and stir until they have dissolved. Warm the mixture until you see steam rising from the top.

3. Meanwhile, prepare an ice bath in a large bowl and set another bowl over it. Set aside.

4. In a medium bowl, with a kitchen towel underneath it to prevent slipping, whisk together the egg yolks with the remaining 6 tablespoons (75 grams) sugar until uniform. While whisking, add a splash of the hot dairy mixture to the yolks. Continue to add the dairy mixture, whisking it in bit by bit, until you've added about half. Add the yolk mixture to the remaining dairy mixture in the double boiler. Set the heat under the double boiler to medium and cook the custard, stirring continuously with a wooden spoon and reducing the heat to medium-low as necessary, until steam begins to rise from the surface and the custard thickens enough to coat the back of the spoon. Hold the spoon horizontally and run your finger through the custard. If the trail left by your finger stays separated, the custard is ready to be cooled.

5. Strain the custard into the bowl sitting over the prepared ice bath and stir in 2 cups of the blueberry compote (reserve any remaining blueberry compote for another use—it will keep in an airtight container in the refrigerator for up to 2 weeks). Stir for 3 to 5 minutes, or until the custard has cooled. Transfer the custard to a

quart-size container, cover, and refrigerate for at least 4 hours or, preferably, overnight.

6. Pour the chilled custard into an ice cream maker and freeze according to the manufacturer's instructions. Place the container in which you refrigerated the custard in the freezer so you can use it to store the finished ice cream. Churn the ice cream until the texture resembles "soft serve." Transfer the ice cream to the chilled storage container and freeze until hardened to your desired consistency. Alternatively, you can serve it immediately—it will be the consistency of gelato. The ice cream will keep, frozen, for up to 7 days.

ROASTED BANANA ICE CREAM

Believe it or not, even people who say they don't like bananas love this ice cream—it tastes just like banana bread pudding. We roast the bananas with dark brown sugar and butter until they are golden and caramelized, and then we fold them into our ice cream base. The ice cream that comes out is elegant and luscious, rich with caramelized bananas, and is one of our favorite winter flavors to make. The roasting of the bananas gives the ice cream such a creamy, almost burnt-caramel flavor; we can't think of a better way to round out a Christmas dinner.

MAKES ABOUT 1 QUART

SPECIAL EQUIPMENT
Immersion blender

FOR THE ROASTED BANANAS

4 medium bananas, preferably somewhat speckled but not brown, peeled and cut into ¼-inch-thick slices

2 tablespoons (28 grams) unsalted butter

2 tablespoons (14 grams) dark brown sugar

Pinch of kosher salt

FOR THE ICE CREAM BASE

2 cups heavy cream

½ cup whole milk

¾ cup (150 grams) granulated sugar

½ teaspoon (2 grams) kosher salt

6 large egg yolks

1. To make the roasted bananas, preheat the oven to 400°F; position the rack in the middle. Line a shallow baking sheet with parchment paper.
2. In a large bowl, toss the bananas, butter, sugar, and salt. Spread the ingredients on the prepared baking sheet and bake for 10 to 15 minutes, or until caramelized. Transfer to a cooling rack and let cool completely.
3. To make the roasted banana ice cream, pour the cream and milk into a double boiler or a heatproof bowl set over a saucepan of simmering water (the bottom of the bowl should not touch the water). Whisk in ½ cup (100 grams) of the sugar and the salt and stir until they have dissolved. Warm the mixture until you see steam rising from the top.
4. Meanwhile, prepare an ice bath in a large bowl and set another bowl over it. Set aside.
5. In a medium bowl, with a kitchen towel underneath it to prevent slipping, whisk together the egg yolks with the remaining ¼ cup (50 grams) sugar until uniform. While whisking, add a splash of the hot dairy mixture to the yolks. Continue to add the dairy mixture, whisking it in bit by bit, until you've added about half. Add the yolk mixture to the remaining dairy mixture in the double boiler. Set the heat under the double boiler to medium and cook the custard, stirring continuously with a wooden spoon and reducing the heat to medium-low as necessary, until steam begins to rise from the surface and the custard thickens enough to coat the back of the spoon. Hold the spoon horizontally and run your finger through the custard. If the trail left by your finger stays separated, the custard is ready to be cooled.
6. Strain the custard into the bowl sitting over the prepared ice bath and stir for 3 to 5 minutes, or until the custard has cooled. Transfer the custard to a quart-size container and add the roasted bananas. Using an immersion blender, buzz the custard until emulsified. Cover the custard and refrigerate for at least 4 hours or, preferably, overnight.

7. Pour the chilled custard into an ice cream maker and freeze according to the manufacturer's instructions. Place the container in which you refrigerated the custard in the freezer so you can use it to store the finished ice cream. Churn the ice cream until the texture resembles "soft serve." Transfer the ice cream to the chilled storage container and freeze until hardened to your desired consistency. Alternatively, you can serve it immediately—it will be the consistency of gelato. The ice cream will keep, frozen, for up to 7 days.

ben's note Keep in mind that bananas will vary in size and moisture content, depending on the season, country of origin, humidity levels in your environment, just to name a few. When dealing with fruit—and we'll say it again and again in this book—you're bound to get differing results, as fruit itself will always vary.

APPLE CRUMBLE WITH CALVADOS AND CRÈME FRAÎCHE ICE CREAM

My favorite apple pie recipe comes from a friend who shares my name, and who was kind enough to share with me a recipe for an apple pie that's practically a work of art. More than a thousand words long, it features little anecdotes here and there, making the recipe valuable for the writing alone, never mind the pie that comes off its pages. We wanted to re-create the flavor of apple pie in ice cream, but pie crust didn't quite work out when tucked into custard—it got too soggy for it to be any good. Instead, we decided to keep the filling and use bits of cooked crumble topping as cookielike bites mixed in with bits of apple. Calvados is a nice way to bump up the apple flavor, but if you don't have that on hand, rum or brandy should do in a pinch.

MAKES ABOUT 1 QUART

FOR THE CRUMBLE

⅔ cup (83 grams) all-purpose flour

6 tablespoons (75 grams) sugar

1 teaspoon baking powder

¼ teaspoon (1 gram) kosher salt

¼ teaspoon (1 gram) freshly grated nutmeg

12 tablespoons (1½ sticks/ 170 grams) unsalted butter, melted and cooled

FOR THE APPLES

2 cups apples (about 2 medium apples, preferably Granny Smiths, cut into ¼-inch dice; see Ben's Notes)

¼ cup (50 grams) sugar

½ teaspoon pure vanilla extract

⅛ teaspoon ground cinnamon

(continued on page 71)

1. To make the crumble, preheat the oven to 350°F; position a rack in the middle. Line a rimmed baking sheet with parchment paper.

2. In a bowl, whisk together the flour, sugar, baking powder, salt, and nutmeg until combined. Add the butter and, using a fork, cut it into the mixture until it resembles wet sand. Refrigerate for about 20 minutes, or until chilled. Sprinkle the chilled crumble mixture over the prepared baking sheet. Bake for 15 minutes, or until golden brown. Transfer the baking sheet to a wire rack and let the crumble cool completely before breaking it into small pieces. Set aside.

3. To make the apples, in a saucepan, combine the apples, sugar, vanilla, cinnamon, salt, and pepper and let the fruit macerate for 30 minutes. Place the saucepan over low heat and cook until the apples are tender, about 10 minutes. Remove from the heat and set aside for 5 minutes. Stir in the calvados; let cool to room temperature.

4. To make the ice cream base, pour the milk into a double boiler or a heatproof bowl set over a saucepan of simmering water (the bottom of the bowl should not touch the water). Whisk in ½ cup (100 grams) of the sugar and the salt and stir until they have dissolved. Warm the mixture until you see steam rising from the top.

5. Meanwhile, prepare an ice bath in a large bowl and set another bowl over it. Set aside.

6. In a medium bowl, with a kitchen towel underneath it to prevent slipping, whisk together the egg yolks with the remaining 2 tablespoons (25 grams) sugar until uniform. While whisking, add a splash of the hot dairy mixture to the yolks. Continue to add the dairy mixture, whisking it in bit by bit, until you've added about half. Add the yolk mixture to the remaining dairy mixture in the double boiler. Set the heat under the double boiler to medium and cook the custard, stirring continuously with a wooden spoon

(continued)

⅛ teaspoon kosher salt

⅛ teaspoon freshly ground
    pink peppercorns

2 tablespoons calvados or
    other brandy

FOR THE ICE CREAM BASE

1½ cups whole milk

½ cup plus 2 tablespoons
    (125 grams) sugar

¼ teaspoon (1 gram) kosher
    salt

6 large egg yolks

2 cups crème fraîche

½ teaspoon pure vanilla
    extract

and reducing the heat to medium-low as necessary, until steam begins to rise from the surface and the custard thickens enough to coat the back of the spoon. Hold the spoon horizontally and run your finger through the custard. If the trail left by your finger stays separated, the custard is ready to be cooled.

7. Strain the custard into a bowl and stir in the crème fraîche. If the mixture seems a bit runny and has lost its thick consistency, return the custard to the double boiler, and cook, stirring, until the custard has thickened enough to coat the back of the spoon. Repeat the finger gap test until the trail left by your finger stays separated. Strain the custard into the bowl sitting over the prepared ice bath, add the vanilla, and stir for 3 to 5 minutes, or until the custard has cooled. Transfer the custard to a quart-size container, cover, and refrigerate for at least 4 hours or, preferably, overnight.

8. Pour the chilled custard into an ice cream maker and freeze according to the manufacturer's instructions. Place the container in which you refrigerated the custard in the freezer so you can use it to store the finished ice cream. Churn the ice cream until the texture resembles "soft serve." In the last 30 seconds of churning, add the crumble and the cooked apples. You can also manually fold the crumble and apples into the ice cream. Transfer the ice cream to the chilled storage container and freeze until hardened to your desired consistency. Alternatively, you can serve it immediately—it will be the consistency of gelato. The ice cream will keep, frozen, for up to 7 days.

ben's notes *Of course, you can use whatever apples you prefer, but we recommend the Granny Smith variety here. They are excellent at holding their shape during cooking, and will stay intact, which is perfect for ice cream. A varietal like McIntosh is too soft and might fall apart, leaving you with applesauce.*

The crumble pieces will soften as the ice cream sits in the freezer—this is supposed to happen.

RHUBARB CRUMBLE ICE CREAM

Rhubarb is one of the harbingers of spring—bringing with it a reprieve from winter citrus. When we spy the green and pink stalks at our local greenmarket, we can't wait to buy some and make ice cream with it. A spin on a traditional rhubarb crumble, an easy and rustic dessert, this flavor pairs rhubarb's tart notes beautifully with creamy sweet custard. Little nibs of the crumble add welcome texture for a lovely spring flavor we're certain you'll love.

MAKES ABOUT 1 QUART

FOR THE RHUBARB COMPOTE

1½ cups (170 grams) chopped rhubarb (from about 4 stalks)

½ cup (100 grams) sugar

4 teaspoons fresh lemon juice

½ plump vanilla bean, split lengthwise and seeds scraped out

FOR THE RHUBARB CRUMBLE ICE CREAM

2 cups heavy cream

1 cup whole milk

½ cup plus 2 tablespoons (125 grams) sugar

¼ teaspoon (1 gram) kosher salt

8 large egg yolks

½ cup Crumble (see page 69; reserve leftovers for another use)

1. To make the rhubarb compote, in a medium saucepan, combine the rhubarb, sugar, lemon juice, and vanilla bean seeds and pod and bring to a simmer over medium heat. Reduce the heat to low and simmer the compote until the rhubarb is soft and almost falling apart, about 8 minutes. Remove from the heat and let cool completely.

2. To make the rhubarb crumble ice cream, pour the cream and milk into a double boiler or a heatproof bowl set over a saucepan of gently simmering water (the bottom of the bowl should not touch the water). Whisk in ½ cup (100 grams) of the sugar and the salt and stir until they have dissolved. Warm the mixture until you see steam rising from the top.

3. Meanwhile, prepare an ice bath in a large bowl and set another bowl over it. Set aside.

4. In a medium bowl, with a kitchen towel underneath it to prevent slipping, whisk together the egg yolks with the remaining 2 tablespoons (25 grams) sugar until uniform. While whisking, add a splash of the hot dairy mixture to the yolks. Continue to add the dairy mixture, whisking it in bit by bit, until you've added about half. Add the yolk mixture to the remaining dairy mixture in the double boiler. Set the heat under the double boiler to medium and cook the custard, stirring continuously with a wooden spoon and reducing the heat to medium-low as necessary, until steam begins to rise from the surface and the custard thickens enough to coat the back of the spoon. Hold the spoon horizontally and run your finger through the custard. If the trail left by your finger stays separated, the custard is ready to be cooled.

5. Strain the custard into the bowl sitting over the prepared ice bath and stir for 3 to 5 minutes, or until the custard has cooled. Transfer the custard to a quart-size container, cover, and refrigerate for at least 4 hours or, preferably, overnight.

6. Pour the chilled custard into an ice cream maker and freeze according to the manufacturer's instructions. Place the container in which you refrigerated the custard in the freezer so you can use it to store the finished ice cream. Churn the ice cream until

the texture resembles "soft serve." Using a spatula, fold in 1 cup of the rhubarb compote and ½ cup of the crumble until combined. Transfer the ice cream to the chilled storage container and freeze until hardened to your desired consistency. Alternatively, you can serve it immediately—it will be the consistency of gelato. The ice cream will keep, frozen, for up to 7 days. You can serve the leftover compote, along with any leftover crumble, as topping for the ice cream, if you wish, or swirl it into your morning yogurt or oatmeal. The compote will keep in an airtight container in the refrigerator for 7 days.

PASSION FRUIT ICE CREAM

One of the things I miss the most about Australia is passion fruit; it's inexpensive and can be found just about everywhere. In fact, I grew up with a passion fruit vine in my parents' garden, and we were always either eating it straight or finding ways to incorporate it into desserts. When I moved to the States, I was sad to learn that passion fruit was considered exotic and was thus quite expensive. Whereas in Australia I could buy three for a dollar, here, at Dean & DeLuca, each passion fruit cost about four dollars! Because the fruit is so much harder to source in the United States, most U.S. pastry chefs turn to a premade, flash-frozen passion fruit puree. A quick web search will point you in the direction of where to find it, and we provide a suggestion at the end of the book (see Sources, page 218).

A few years ago when I was visiting my family in Australia, my dad asked me to make some ice cream, and I decided to give passion fruit ice cream a try, using the fresh fruit so readily available back home. I loved the tartness of the fruit against the cool, creamy custard, and while we also provide a recipe for Passion Fruit Sorbet (page 169)—a more common iteration of this fruit in dessert—I think the ice cream version is not to be missed.

Passion fruit is also prominently featured in our Pavlova (page 204), a popular dessert thought to have originated in Australia or New Zealand and named for the famed Russian ballet dancer Anna Pavlova. It's a meringue with a crispy outer shell and a soft, gooey inside, and is generously topped with strawberries, passion fruit, mango, and kiwi and topped with lightly sweetened whipped cream.

MAKES ABOUT 1 QUART

2 cups heavy cream

¼ cup whole milk

¾ cup (150 grams) sugar

½ teaspoon (2 grams)
    kosher salt

8 large egg yolks

1 cup passion fruit puree
    (see Sources, page 218)

1. Pour the cream and milk into a double boiler or a heatproof bowl set over a saucepan of gently simmering water (the bottom of the bowl should not touch the water). Whisk in ½ cup (100 grams) of the sugar and the salt and stir until they have dissolved. Warm the mixture until you see steam rising from the top.

2. Meanwhile, prepare an ice bath in a large bowl and set another bowl over it. Set aside.

3. In a medium bowl, with a kitchen towel underneath it to prevent slipping, whisk together the egg yolks with the remaining ¼ cup (50 grams) sugar until uniform. While whisking, add a splash of the hot dairy mixture to the yolks. Continue to add the dairy mixture, whisking it in bit by bit, until you've added about half. Add the yolk mixture to the remaining dairy mixture in the double boiler. Set the heat under the double boiler to medium and cook the custard, stirring continuously with a wooden spoon and reducing the heat to medium-low as necessary, until steam begins to rise from the surface and the custard thickens enough to coat the back of the spoon. Hold the spoon horizontally and run your finger through the custard. If the trail left by your finger stays separated, the custard is ready to be cooled.

4. Strain the custard into the bowl sitting over the prepared ice bath and stir for 3 to 5 minutes, or until the custard has cooled; stir in the passion fruit puree. Transfer the custard to a quart-size container, cover, and refrigerate for at least 4 hours or, preferably, overnight.

5. Pour the chilled custard into an ice cream maker and freeze according to the manufacturer's instructions. Place the container in which you refrigerated the custard in the freezer so you can use it to store the finished ice cream. Churn the ice cream until the texture resembles "soft serve." Transfer the ice cream to the chilled storage container and freeze until hardened to your desired consistency. Alternatively, you can serve it immediately—it will be the consistency of gelato. The ice cream will keep, frozen, for up to 7 days.

ben's note *Bear in mind that passion fruit puree is quite loose, not thick like applesauce, but more like a thick nectar. When we first saw it we were surprised by how "liquid" it was—we were imagining something thicker.*

HONEY ICE CREAM WITH ROASTED FIGS AND WALNUTS

This flavor exists because we wanted to make use of the most local honey we've ever gotten our hands on—the one made in Pete's backyard! Beekeeping is nothing new to the Van Leeuwen family—they have a long history as amateur beekeepers: Ben and Pete's dad, and their sister, both keep bees in Connecticut. So, we decided to use Pete's wonderful honey and pair it with some ripe, roasted figs and toasted walnuts. We recommend you experiment with different kinds of honey—from a mild clover to a deep, rich buckwheat—and different types of figs (from green to black), and swap in a nut of your choosing. We recommend using raw, local honey, as it packs a bigger nutritional punch than pasteurized honey from far away. Before adding honey to the custard, be sure to let the custard cool some—heat destroys honey's nutritional properties.

MAKES ABOUT 1 QUART

½ cup (64 grams) chopped walnuts

8 ounces (227 grams) fresh black figs, halved

¼ cup (55 grams) light brown sugar

¼ teaspoon (1 gram) kosher salt, plus more as needed

2 cups heavy cream

1 cup whole milk

6 large egg yolks

½ cup (170 grams) mild honey

1. Preheat the oven to 300°F; position a rack in the middle. Line a rimmed baking sheet with parchment paper. Spread the nuts in a single layer on the prepared baking sheet and toast the nuts in the oven for 5 to 10 minutes, until fragrant. Transfer to a plate to cool and set aside. Raise the oven temperature to 400°F.

2. Line a second baking sheet with parchment paper. In a medium bowl, combine the figs with the brown sugar and a pinch of salt and spread them on the prepared baking sheet. Slice figs in half. Bake for 15 to 20 minutes, or until the figs slump and are tender. Set aside to cool. Roughly chop the figs and set aside.

3. Pour the cream and milk into a double boiler or a heatproof bowl set over a saucepan of gently simmering water (the bottom of the bowl should not touch the water). Whisk in ¼ teaspoon of the salt and warm the mixture until you see steam rising from the top.

4. Meanwhile, prepare an ice bath in a large bowl and set another bowl over it. Set aside.

5. In a medium bowl, with a kitchen towel underneath it to prevent slipping, whisk together the egg yolks until uniform. While whisking, add a splash of the hot dairy mixture to the yolks. Continue to add the dairy mixture, whisking it in bit by bit, until you've added about half. Add the yolk mixture to the remaining dairy mixture in the double boiler. Set the heat under the double boiler to medium and cook the custard, stirring continuously with a wooden spoon and reducing the heat to medium-low as necessary, until steam begins to rise from the surface and the custard thickens enough to coat the back of the spoon. Hold the spoon horizontally and run your finger through the custard. If the trail left by your finger stays separated, the custard is ready to be cooled.

6. Strain the custard into the bowl sitting over the prepared ice bath and stir for 3 to 5 minutes, or until the custard has cooled. Stir in

the honey until incorporated. Transfer the custard to a quart-size container, cover, and refrigerate for at least 4 hours or, preferably, overnight.

7. Pour the chilled custard into an ice cream maker and freeze according to the manufacturer's instructions. Place the container in which you refrigerated the custard in the freezer so you can use it to store the finished ice cream. Churn the ice cream until the texture resembles "soft serve." Using a spatula, fold in the figs and walnuts until incorporated. Transfer the ice cream to the chilled storage container and freeze until hardened to your desired consistency. Alternatively, you can serve it immediately—it will be the consistency of gelato. The ice cream will keep, frozen, for up to 7 days.

MAPLE-WALNUT ICE CREAM

We love the warm, fall flavor imparted by pure Vermont maple syrup and wanted to make it a part of our fall ice cream lineup. Along with Pumpkin Ice Cream (page 103), Maple-Walnut might be in a tie for our favorite ice cream to serve at the end of a Thanksgiving meal. It's a nice way to bring a little bit of Vermont into your home if you can't be there in person; it's hard to beat a scoop of this ice cream over a slice of apple pie.

MAKES ABOUT 1 QUART

2 cups heavy cream

1 cup whole milk

1 cup (140 grams) maple sugar

½ teaspoon (2 grams) kosher salt

8 large egg yolks

¼ cup (32 grams) chopped raw walnuts

1. Pour the cream and milk into a double boiler or a heatproof bowl set over a saucepan of gently simmering water (the bottom of the bowl should not touch the water). Whisk in ¾ cup (105 grams) of the maple sugar and the salt and stir until they have dissolved. Warm the mixture until you see steam rising from the top.

2. Meanwhile, prepare an ice bath in a large bowl and set another bowl over it. Set aside.

3. In a medium bowl, with a kitchen towel underneath it to prevent slipping, whisk together the egg yolks with the remaining ¼ cup (35 grams) maple sugar until uniform. While whisking, add a splash of the hot dairy mixture to the yolks. Continue to add the dairy mixture, whisking it in bit by bit, until you've added about half. Add the yolk mixture to the remaining dairy mixture in the double boiler. Set the heat under the double boiler to medium and cook the custard, stirring continuously with a wooden spoon and reducing the heat to medium-low as necessary, until steam begins to rise from the surface and the custard thickens enough to coat the back of the spoon. Hold the spoon horizontally and run your finger through the custard. If the trail left by your finger stays separated, the custard is ready to be cooled.

4. Strain the custard into the bowl sitting over the prepared ice bath and stir for 3 to 5 minutes, or until the custard has cooled. Transfer the custard to a quart-size container, cover, and refrigerate for at least 4 hours or, preferably, overnight.

5. Pour the chilled custard into an ice cream maker and freeze according to the manufacturer's instructions. Place the container in which you refrigerated the custard in the freezer so you can use it to store the finished ice cream. Churn the ice cream until the texture resembles "soft serve." In the last minute of churning, add the walnuts and churn to incorporate. Transfer the ice cream to the chilled storage container and freeze until hardened to your desired consistency. Alternatively, you can serve it immediately—it will be the consistency of gelato. The ice cream will keep, frozen, for up to 7 days.

HAZELNUTS

Hazelnuts, loosely resembling acorns, are tree nuts that enjoy immense popularity globally, no doubt facilitated by their fraternization with chocolate (which gives us things like Nutella, for instance). We're pretty sure they make all the other nuts out there jealous, except maybe the peanut, since it's also pretty popular!

Primarily grown in Turkey, Italy, Greece, Georgia, Azerbaijan, south of Catalonia in Spain, Kent in the United Kingdom, as well as in Oregon and Washington in the United States, hazelnuts are usually harvested in midautumn after the trees have shed their leaves and nuts. Filberts, by the way, are technically a type of hazelnut cultivar, but the name is often used interchangeably with *hazelnut*.

The largest producer of hazelnuts, by far, is Turkey, with approximately 75 percent of worldwide production. However, our favorite hazelnuts come from the Piedmont region in Italy, as well as Sicily, where the hazelnuts seem to have the most complex flavor. Because of differences in the soil, climate, moisture levels, and other environmental factors, the nuts from these regions have slightly different qualities. It is remarkable just how much these factors will affect the underlying taste of the nut, but they do!

In searching for our favorite hazelnuts for our Hazelnut Ice Cream (page 82) and Gianduja Ice Cream (page 22), we managed to find a hazelnut-processing facility in Italy that not only produces some of the best-tasting hazelnuts we've ever eaten but also operates in an ecologically friendly manner by generating electricity at the plant using discarded hazelnut shells. The Piedmont hazelnut, or *la nocciola Piemonte,* with its smoky, buttery flavor, is origin-certified by the Italian government. We use Piedmont hazelnuts in combination with Sicilian ones that we also love. Together, the nuts are ground into a paste that is perfectly suited to flavor our ice cream.

HAZELNUT ICE CREAM

To make true nut-flavored ice cream, you need to use supersmooth ground-nut pastes, or nut butters, which can be easily found online. While they're a little pricey, the results are far superior to those you'd get using the sugar-laden supermarket versions of these pastes.

We source our hazelnuts from Piedmont and Sicily; both are wonderful but very different. Oregon and Turkey also produce nice hazelnuts, though in our experience, the Italian nuts have the richest, deepest flavor. Whichever hazelnut paste you wind up using, just try to find the best quality available to you—it will make a world of difference.

MAKES ABOUT 1 QUART

1½ cups heavy cream

1¼ cups whole milk

½ cup plus 2 tablespoons (125 grams) sugar

¼ teaspoon (1 gram) kosher salt

6 large egg yolks

¼ cup (60 grams) hazelnut paste (see Sources, page 218)

½ cup (60 grams) hazelnuts (optional)

1. Pour the cream and milk into a double boiler or a heatproof bowl set over a saucepan of gently simmering water (the bottom of the bowl should not touch the water). Whisk in ½ cup (100 grams) of the sugar and the salt and stir until they have dissolved. Warm the mixture until you see steam rising from the top.

2. Meanwhile, prepare an ice bath in a large bowl and set another bowl over it. Set aside.

3. In a medium bowl, with a kitchen towel underneath it to prevent slipping, whisk together the egg yolks with the remaining 2 tablespoons (25 grams) sugar until uniform. While whisking, add a splash of the hot dairy mixture to the yolks. Continue to add the dairy mixture, whisking it in bit by bit, until you've added about half. Add the yolk mixture to the remaining dairy mixture in the double boiler. Set the heat under the double boiler to medium and cook the custard, stirring continuously with a wooden spoon and reducing the heat to medium-low as necessary, until steam begins to rise from the surface and the custard thickens enough to coat the back of the spoon. Hold the spoon horizontally and run your finger through the custard. If the trail left by your finger stays separated, the custard is ready to be cooled. Whisk in the hazelnut paste until it has melted and the custard is uniform.

4. Strain the custard into the bowl sitting over the prepared ice bath and stir for 3 to 5 minutes, or until the custard has cooled. Transfer the custard to a quart-size container, cover, and refrigerate for at least 4 hours or, preferably, overnight.

5. If using the hazelnuts, preheat the oven to 325°F; position a rack in the middle. Spread the hazelnuts on a rimmed baking sheet and toast in the oven until crisp and fragrant, 5 to 10 minutes. Transfer the baking sheet to a wire rack to cool. Using a clean kitchen towel, rub the skins off the hazelnuts, finely chop the nuts, and set them aside to fold into the ice cream or use as a garnish.

6. Pour the chilled custard into an ice cream maker and freeze according to the manufacturer's instructions. Place the container in which you refrigerated the custard in the freezer so you can use it to store the finished ice cream. Churn the ice cream until the tex-

ture resembles "soft serve." At the last minute, add the chopped hazelnuts, if desired, and churn for 1 minute. Transfer the ice cream to the chilled storage container and freeze until hardened to your desired consistency. Alternatively, you can serve it immediately—it will be the consistency of gelato. If you didn't use the toasted hazelnuts in the ice cream, you can use them as a topping. The ice cream will keep, frozen, for up to 7 days.

PISTACHIO ICE CREAM

Pistachio was one of our original ten flavors when we launched, and one we're particularly proud of getting right. Most pistachio ice cream we've encountered is vanilla ice cream with pistachios mixed in or topped with almonds. We don't think this counts as pistachio ice cream.

We decided to hunt down the best pistachio paste we could get our hands on. Unfortunately, what is widely available at grocery stores is a confectionary product that hardly resembles pistachios. Finally we found beautiful Sicilian pistachio paste of such a rich dark green color, it looks almost unreal—we'd never seen anything like it.

It took us quite a few rounds of testing to get the flavor just right. For a nut ice cream to taste good, you must be mindful of the fat levels in the paste, cream, milk, and egg yolks to end up with smooth and luscious ice cream, not chalky.

MAKES ABOUT 1 QUART

SPECIAL EQUIPMENT
Immersion blender

2 cups heavy cream

1½ cups whole milk

¾ cup (150 grams) sugar

¼ teaspoon (1 gram) kosher salt

6 large egg yolks

¼ cup (50 grams) pistachio paste (see Sources, page 218)

1. Pour the cream and milk into a double boiler or a heatproof bowl set over a saucepan of gently simmering water (the bottom of the bowl should not touch the water). Whisk in ½ cup (100 grams) of the sugar and the salt and stir until they have dissolved. Warm the mixture until you see steam rising from the top.

2. Meanwhile, prepare an ice bath in a large bowl and set another bowl over it. Set aside.

3. In a medium bowl, with a kitchen towel underneath it to prevent slipping, whisk together the egg yolks with the remaining ¼ cup (50 grams) sugar until uniform. While whisking, add a splash of the hot dairy mixture to the yolks. Continue to add the dairy mixture, whisking it in bit by bit, until you've added about half. Add the yolk mixture to the remaining dairy mixture in the double boiler. Set the heat under the double boiler to medium and cook the custard, stirring continuously with a wooden spoon and reducing the heat to medium-low as necessary, until steam begins to rise from the surface and the custard thickens enough to coat the back of the spoon. Hold the spoon horizontally and run your finger through the custard. If the trail left by your finger stays separated, the custard is ready to be cooled. Remove from the heat and whisk in the pistachio paste. Using your immersion blender, buzz the custard until emulsified and uniform.

4. Strain the custard into the bowl sitting over the prepared ice bath and stir for 3 to 5 minutes, or until the custard has cooled. Transfer the custard to a quart-size container, cover, and refrigerate for at least 4 hours or, preferably, overnight.

5. Pour the chilled custard into an ice cream maker and freeze according to the manufacturer's instructions. Place the container in which you refrigerated the custard in the freezer so you can use it to store the finished ice cream. Churn the ice cream until the texture resembles "soft serve." Transfer the ice cream to the chilled storage container and freeze until hardened to your desired consistency. Alternatively, you can serve it immediately—it will be the consistency of gelato. The ice cream will keep, frozen, for up to 7 days.

BROWN BUTTER PECAN ICE CREAM

During the first year I lived in the United States, I had planned to go back to Australia to visit my family, except I had planned to go over Thanksgiving and was going to miss my first experience of this amazing holiday. I had heard so much about Thanksgiving, and I was incredibly sad to be missing out.

So, Ben and Pete organized an early Thanksgiving for me and invited a bunch of friends. I made pumpkin pie, which eventually became the inspiration behind our Pumpkin Ice Cream (page 103), and Ben made butter pecan ice cream. Through the years he tweaked and tweaked the recipe, eventually browning the butter for a nuttier and more developed ice cream flavor, which we're thrilled to share with you here.

MAKES ABOUT 1 QUART

SPECIAL EQUIPMENT
Immersion blender

8 tablespoons (1 stick/
    113 grams) unsalted butter

1 cup heavy cream

1½ cups whole milk

½ cup plus 2 tablespoons
    (125 grams) sugar

½ teaspoon (2 grams)
    kosher salt

8 large egg yolks

½ cup (64 grams) chopped
    raw pecans

1. In a medium skillet or saucepan, melt the butter over medium heat. Continue to heat the butter until it turns chestnut brown and smells nutty, about 4 minutes. Remove from the heat and set aside.

2. Pour the cream and milk into a double boiler or a heatproof bowl set over a saucepan of gently simmering water (the bottom of the bowl should not touch the water). Whisk in ½ cup (100 grams) of the sugar, the salt, and the browned butter and stir until the sugar and salt have dissolved. Warm the mixture until you see steam rising from the top.

3. Meanwhile, prepare an ice bath in a large bowl and set another bowl over it. Set aside.

4. In a medium bowl, with a kitchen towel underneath it to prevent slipping, whisk together the egg yolks with the remaining 2 tablespoons (25 grams) sugar until uniform. While whisking, add a splash of the hot dairy mixture to the yolks. Continue to add the dairy mixture, whisking it in bit by bit, until you've added about half. Add the yolk mixture to the remaining dairy mixture in the double boiler. Set the heat under the double boiler to medium and cook the custard, stirring continuously with a wooden spoon and reducing the heat to medium-low as necessary, until steam begins to rise from the surface and the custard thickens enough to coat the back of the spoon. Hold the spoon horizontally and run your finger through the custard. If the trail left by your finger stays separated, the custard is ready to be cooled.

5. Strain the custard into the bowl sitting over the prepared ice bath, and, using an immersion blender, buzz the liquid until the mixture is emulsified. Stir for 3 to 5 minutes, or until the custard has cooled. Transfer the custard to a quart-size container, cover, and refrigerate for at least 4 hours or, preferably, overnight.

6. Pour the chilled custard into an ice cream maker and freeze according to the manufacturer's instructions. Place the container in

which you refrigerated the custard in the freezer so you can use it to store the finished ice cream. Churn the ice cream until the texture resembles "soft serve." In the last minute of churning, add the pecans and churn for 1 minute to incorporate. Transfer the ice cream to the chilled storage container and freeze until hardened to your desired consistency. Alternatively, you can serve it immediately—it will be the consistency of gelato. The ice cream will keep, frozen, for up to 7 days.

ben's note We were quite surprised, when we looked at the back of our butter carton, that there were more ingredients listed than just cream. Something mysteriously called "flavoring" is also added. We recommend seeking out a high-quality butter in which the only ingredient is cream. It will likely be made with cream from grass-fed cows and have delicious flavor without additives.

GOAT CHEESE WITH BLACKBERRY-RED CURRANT COMPOTE ICE CREAM

You might be surprised to find that goat cheese makes ice cream taste just like an incredible, creamy cheesecake. It's also a perfect complement to the tart blackberry-red currant compote. Our favorite is the fresh goat cheese from Sprout Creek Farm in Poughkeepsie, New York, and it doesn't hurt that the farm has the cutest goats we've ever seen! This seasonal flavor shines the most during spring and summer when goats have access to green pastures making fresh goat cheese more flavorful.

MAKES ABOUT 1 QUART

1½ cups heavy cream

2 cups whole milk

½ cup plus 2 tablespoons (125 grams) sugar

¼ teaspoon (1 gram) kosher salt

⅛ teaspoon ground nutmeg

6 large egg yolks

6 ounces (170 grams) fresh goat cheese

1 cup Blackberry-Red Currant Compote (page 198)

1. Pour the cream and milk into a double boiler or a heatproof bowl set over a saucepan of simmering water (the bottom of the bowl should not touch the water). Whisk in ½ cup (100 grams) of the sugar, the salt, and the nutmeg, and stir until the sugar and salt have dissolved. Warm the mixture until you see steam rising from the top.

2. Meanwhile, prepare an ice bath in a large bowl and set another bowl over it. Set aside.

3. In a medium bowl, with a kitchen towel underneath it to prevent slipping, whisk together the egg yolks with the remaining 2 tablespoons (25 grams) sugar until uniform. While whisking, add a splash of the hot dairy mixture to the yolks. Continue to add the dairy mixture, whisking it in bit by bit, until you've added about half. Add the yolk mixture to the remaining dairy mixture in the double boiler. Set the heat under the double boiler to medium and cook the custard, stirring continuously with a wooden spoon and reducing the heat to medium-low as necessary, until steam begins to rise from the surface and the custard thickens enough to coat the back of the spoon. Hold the spoon horizontally and run your finger through the custard. If the trail left by your finger stays separated, the custard is ready to be cooled.

4. Strain the custard into the bowl sitting over the prepared ice bath and whisk in the goat cheese. Using an immersion blender, buzz the custard until the mixture is combined and the custard is uniform. Stir for 3 to 5 minutes, or until the custard has cooled. Transfer the custard to a quart-size container, cover, and refrigerate for at least 4 hours or, preferably, overnight.

5. Pour the chilled custard into an ice cream maker and freeze according to the manufacturer's instructions. Place the container in which you refrigerated the custard in the freezer so you can use it to store the finished ice cream. Churn the ice cream until the texture resembles "soft serve." During the last minute of churning, fold in the blackberry-red currant compote until combined. Transfer the ice cream to the chilled storage container and freeze until hardened to your desired consistency. Alternatively, you can serve it immediately—it will be the consistency of gelato. The ice cream will keep, frozen, for up to 7 days.

CURRANTS AND CREAM ICE CREAM

In our quest to source only the very best ingredients, sometimes we have to search the globe for the very best flavors: Vanilla, chocolate, and pistachios are all ingredients that are imported to the United States. With certain ingredients, however, local is best, as is the case with our red currants.

Hudson Valley is home to some of the best berries, and we were lucky to find a farm that grew enough beautiful red currants for us to use in our ice cream. Ben's friend Sarah spent some time in Scandinavia, where red currants are prominent in cooking, and suggested we use them in our ice cream. We loved the idea of highlighting these tart berries in sweet custard, and the resulting ice cream is one of our, and our customers', favorites, especially in the summertime.

MAKES ABOUT 1 QUART

FOR THE RED CURRANT COMPOTE

2 cups (400 grams) red currants

½ cup plus 2 tablespoons (125 grams) sugar

Pinch of kosher salt

FOR THE ICE CREAM BASE

2 cups heavy cream

½ cup whole milk

½ cup plus 2 tablespoons (125 grams) sugar

¼ teaspoon (1 gram) kosher salt

6 large egg yolks

1. To make the red currant compote, in a nonreactive bowl, combine the currants, sugar, and salt and let stand at room temperature for at least 2 hours. Strain into a bowl and measure out 1 cup of the syrup from the bowl; set aside (reserve any remaining syrup for another use). Transfer the berries to a separate bowl and set aside as well.

2. To make the currants and cream ice cream, pour the cream and milk into a double boiler or a heatproof bowl set over a saucepan of simmering water (the bottom of the bowl should not touch the water). Whisk in ½ cup (100 grams) of the sugar and the salt and stir until they have dissolved. Warm the mixture until you see steam rising from the top.

3. Meanwhile, prepare an ice bath in a large bowl and set another bowl over it. Set aside.

4. In a medium bowl, with a kitchen towel underneath it to prevent slipping, whisk together the egg yolks with the remaining 2 tablespoons (25 grams) sugar until uniform. While whisking, add a splash of the hot dairy mixture to the yolks. Continue to add the dairy mixture, whisking it in bit by bit, until you've added about half. Add the yolk mixture to the remaining dairy mixture in the double boiler. Set the heat under the double boiler to medium and cook the custard, stirring continuously and reducing the heat to medium-low as necessary, until steam begins to rise from the surface and the custard thickens enough to coat the back of the spoon. Hold the spoon horizontally and run your finger through the custard. If the trail left by your finger stays separated, the custard is ready to be cooled.

5. Strain the custard into the bowl sitting over the prepared ice bath and stir for 3 to 5 minutes, or until the custard has cooled. Stir in the reserved 1 cup currant syrup until incorporated. Transfer the custard to a quart-size container, cover, and refrigerate for at least 4 hours or, preferably, overnight.

6. Pour the chilled custard into an ice cream maker and freeze according to the manufacturer's instructions. Place the container in

which you refrigerated the custard in the freezer so you can use it to store the finished ice cream. Churn the ice cream until the texture resembles "soft serve." Add all of the reserved currants, and churn for about 30 seconds, until just combined. Transfer the ice cream to the chilled storage container and freeze until hardened to your desired consistency. Alternatively, you can serve it immediately—it will be the consistency of gelato. The ice cream will keep, frozen, for up to 7 days.

CHERRY CHEESECAKE ICE CREAM

We love a good, New York-style cheesecake: luxurious, creamy, and redolent of cherries. In this recipe, we throw in some boozy cherries to complement the creaminess of the ice cream base. In our stores we use *Griottines*, cherries macerated in eau-de-vie or kirsch, but you can just as successfully use morello cherries or any brandied cherries you have on hand. If you've never made brandied cherries, we can't recommend it enough; it's easy and so satisfying to have a batch of your own in the fridge. You'll have brandied cherries left over—a high-quality problem to have. Fold them into ice cream, tuck them into bread pudding, or add them to a much-needed old-fashioned at the end of the week. If you choose not to make your own brandied cherries, substitute ½ cup store-bought brandied cherries—drain them, reserving the liquid, and chop before adding to the ice cream as directed.

MAKES ABOUT 1 QUART

SPECIAL EQUIPMENT
Immersion blender

FOR THE BRANDIED CHERRIES

½ cup (100 grams) sugar

¼ plump vanilla bean, split lengthwise and seeds scraped out

Generous pinch of freshly grated nutmeg

Pinch of ground cinnamon

Pinch of kosher salt

½ cup cherry juice or water (see Ben's Note)

1 cup kirsch or brandy

1 pound (454 grams) cherries, stemmed and pitted, if you like

FOR THE CHERRY CHEESECAKE ICE CREAM

1½ cups heavy cream

2 cups plus 2 tablespoons whole milk

½ cup (100 grams) sugar

1. To make the brandied cherries, in a medium saucepan, combine the sugar, vanilla bean seeds and pod, nutmeg, cinnamon, salt, and cherry juice. Bring the liquid to a low simmer over medium heat, then reduce the heat to low and cook, stirring, until the sugar has fully dissolved. Let simmer for 5 minutes. Remove from the heat and stir in the kirsch followed by the cherries. Transfer the cherries and their liquid to canning jars. Let cool to room temperature, then seal the jars and refrigerate for at least 48 hours (these cherries may be stored in the fridge for several months) before using.

2. To make the cherry cheesecake ice cream, pour the cream and milk into a double boiler or a heatproof bowl set over a saucepan of gently simmering water (the bottom of the bowl should not touch the water). Whisk in the sugar and the salt and stir until they have dissolved. Warm the mixture until you see steam rising from the top.

3. Meanwhile, prepare an ice bath in a large bowl. Set aside.

4. In a medium bowl, with a kitchen towel underneath it to prevent slipping, whisk together the egg yolks until uniform. While whisking, add a splash of the hot dairy mixture to the yolks. Continue to add the dairy mixture, whisking it in bit by bit, until you've added about half. Add the yolk mixture to the remaining dairy mixture in the double boiler. Set the heat under the double boiler to medium and cook the custard, stirring continuously with a wooden spoon and reducing the heat to medium-low as necessary, until steam begins to rise from the surface and the custard thickens enough to coat the back of the spoon. Hold the spoon horizontally and run your finger through the custard. If the trail left by your finger stays separated, the custard is ready to be cooled.

¼ teaspoon (1 gram) kosher
  salt

6 large egg yolks

½ cup cream cheese

½ teaspoon pure vanilla
  extract

. . . .

*It might seem annoying
that we give you such odd
measurements, like "2
cups and 2 tablespoons."
But having tested and
retested small batches
of these ice creams, we
found certain measure-
ments consistently give
just about the perfect
ice cream. And while it
seems like a pain to add
another 2 tablespoons of
milk to your liquids, it's a
small step to take to get
your ice cream from a bit
too "chewy" to perfectly
toothsome. We hope you
agree.*

. . . .

5. Strain the custard into a bowl and add in the cream cheese and vanilla, stirring until the cream cheese has melted. Using an immersion blender, buzz the custard until emulsified. Place the bowl over the prepared ice bath and stir for 3 to 5 minutes, or until the custard has cooled. Transfer the custard to a quart-size container, cover, and refrigerate for at least 4 hours or, preferably, overnight.

6. Meanwhile, measure out ½ cup of the brandied cherries with their liquid. Drain the cherries, reserving the liquid, and chop them. Set aside the chopped cherries and the liquid separately.

7. Pour the chilled custard into an ice cream maker and freeze according to the manufacturer's instructions. Place the container in which you refrigerated the custard in the freezer so you can use it to store the finished ice cream. Churn the ice cream until the texture resembles "soft serve." In the last minute of churning, add the reserved ½ cup chopped cherries and churn for 1 minute to incorporate. Transfer the ice cream to the chilled storage container and freeze until hardened to your desired consistency. Alternatively, you can serve it immediately—it will be the consistency of gelato.

8. In a small saucepan, bring ½ cup of the cherry liquid to a simmer over medium heat and cook until reduced and thickened, 4 to 5 minutes. Remove from the heat and let cool to room temperature. Drizzle the syrup over the ice cream before serving. The ice cream will keep, frozen, for up to 7 days.

ben's note *When you pit cherries (or defrost frozen cherries), you wind up with some cherry juice as a result. Instead of discarding it, you should use it for these brandied cherries—it will give more of that cherry flavor to the final product. Whatever you lack in juice, you can make up with water.*

SOUR CREAM WITH BLUEBERRY SWIRL ICE CREAM

For quite some time, Ben has been keen on trying to make ice cream using sour cream, and when we started working on this book and were discussing the recipes we wanted to include, sour cream was at the top of the list as an ingredient we wanted to work with. Our coauthor, Olga, who is Russian and loves all things sour cream, couldn't agree more.

Sour cream is created by introducing cream to certain kinds of lactic bacteria and allowing the cream to "sour," or ferment. Often, sour cream is confused with its fattier cousin, crème fraîche, but unlike sour cream, crème fraîche doesn't curdle when you cook with it, thanks to its higher fat content, and sour cream is tangier on your palate than crème fraîche is. It's that second quality that made us think of sour cream as a flavoring for ice cream. We complement the sour cream by adding a swirl of homemade blueberry compote at the end.

MAKES ABOUT 1 QUART

SPECIAL EQUIPMENT
Immersion blender

FOR THE BLUEBERRY COMPOTE

½ cup fresh or frozen blueberries

2 tablespoons (25 grams) sugar

A drop or two of fresh lemon juice

FOR THE SOUR CREAM ICE CREAM

1½ cups heavy cream

2 tablespoons whole milk

½ cup plus 2 tablespoons (125 grams) sugar

¼ teaspoon (1 gram) kosher salt

8 large egg yolks

1½ cups sour cream

1. To make the blueberry compote, in a small saucepan, combine the blueberries, sugar, and lemon juice and bring to a gentle simmer over medium heat. Cook the berries until they slump and the syrup thickens, 5 to 7 minutes. (If you are using frozen berries, this process could take a bit longer, since the berries start out with more moisture.) Remove from the heat and set aside to cool to room temperature. Transfer to an airtight container and refrigerate until ready to use.

2. To make the sour cream ice cream, pour the cream and milk into a double boiler or a heatproof bowl set over a saucepan of simmering water (the bottom of the bowl should not touch the water). Whisk in ½ cup (100 grams) of the sugar and the salt and stir until they have dissolved. Warm the mixture until you see steam rising from the top.

3. Meanwhile, prepare an ice bath in a large bowl. Set aside.

4. In a medium bowl, with a kitchen towel underneath it to prevent slipping, whisk together the egg yolks with the remaining 2 tablespoons (25 grams) sugar until uniform. While whisking, add a splash of the hot dairy mixture to the yolks. Continue to add the dairy mixture, whisking it in bit by bit, until you've added about half. Add the yolk mixture to the remaining dairy mixture in the double boiler. Set the heat under the double boiler to medium and cook the custard, stirring continuously with a wooden spoon and reducing the heat to medium-low as necessary, until steam begins to rise from the surface and the custard thickens enough to coat the back of the spoon. Hold the spoon horizontally and run your finger through the custard. If the trail left by your finger stays separated, the custard is ready to be cooled.

5. Strain the custard into a bowl and stir in the sour cream until incorporated. Using an immersion blender, buzz the mixture until

emulsified. Place the bowl over the prepared ice bath and stir for 3 to 5 minutes, or until the custard has cooled. Transfer the custard to a quart-size container, cover, and refrigerate for at least 4 hours or, preferably, overnight.

6. Pour the chilled custard into an ice cream maker and freeze according to the manufacturer's instructions. Place the container in which you refrigerated the custard in the freezer so you can use it to store the finished ice cream. Churn the ice cream until the texture resembles "soft serve." Fold in the blueberry compote until there are pockets of plain ice cream and ripples of blueberry swirl. Transfer the ice cream to the chilled storage container and freeze until hardened to your desired consistency. Alternatively, you can serve it immediately—it will be the consistency of gelato. The ice cream will keep, frozen, for up to 7 days.

ben's note Most industrially produced sour cream will contain thickening agents: guar, rennet, carrageenan—even gelatin! Real sour cream, which contains only cream and lactic bacteria, shouldn't have any of those things; we urge you to seek out the best-quality sour cream you can find—it will make a great difference in your ice cream.

CASSATA SICILIANA ICE CREAM

Cassata siciliana is a cakelike dessert from Palermo, Sicily, that often contains dried fruit, nuts, and chocolate chips. There are as many variations of it as there are cooks who make it, but two of the key ingredients are fresh ricotta and candied citrus peel. Sheep's milk ricotta is ideal to use for this recipe, but fresh cow's milk ricotta is also fine, as it's more readily available (just make sure you're using fresh ricotta and not the stuff that comes in a plastic pint-size container). Making your own fresh ricotta is also fast and easy—and it's nice to have what's left over to spread on toast or to top your pasta.

MAKES ABOUT 1 QUART

FOR THE FRESH RICOTTA

2 cups whole milk

¾ cup heavy cream

¼ teaspoon (1 gram) kosher salt

1½ tablespoons fresh lemon juice

FOR THE CASSATA SICILIANA ICE CREAM

2 cups heavy cream

½ cup whole milk

½ cup plus 2 tablespoons (125 grams) sugar

½ teaspoon (2 grams) kosher salt

6 large egg yolks

2 tablespoons fresh orange juice

2 tablespoons fresh lemon juice

Candied lemon, orange, or grapefruit peel (see page 199), left whole or chopped

1. To make the fresh ricotta, combine the milk, cream, and salt in a medium nonreactive saucepan. Clip a candy thermometer to the pan, and heat the milk over medium heat, stirring occasionally, until it reaches 190°F. Remove from the heat, add the lemon juice, and gently stir once or twice. Let the pan sit, undisturbed, for 5 minutes.

2. Line a large strainer with several layers of cheesecloth and place it over a large bowl. Pour the curds and whey into the colander and let the curds strain for at least 1 hour. Depending on the age of your milk and cream, the curds might be looser or tighter, which will affect your ricotta. Let the ricotta drain until it's the consistency of mascarpone cheese. Transfer the ricotta from the cheesecloth to a container, cover, and refrigerate until needed. You will have about 1½ cups ricotta; set aside 1 cup to be used in this recipe and reserve the remainder for another use. Fresh ricotta will keep, refrigerated, for up to 1 week.

3. To make the cassata siciliana ice cream, pour the cream and milk into a double boiler or a heatproof bowl set over a saucepan of gently simmering water (the bottom of the bowl should not touch the water). Whisk in ½ cup (100 grams) of the sugar and the salt and stir until they have dissolved. Warm the mixture until you see steam rising from the top.

4. Meanwhile, prepare an ice bath in a large bowl and set another bowl over it. Set aside.

5. In a medium bowl, with a kitchen towel underneath it to prevent slipping, whisk together the egg yolks with the remaining 2 tablespoons (25 grams) sugar until uniform. While whisking, add a splash of the hot dairy mixture to the yolks. Continue to add the dairy mixture, whisking it in bit by bit, until you've added about half. Add the yolk mixture to the remaining dairy mixture in the double boiler. Set the heat under the double boiler to medium and cook the custard, stirring continuously with a wooden spoon and reducing the heat to medium-low as necessary, until steam begins to rise from the surface and the custard thickens enough

to coat the back of the spoon. Hold the spoon horizontally and run your finger through the custard. If the trail left by your finger stays separated, the custard is ready to be cooled.

6. Strain the custard into the bowl sitting over the prepared ice bath and stir for 3 to 5 minutes, or until the custard has cooled. Stir in the reserved 1 cup fresh ricotta, the orange juice, and the lemon juice. Transfer the custard to a quart-size container, cover, and refrigerate for at least 4 hours or, preferably, overnight.

7. Pour the chilled custard into an ice cream maker and freeze according to the manufacturer's instructions. Place the container in which you refrigerated the custard in the freezer so you can use it to store the finished ice cream. Churn the ice cream until the texture resembles "soft serve." Transfer the ice cream to the chilled storage container and freeze until hardened to your desired consistency. Alternatively, you can serve it immediately—it will be the consistency of gelato. Serve, garnished with candied citrus peels. The ice cream will keep, frozen, for up to 7 days.

EGGNOG ICE CREAM

As you would expect, in the winter, with its snowbanks and subfreezing temperatures, sales of our ice cream decline as fewer people are craving anything cold, never mind frozen. We get it—although if left to our own devices, we can, and do, eat ice cream year-round.

To make ice cream sound more enticing during the colder months, we create seasonally driven, limited-edition batches to mark the holiday season: Pumpkin (page 103) and Apple Crumble with Calvados and Crème Fraîche (page 69) for Thanksgiving and this Eggnog Ice Cream for Christmas. Grinding all the spices fresh makes this ice cream truly shine. Because the cold dulls flavors a bit, you want the freshest spices ground right before you need them for the biggest flavor impact.

MAKES ABOUT 1 QUART

2 cups heavy cream

1 cup whole milk

1/2 cup plus 2 tablespoons (125 grams) sugar

2 teaspoons freshly grated nutmeg

1/2 teaspoon freshly ground Sichuan pepper

1/4 teaspoon freshly ground allspice

1/2 plump vanilla bean, split lengthwise and seeds scraped out

3/4 teaspoon (3 grams) kosher salt

8 large egg yolks

2 tablespoons rum, bourbon, or regular or apple brandy

1. Pour the cream and milk into a double boiler or a heatproof bowl set over a saucepan of gently simmering water (the bottom of the bowl should not touch the water). Whisk in 1/2 cup (100 grams) of the sugar, the nutmeg, pepper, allspice, vanilla bean seeds and pod, and salt and stir until the sugar and salt have dissolved. Warm the mixture until you see steam rising from the top. Remove the vanilla bean pod (see page 34 for ideas on what you can do with it).

2. Meanwhile, prepare an ice bath in a large bowl and set another bowl over it. Set aside.

3. In a medium bowl, with a kitchen towel underneath it to prevent slipping, whisk together the egg yolks with the remaining 2 tablespoons (25 grams) sugar until uniform. While whisking, add a splash of the hot dairy mixture to the yolks. Continue to add the dairy mixture, whisking it in bit by bit, until you've added about half. Add the yolk mixture to the remaining dairy mixture in the double boiler. Set the heat under the double boiler to medium and cook the custard, stirring continuously with a wooden spoon and reducing the heat to medium-low as necessary, until steam begins to rise from the surface and the custard thickens enough to coat the back of the spoon. Hold the spoon horizontally and run your finger through the custard. If the trail left by your finger stays separated, the custard is ready to be cooled.

4. Strain the custard into the bowl sitting over the prepared ice bath and add the rum. Stir for 3 to 5 minutes, or until the custard has cooled. Transfer the custard to a quart-size container, cover, and refrigerate for at least 4 hours or, preferably, overnight.

5. Pour the chilled custard into an ice cream maker and freeze according to the manufacturer's instructions. Place the container in which you refrigerated the custard in the freezer so you can use it to store the finished ice cream. Churn the ice cream until the texture resembles "soft serve." Transfer the ice cream to the chilled storage container and freeze until hardened to your desired consistency. Alternatively, you can serve it immediately—it will be the consistency of gelato. The ice cream will keep, frozen, for up to 7 days.

STOUT ICE CREAM

Beer ice cream can be tricky. You are adding a lot of liquid (and no fat), so you need to make sure the ice cream doesn't end up icy. We use a lot of egg yolks and all heavy cream (no milk) to get a smooth and full body. Besides eating it, our other favorite thing to do with stout ice cream is to add it to root beer floats.

You'll notice that this ice cream has no chocolate, a traditional pairing for stout. Too often, we feel, stout is paired with chocolate—not a bad idea overall, but the stout's wonderful, malty flavor tastes muddled, and we like the idea of letting the stout taste shine on its own in this grown-up ice cream flavor.

MAKES ABOUT 1 QUART

2 cups heavy cream

½ cup plus 2 tablespoons (125 grams) sugar

¼ teaspoon (1 gram) kosher salt

8 large egg yolks

1 cup stout beer, such as Guinness

1. Pour the cream into a double boiler or a heatproof bowl set over a saucepan of gently simmering water (the bottom of the bowl should not touch the water). Whisk in ½ cup (100 grams) of the sugar and the salt and stir until they have dissolved. Warm the mixture until you see steam rising from the top.

2. Meanwhile, prepare an ice bath in a large bowl and set another bowl over it. Set aside.

3. In a medium bowl, with a kitchen towel underneath it to prevent slipping, whisk together the egg yolks with the remaining 2 tablespoons (25 grams) sugar until uniform. While whisking, add a splash of the hot dairy mixture to the yolks. Continue to add the dairy mixture, whisking it in bit by bit, until you've added about half. Add the yolk mixture to the remaining dairy mixture in the double boiler. Set the heat under the double boiler to medium and cook the custard, stirring continuously with a wooden spoon and reducing the heat to medium-low as necessary, until steam begins to rise from the surface and the custard thickens enough to coat the back of the spoon. Hold the spoon horizontally and run your finger through the custard. If the trail left by your finger stays separated, the custard is ready to be cooled.

4. Strain the custard into the bowl sitting over the prepared ice bath and stir in the stout; stir for 3 to 5 minutes, or until the custard has cooled. Transfer the custard to a quart-size container, cover, and refrigerate for at least 4 hours or, preferably, overnight.

5. Pour the chilled custard into an ice cream maker and freeze according to the manufacturer's instructions. Place the container in which you refrigerated the custard in the freezer so you can use it to store the finished ice cream. Churn the ice cream until the texture resembles "soft serve." Transfer the ice cream to the chilled storage container and freeze until hardened to your desired consistency. Alternatively, you can serve it immediately—it will be the consistency of gelato. The ice cream will keep, frozen, for up to 7 days.

PUMPKIN ICE CREAM

We tried all these organic pumpkin purees; we tried *making* our own pumpkin puree—and in the end, we realized that the most consistent product for pumpkin pie, and pumpkin pie ice cream, was Libby's canned pumpkin. With perfect texture and the right amount of moisture, it's such a consistent product that you're guaranteed a predictable outcome with your pie, pumpkin bread, or ice cream—which goes a long way, especially when you are making large batches over and over.

While pumpkin pie is one of our favorite desserts, we didn't like how it translated to ice cream— it tasted overwhelmingly sweet. After playing around with the recipe, we decided to remove all but a trace of the spices and let the pumpkin speak for itself. We loved the elegant, clean fall flavor and are so happy to share it with you.

MAKES ABOUT 1 QUART

2 cups heavy cream

½ cup whole milk

¾ cup (150 grams) sugar

½ teaspoon (2 grams) kosher salt

⅛ teaspoon ground cinnamon

⅛ teaspoon freshly grated nutmeg

6 large egg yolks

⅔ cup (160 grams) canned pure pumpkin puree

1. Pour the cream and milk into a double boiler or a heatproof bowl set over a saucepan of gently simmering water (the bottom of the bowl should not touch the water). Whisk in ½ cup (100 grams) of the sugar, the salt, cinnamon, and nutmeg, and stir until the sugar and salt have dissolved. Warm the mixture until you see steam rising from the top.

2. Meanwhile, prepare an ice bath in a large bowl and set another bowl over it. Set aside.

3. In a medium bowl, with a kitchen towel underneath it to prevent slipping, whisk together the egg yolks with the remaining ¼ cup (50 grams) sugar until uniform. While whisking, add a splash of the hot dairy mixture to the yolks. Continue to add the dairy mixture, whisking it in bit by bit, until you've added about half. Add the yolk mixture to the remaining dairy mixture in the double boiler. Set the heat under the double boiler to medium and cook the custard, stirring continuously with a wooden spoon and reducing the heat to medium-low as necessary, until steam begins to rise from the surface and the custard thickens enough to coat the back of the spoon. Hold the spoon horizontally and run your finger through the custard. If the trail left by your finger stays separated, the custard is ready to be cooled.

4. Strain the custard into the bowl sitting over the prepared ice bath; stir in the pumpkin until the custard is uniform. Stir for 3 to 5 minutes more, or until the custard has cooled. Transfer the custard to a quart-size container, cover, and refrigerate for at least 4 hours or, preferably, overnight.

5. Pour the chilled custard into an ice cream maker and freeze according to the manufacturer's instructions. Place the container in which you refrigerated the custard in the freezer so you can use it to store the finished ice cream. Churn the ice cream until the texture resembles "soft serve." Transfer the ice cream to the chilled storage container and freeze until hardened to your desired consistency. Alternatively, you can serve it immediately—it will be the consistency of gelato. The ice cream will keep, frozen, for up to 7 days.

SWEET CORN ICE CREAM

We first made this ice cream one summer for the New Amsterdam Market in New York City. And we did it again for a Taste Talks event, a three-day food festival celebrating artisans and innovators in the food community, with Dan Barber, the chef of Blue Hill at Stone Barns restaurant and one of the preeminent forces behind the local and seasonal food movement. It's important that you use excellent, in-season corn. Taste a kernel of the corn beforehand to see if the corn is truly sweet.

MAKES ABOUT 1 QUART

4 ears fresh corn, husked

2 cups heavy cream

½ cup whole milk

¾ cup (150 grams) sugar

¼ teaspoon (1 gram) kosher salt

6 large egg yolks

1. Slice the kernels off the cobs; you should have about 2 cups kernels. Set the kernels aside; break each corncob in half. Pour the cream and milk into a double boiler or a heatproof bowl set over a saucepan of gently simmering water (the bottom of the bowl should not touch the water). Add the corncobs; whisk in ½ cup (100 grams) of the sugar and the salt and stir until they have dissolved. Warm the mixture until you see steam rising from the top.

2. Meanwhile, prepare an ice bath in a large bowl and set another bowl over it. Set aside.

3. In a medium bowl, with a kitchen towel underneath it to prevent slipping, whisk together the egg yolks with the remaining ¼ cup (50 grams) sugar until uniform. While whisking, add a splash of the hot dairy mixture to the yolks. Continue to add the dairy mixture, whisking it in bit by bit, until you've added about half. Add the yolk mixture to the remaining dairy mixture in the double boiler. Set the heat under the double boiler to medium and cook the custard, stirring continuously with a wooden spoon and reducing the heat to medium-low as necessary, until steam begins to rise from the surface and the custard thickens enough to coat the back of the spoon. Hold the spoon horizontally and run your finger through the custard. If the trail left by your finger stays separated, the custard is ready to be cooled. Remove and discard the corncobs and transfer the custard to a blender. Add the reserved kernels and process until smooth.

4. Strain the custard into the bowl sitting over the prepared ice bath and stir for 3 to 5 minutes, or until the custard has cooled. Transfer the custard to a quart-size container, cover, and refrigerate for at least 4 hours or, preferably, overnight.

5. Pour the chilled custard into an ice cream maker and freeze according to the manufacturer's instructions. Place the container in which you refrigerated the custard in the freezer so you can use it to store the finished ice cream. Churn the ice cream until the texture resembles "soft serve." Transfer the ice cream to the chilled storage container and freeze until hardened to your desired consistency. Alternatively, you can serve it immediately—it will be the consistency of gelato. The ice cream will keep, frozen, for up to 7 days.

TARRAGON ICE CREAM

Tarragon, one of Ben's favorite herbs, is woefully underused in American kitchens. Its mild anise flavor yields an elegant ice cream, which can stand on its own as well as complement a fruit-focused dessert. Instead of just infusing the base with tarragon, we blend it into the custard for a deeper flavor and a beautiful green color. In general, herb- and tea-infused ice creams are a good place to experiment with flavors—you don't have to fiddle around with fat percentages, since tarragon doesn't increase the overall mass much, and the adjustments can be fairly minor.

MAKES ABOUT 1 QUART

2 cups heavy cream

1 cup whole milk

½ cup plus 2 tablespoons (125 grams) sugar

¼ teaspoon (1 gram) kosher salt

6 large egg yolks

⅓ cup generously packed fresh tarragon leaves

1. Pour the cream and milk into a double boiler or a heatproof bowl set over a saucepan of gently simmering water (the bottom of the bowl should not touch the water). Whisk in ½ cup (100 grams) of the sugar and the salt and stir until they have dissolved. Warm the mixture until you see steam rising from the top.

2. Meanwhile, prepare an ice bath in a large bowl and set another bowl over it. Set aside.

3. In a medium bowl, with a kitchen towel underneath it to prevent slipping, whisk together the egg yolks with the remaining 2 tablespoons (25 grams) sugar until uniform. While whisking, add a splash of the hot dairy mixture to the yolks. Continue to add the dairy mixture, whisking it in bit by bit, until you've added about half. Add the yolk mixture to the remaining dairy mixture in the double boiler. Set the heat under the double boiler to medium and cook the custard, stirring continuously with a wooden spoon and reducing the heat to medium-low as necessary, until steam begins to rise from the surface and the custard thickens enough to coat the back of the spoon. Hold the spoon horizontally and run your finger through the custard. If the trail left by your finger stays separated, the custard is ready to be cooled.

4. Strain the custard into the bowl sitting over the prepared ice bath and stir for 3 to 5 minutes, or until the custard has cooled. Transfer the cooled custard to a blender and add the tarragon; blend until completely uniform. (If the custard has tiny green flecks, that's okay—it will make for prettier ice cream.) Transfer the custard to a quart-size container, cover, and refrigerate for at least 4 hours or, preferably, overnight.

5. Pour the chilled custard into an ice cream maker and freeze according to the manufacturer's instructions. Place the container in which you refrigerated the custard in the freezer so you can use it to store the finished ice cream. Churn the ice cream until the texture resembles "soft serve." Transfer the ice cream to the chilled storage container and freeze until hardened to your desired consistency. Alternatively, you can serve it immediately—it will be the consistency of gelato. The ice cream will keep, frozen, for up to 7 days.

OLIVE OIL ICE CREAM

Olive oil ice cream might sound exotic in the States, but it's pretty commonplace in Italy. If you think olive oil doesn't belong in ice cream, we beg you to reconsider. Olive oil lends a subtle savory note to sweet custard, creating a gentle, pleasing contrast on the palate—the sweet and the savory playing against each other simultaneously. For this ice cream, we like to use a peppery olive oil from Sicily, but if you're looking for olive oil with more floral, fruity notes, consider oils from Liguria, Tuscany, or Spain. Serve this ice cream topped with a tiny drizzle of olive oil and a pinch or two of flaky sea salt.

MAKES ABOUT 1 QUART

SPECIAL EQUIPMENT
Immersion blender

1¼ cups heavy cream

1½ cups plus 2 tablespoons whole milk

½ cup plus 2 tablespoons (125 grams) sugar

¼ teaspoon (1 gram) kosher salt

8 large egg yolks

½ cup extra-virgin olive oil, plus more for serving (optional)

Flaky sea salt, such as Maldon (optional)

ben's note When making this ice cream, we recommend you go with your finest olive oil, the kind you reserve for dressings and finishing a dish. Boring olive oil will guarantee boring ice cream.

1. Pour the cream and milk into a double boiler or a heatproof bowl set over a saucepan of gently simmering water (the bottom of the bowl should not touch the water). Whisk in ½ cup (100 grams) of the sugar and the salt and stir until they have dissolved. Warm the mixture until you see steam rising from the top.

2. Meanwhile, prepare an ice bath in a large bowl. Set aside.

3. In a medium bowl, with a kitchen towel underneath it to prevent slipping, whisk together the egg yolks with the remaining 2 tablespoons (25 grams) sugar until uniform. While whisking, add a splash of the hot dairy mixture to the yolks. Continue to add the dairy mixture, whisking it in bit by bit, until you've added about half. Add the yolk mixture to the remaining dairy mixture in the double boiler. Set the heat under the double boiler to medium and cook the custard, stirring continuously with a wooden spoon and reducing the heat to medium-low as necessary, until steam begins to rise from the surface and the custard thickens enough to coat the back of the spoon. Hold the spoon horizontally and run your finger through the custard. If the trail left by your finger stays separated, the custard is ready to be cooled.

4. Strain the custard into a bowl and stir in the ½ cup of olive oil. Using an immersion blender, buzz the custard until emulsified. Set the bowl over the prepared ice bath and stir for 3 to 5 minutes, or until the custard has cooled. Transfer the custard to a quart-size container, cover, and refrigerate for at least 4 hours or, preferably, overnight.

5. Pour the chilled custard into an ice cream maker and freeze according to the manufacturer's instructions. Place the container in which you refrigerated the custard in the freezer so you can use it to store the finished ice cream. Churn the ice cream until the texture resembles "soft serve." Transfer the ice cream to the chilled storage container and freeze until hardened to your desired consistency. Alternatively, you can serve it immediately—it will be the consistency of gelato. If you like, serve the ice cream topped with a drizzle of olive oil and a few flakes of sea salt. The ice cream will keep, frozen, for up to 7 days.

COCONUT ICE CREAM

Coconut is a perfect vehicle for ice cream because it's naturally fatty, and fat gives ice cream its structure and body. We use a blend of heavy cream and coconut milk, and we amp up the coconut flavor by adding some shredded, sweetened dried coconut. If you can't find the desiccated kind with just sugar (most sweetened coconut is wet and sticky), use unsweetened coconut chips—they'll work much better than the sticky, wet, shredded sweetened coconut sold at most supermarkets.

MAKES ABOUT 1 QUART

1½ cups heavy cream

1½ cups coconut milk, preferably organic and without stabilizers

½ cup plus 2 tablespoons (125 grams) sugar

½ cup finely shredded desiccated sweetened coconut

½ teaspoon (2 grams) kosher salt

8 large egg yolks

1. Pour the cream and coconut milk into a double boiler or a heat-proof bowl set over a saucepan of simmering water (the bottom of the bowl should not touch the water). Whisk in ½ cup (100 grams) of the sugar, the shredded coconut, and the salt, and stir until the sugar and salt have dissolved. Warm the mixture until you see steam rising from the top.

2. Meanwhile, prepare an ice bath in a large bowl and set another bowl over it. Set aside.

3. In a medium bowl, with a kitchen towel underneath it to prevent slipping, whisk together the egg yolks with the remaining 2 tablespoons (25 grams) sugar until uniform. While whisking, add a splash of the hot dairy mixture to the yolks. Continue to add the dairy mixture, whisking it in bit by bit, until you've added about half. Add the yolk mixture to the remaining dairy mixture in the double boiler. Set the heat under the double boiler to medium and cook the custard, stirring continuously with a wooden spoon and reducing the heat to medium-low as necessary, until steam begins to rise from the surface and the custard thickens enough to coat the back of the spoon. Hold the spoon horizontally and run your finger through the custard. If the trail left by your finger stays separated, the custard is ready to be cooled.

4. Strain the custard into the bowl sitting over the prepared ice bath and stir for 3 to 5 minutes, or until the custard has cooled. Transfer the custard to a quart-size container, cover, and refrigerate for at least 4 hours or, preferably, overnight.

5. Pour the chilled custard into an ice cream maker and freeze according to the manufacturer's instructions. Place the container in which you refrigerated the custard in the freezer so you can use it to store the finished ice cream. Churn the ice cream until the texture resembles "soft serve." Transfer the ice cream to the chilled storage container and freeze until hardened to your desired consistency. Alternatively, you can serve it immediately—it will be the consistency of gelato. The ice cream will keep, frozen, for up to 7 days.

COCONUT-AVOCADO ICE CREAM

In Southeast Asia, avocado is often served as a dessert, typically over shaved ice and sweetened evaporated milk, and in the Philippines, avocado ice cream is not uncommon, either. This flavor was the brainchild of our head of production, Jane, whose Vietnamese roots often bring us delightful and exotic treats. We loved the idea of combining these two complementary flavors. Avocados' natural creaminess and fat content are a perfect canvas for ice cream and yield a sumptuous texture that is a perfect pairing for coconut.

MAKES ABOUT 1 QUART

SPECIAL EQUIPMENT
Immersion blender

1½ cups heavy cream

1 cup whole milk

½ cup plus 2 tablespoons (125 grams) sugar

1 plump vanillla bean, split lengthwise and seeds scraped out

¼ teaspoon (1 gram) kosher salt

6 large egg yolks

½ cup plus 2 tablespoons mashed avocado (from about 1 avocado)

¼ cup sweetened coconut or unsweetened coconut flakes, toasted

1. Pour the cream and milk into a double boiler or a heatproof bowl set over a saucepan of simmering water (the bottom of the bowl should not touch the water). Whisk in ½ cup (100 grams) of the sugar, the vanilla bean seeds and pod, and the salt, and stir until the sugar and salt have dissolved. Warm the mixture until you see steam rising from the top.

2. Meanwhile, prepare an ice bath in a large bowl. Set aside.

3. In a medium bowl, with a kitchen towel underneath it to prevent slipping, whisk together the egg yolks with the remaining 2 tablespoons (25 grams) sugar until uniform. While whisking, add a splash of the hot dairy mixture to the yolks. Continue to add the dairy mixture, whisking it in bit by bit, until you've added about half. Add the yolk mixture to the remaining dairy mixture in the double boiler. Set the heat under the double boiler to medium and cook the custard, stirring continuously with a wooden spoon and reducing the heat to medium-low as necessary, until steam begins to rise from the surface and the custard thickens enough to coat the back of the spoon. Hold the spoon horizontally and run your finger through the custard. If the trail left by your finger stays separated, the custard is ready to be cooled.

4. Strain the custard into a bowl and add the avocado. Using an immersion blender, buzz the mixture until smooth and emulsified; stir in the coconut flakes. Set the bowl over the prepared ice bath and stir for 3 to 5 minutes, or until the custard has cooled. Transfer the custard to a quart-size container, cover, and refrigerate for at least 4 hours or, preferably, overnight.

5. Pour the chilled custard into an ice cream maker and freeze according to the manufacturer's instructions. Place the container in which you refrigerated the custard in the freezer so you can use it to store the finished ice cream. Churn the ice cream until the texture resembles "soft serve." Transfer the ice cream to the chilled storage container and freeze until hardened to your desired consistency. Alternatively, you can serve it immediately—it will be the consistency of gelato. The ice cream will keep, frozen, for up to 7 days.

GINGER ICE CREAM

Our ginger ice cream came to be as a result of a happy accident. Originally aiming for a Dark 'n' Stormy flavor, we were finding that working with alcohol in ice cream was a pretty frustrating experience. The test batches either showed no signs of having rum in it or was far too soft and lacking any bite whatsoever. At some point, we decided to make ice cream flavored only with ginger, and were blown away by how good it tasted. We realized then and there that we had a hit on our hands, and included it as one of our original flavors.

It also happened to be the first Van Leeuwen ice cream flavor our coauthor, Olga, sampled when she first spotted our yellow truck in Battery Park in late June 2008. It was our very first trial run, before we officially launched, and we still marvel at the coincidence that our future coauthor happened to be at the very location where we were first scooping. The way Olga tells the story, she was immediately drawn to the beautiful yellow truck and the classic botanical drawings. Since she had never tasted ginger ice cream, the flavor immediately caught her eye. And with that first scoop, her love for Van Leeuwen ice cream was born. Clearly, this was fate working its magic.

MAKES ABOUT 1 QUART

SPECIAL EQUIPMENT
Candy thermometer

FOR THE GINGER SIMPLE SYRUP

1 cup (200 grams) sugar, plus more for coating

1 3-inch knob fresh ginger, diced small (see Ben's Note)

FOR THE GINGER ICE CREAM

2½ cups heavy cream

1 cup whole milk

8 large egg yolks

½ cup (100 grams) sugar

¼ cup fresh ginger juice (from about a 4-inch knob of ginger; see Ben's Notes on pages 112 and 171)

1. To make the ginger simple syrup, in a saucepan, combine 1 cup of the sugar, the ginger, and ¼ cup water and bring to a simmer over medium heat. Clip a candy thermometer to the side of the pan. Once the liquid reaches 225°F, simmer for 10 minutes more. Remove from the heat, strain into a bowl, and let cool. You should have about ⅔ cup of syrup. Transfer the ginger pieces from the strainer to a bowl and toss them with additional sugar until coated. Set aside the syrup and candied ginger.

2. To make the ginger ice cream, pour the cream and milk into a double boiler or a heatproof bowl set over a saucepan of simmering water (the bottom of the bowl should not touch the water). Whisk in the ginger syrup and warm the mixture until you see steam rising from the top.

3. Meanwhile, prepare an ice bath in a large bowl and set another bowl over it. Set aside.

4. In a medium bowl, with a kitchen towel underneath it to prevent slipping, whisk together the egg yolks with the sugar until uniform. While whisking, add a splash of the hot dairy mixture to the yolks. Continue to add the dairy mixture, whisking it in bit by bit, until you've added about half. Add the yolk mixture to the remaining dairy mixture in the double boiler. Set the heat under the double boiler to medium and cook the custard, stirring continuously with a wooden spoon and reducing the heat to medium-low as necessary, until steam begins to rise from the surface and the custard thickens enough to coat the back of the spoon. Hold the spoon horizontally and run your finger through the custard. If the trail left by your finger stays separated, the custard is ready to be cooled.

5. Strain the custard into the bowl sitting over the prepared ice bath and stir for 3 to 5 minutes, or until the custard has cooled. Add in the ginger juice. Transfer the custard to a quart-size container, cover, and refrigerate for at least 4 hours or, preferably, overnight.

6. Pour the chilled custard into an ice cream maker and freeze according to the manufacturer's instructions. Place the container in which you refrigerated the custard in the freezer so you can use it to store the finished ice cream. Churn the ice cream until the texture resembles "soft serve." Transfer the ice cream to the chilled storage container and freeze until hardened to your desired consistency. Alternatively, you can serve it immediately—it will be the consistency of gelato. If you like, use the candied ginger as a garnish—otherwise, transfer it to an airtight container and reserve it for another use; it will keep for up to 1 week. The ice cream will keep, frozen, for up to 7 days.

ben's note *If you can find it, baby ginger is absolutely perfect here; it's juicier and less stringy than the adult version. Organic markets often stock it. Look for smaller tubers—it's a good sign the ginger will be less stringy or fibrous.*

KAFFIR LIME LEAF ICE CREAM

Kaffir lime leaves may be a little difficult to procure—you can find them in specialty and Asian grocery stores—but their flavor and fragrance are inimitable and very much worth seeking out. This is a great ice cream flavor to pair with a Southeast Asian-themed menu. The leaves are often sold frozen, and it's best to keep them that way until you are ready to use them. Stored properly, their shelf life can be extended far beyond that produced by mere refrigeration. Because the leaves can be tough and stringy, we recommend straining the custard after blending the leaves into it.

MAKES ABOUT 1 QUART

2 cups heavy cream

1 cup whole milk

½ cup plus 2 tablespoons (125 grams) sugar

¼ teaspoon (1 gram) kosher salt

6 large egg yolks

9 medium kaffir lime leaves (see Sources, page 218)

1. Pour the cream and milk into a double boiler or a heatproof bowl set over a saucepan of gently simmering water (the bottom of the bowl should not touch the water). Whisk in ½ cup (100 grams) of the sugar and the salt and stir until they have dissolved. Warm the mixture until you see steam rising from the top.

2. Meanwhile, prepare an ice bath in a large bowl and set another bowl over it. Set aside.

3. In a medium bowl, with a kitchen towel underneath it to prevent slipping, whisk together the egg yolks with the remaining 2 tablespoons (25 grams) sugar until uniform. While whisking, add a splash of the hot dairy mixture to the yolks. Continue to add the dairy mixture, whisking it in bit by bit, until you've added about half. Add the yolk mixture to the remaining dairy mixture in the double boiler. Set the heat under the double boiler to medium and cook the custard, stirring continuously with a wooden spoon and reducing the heat to medium-low as necessary, until steam begins to rise from the surface and the custard thickens enough to coat the back of the spoon. Hold the spoon horizontally and run your finger through the custard. If the trail left by your finger stays separated, the custard is ready to be cooled.

4. Strain the custard into the bowl sitting over the prepared ice bath and stir for 3 to 5 minutes, or until the custard has cooled. Transfer the cooled custard to a blender and add the kaffir lime leaves; blend until completely uniform. Strain the custard into a bowl to get rid of some of the kaffir lime leaf fibers. Transfer the custard to a quart-size container, cover, and refrigerate for at least 4 hours or, preferably, overnight.

5. Pour the chilled custard into an ice cream maker and freeze according to the manufacturer's instructions. Place the container in which you refrigerated the custard in the freezer so you can use it to store the finished ice cream. Churn the ice cream until the texture resembles "soft serve." Transfer the ice cream to the chilled storage container and freeze until hardened to your desired consistency. Alternatively, you can serve it immediately—it will be the consistency of gelato. The ice cream will keep, frozen, for up to 7 days.

LAVENDER AND HONEY ICE CREAM

Lavender makes us dream of summers in Provence (wouldn't that be nice?) where fields of lavender go on and on, as far as the eye can see, and the flowers' intoxicating perfume soaks the air. Sweetened with honey, lavender ice cream is subtle and restrained—it doesn't taste soapy as sometimes lavender-flavored foods can (this happens when low-grade or artificial lavender is used). It's important that you find the freshest dried lavender flowers available, and make sure the flowers are food grade.

MAKES ABOUT 1 QUART

2 cups heavy cream

2 cups whole milk

½ cup (16 grams) food-grade
    lavender flowers

3 tablespoons (54 grams)
    mild honey

½ teaspoon (2 grams)
    kosher salt

6 large egg yolks

½ cup (100 grams) sugar

1. Pour the cream and milk into a double boiler or a heatproof bowl set over a saucepan of gently simmering water (the bottom of the bowl should not touch the water). Whisk in the lavender, honey, and salt, and stir until combined. Warm the mixture until you see steam rising from the top. Remove from the heat and strain the liquid into a bowl, pressing on the solids; discard the lavender flowers in the strainer. Return the dairy mixture to the double boiler.

2. Meanwhile, prepare an ice bath in a large bowl and set another bowl over it. Set aside.

3. In a medium bowl, with a kitchen towel underneath it to prevent slipping, whisk together the egg yolks with the sugar until uniform. While whisking, add a splash of the hot dairy mixture to the yolks. Continue to add the dairy mixture, whisking it in bit by bit, until you've added about half. Add the yolk mixture to the remaining dairy mixture in the double boiler. Set the heat under the double boiler to medium and cook the custard, stirring continuously with a wooden spoon and reducing the heat to medium-low as necessary, until steam begins to rise from the surface and the custard thickens enough to coat the back of the spoon. Hold the spoon horizontally and run your finger through the custard. If the trail left by your finger stays separated, the custard is ready to be cooled.

4. Strain the custard into the bowl sitting over the prepared ice bath and stir for 3 to 5 minutes, or until the custard has cooled. Transfer the custard to a quart-size container, cover, and refrigerate for at least 4 hours or, preferably, overnight.

5. Pour the chilled custard into an ice cream maker and freeze according to the manufacturer's instructions. Place the container in which you refrigerated the custard in the freezer so you can use it to store the finished ice cream. Churn the ice cream until the texture resembles "soft serve." Transfer the ice cream to the chilled storage container and freeze until hardened to your desired consistency. Alternatively, you can serve it immediately—it will be the consistency of gelato. The ice cream will keep, frozen, for up to 7 days.

ROSE WATER–CARDAMOM ICE CREAM

Rose water–cardamom is such a lovely flavor combination, and since all three of us love a good Indian dessert where it's prominently featured, we thought, *Why not try it in ice cream?* The trick to balancing the flavors is to show restraint with the rose water; it's easy to go from a dessert that's delicately perfumed to one that smells like a Victorian grandmother. Rose water can be found in Middle Eastern grocery stores, but more and more grocery stores carry it now. If all else fails, you can always order it online.

MAKES ABOUT 1 QUART

2 cups heavy cream

1 cup whole milk

½ cup plus 2 tablespoons (125 grams) sugar

1 tablespoon ground cardamom

½ teaspoon (2 grams) kosher salt

8 large egg yolks

2 teaspoons rose water, or to taste

1. Pour the cream and milk into a double boiler or a heatproof bowl set over a saucepan of gently simmering water (the bottom of the bowl should not touch the water). Whisk in ½ cup (100 grams) of the sugar, the cardamom, and the salt and stir until the sugar and salt have dissolved. Warm the mixture until you see steam rising from the top.

2. Meanwhile, prepare an ice bath in a large bowl and set another bowl over it. Set aside.

3. In a medium bowl, with a kitchen towel underneath it to prevent slipping, whisk together the egg yolks with the remaining 2 tablespoons (50 grams) sugar until uniform. While whisking, add a splash of the hot dairy mixture to the yolks. Continue to add the dairy mixture, whisking it in bit by bit, until you've added about half. Add the yolk mixture to the remaining dairy mixture in the double boiler. Set the heat under the double boiler to medium and cook the custard, stirring continuously with a wooden spoon and reducing the heat to medium-low as necessary, until steam begins to rise from the surface and the custard thickens enough to coat the back of the spoon. Hold the spoon horizontally and run your finger through the custard. If the trail left by your finger stays separated, the custard is ready to be cooled.

4. Strain the custard into the bowl sitting over the prepared ice bath and stir for 3 to 5 minutes, or until the custard has cooled. Transfer the custard to a quart-size container, cover, and refrigerate for at least 4 hours or, preferably, overnight.

5. Stir the rose water into the chilled custard, starting with half the amount called for and adding more as you like. Pour the custard into an ice cream maker and freeze according to the manufacturer's instructions. Place the container in which you refrigerated the custard in the freezer so you can use it to store the finished ice cream. Churn the ice cream until the texture resembles "soft serve." Transfer the ice cream to the chilled storage container and freeze until hardened to your desired consistency. Alternatively, you can serve it immediately—it will be the consistency of gelato. The ice cream will keep, frozen, for up to 7 days.

ORANGE BLOSSOM WATER ICE CREAM WITH PISTACHIO SHORTBREAD

One of our favorite things about making ice cream is the ability to combine your most beloved flavors: Butterscotch and Brownies (page 123), Apple Crumble with Calvados and Crème Fraîche (page 69), Curried Nuts with Salted Caramel Swirl (page 141)—the list goes on. It seems like there's virtually no limit to the wonderful flavor combinations, but we're still prone to shying away from certain ones. This flavor is proof positive that we should always strive to challenge ourselves in the kitchen.

Ben had this idea that we should combine shortbread with ice cream but, being Ben, he was very specific: pistachio–orange blossom water shortbread combined with orange blossom water ice cream. When Pete and I heard that idea, we thought it was a bit much, perhaps a little too involved for a home cook, but Ben dug his heels in and urged us to give this flavor a try. We are so glad we listened to him— the ice cream reminds us of cookies-and-cream ice cream with a Persian twist. You can always use store-bought shortbread, but the homemade version has a wonderful chewiness that's unparalleled in prepackaged varieties.

MAKES ABOUT 1 QUART

FOR THE PISTACHIO SHORTBREAD

2 cups (250 grams) all-purpose flour

2/3 cup (133 grams) granulated sugar

1/2 teaspoon (2 grams) kosher salt

1 cup (2 sticks/226 grams) unsalted butter, cut into 1/2-inch cubes

1 large egg yolk

1/2 cup (63 grams) whole pistachios, toasted and roughly chopped

1 teaspoon orange blossom water

FOR THE ORANGE BLOSSOM WATER ICE CREAM

2 cups heavy cream

1 cup whole milk

(continued on next page)

1. To make the pistachio shortbread, preheat the oven to 325°F; position a rack in the middle. Line a 9-inch square baking pan with overlapping, perpendicular pieces of parchment paper trimmed to fit the pan with about a 2- to 3-inch overhang (so that you can easily pull the shortbread out when you are ready to cut it).

2. In a food processor, pulse together the flour, sugar, and salt until combined. Add the butter, egg yolk, pistachios, and orange blossom water and pulse until a scraggly, loose dough comes together. Dump out the dough, loose bits and all, onto the counter and knead until combined. Press the dough into the baking pan and score it all over with a fork. Transfer the pan to the oven and bake for 40 to 45 minutes, or until the shortbread is golden and firm. Transfer the pan to a wire rack and let cool completely. Using the overhanging parchment paper, lift the shortbread out of the pan and cut into pieces (we like 1-inch squares) on a cutting board. You will need 1/4 to 1/3 cup of cubed shortbread for the ice cream; transfer the remaining shortbread to a cookie tin and enjoy it as you like.

3. To make the orange blossom water ice cream, pour the cream and milk into a double boiler or a heatproof bowl set over a saucepan of gently simmering water (the bottom of the bowl should not touch the water). Whisk in 1/2 cup (100 grams) of the sugar and the salt and stir until they have dissolved. Warm the mixture until you see steam rising from the top.

4. Meanwhile, prepare an ice bath in a large bowl and set another bowl over it. Set aside.

5. In a medium bowl, with a kitchen towel underneath it to prevent

(continued)

½ cup plus 2 tablespoons
(125 grams) sugar

½ teaspoon (2 grams)
kosher salt

8 large egg yolks

2 tablespoons orange
blossom water, or to taste

slipping, whisk together the egg yolks with the remaining 2 tablespoons (25 grams) sugar until uniform. While whisking, add a splash of the hot dairy mixture to the yolks. Continue to add the dairy mixture, whisking it in bit by bit, until you've added about half. Add the yolk mixture to the remaining dairy mixture in the double boiler. Set the heat under the double boiler to medium and cook the custard, stirring continuously with a wooden spoon and reducing the heat to medium-low as necessary, until steam begins to rise from the surface and the custard thickens enough to coat the back of the spoon. Hold the spoon horizontally and run your finger through the custard. If the trail left by your finger stays separated, the custard is ready to be cooled.

6. Strain the custard into the bowl sitting over the prepared ice bath and stir for 3 to 5 minutes, or until the custard has cooled. Transfer the custard to a quart-size container, cover, and refrigerate for at least 4 hours or, preferably, overnight.

7. Stir the orange blossom water into the chilled custard. Pour the custard into an ice cream maker and freeze according to the manufacturer's instructions. Place the container in which you refrigerated the custard in the freezer so you can use it to store the finished ice cream. Churn the ice cream until the texture resembles "soft serve." Using a spatula, fold in the shortbread cubes until incorporated. Transfer the ice cream to the chilled storage container and freeze until hardened to your desired consistency. Alternatively, you can serve it immediately—it will be the consistency of gelato. The ice cream will keep, frozen, for up to 7 days.

PALM SUGAR

Palm sugar might be new to some readers, but it's been steadily gaining in popularity in recent years. We love palm sugar so much that we've dedicated a whole singular flavor of ice cream to it.

Palm sugar is sugar made from the sap of a number of palm trees such as date, coconut, and a few others. Often, you will see a label noting which type of tree the palm sugar came from, but sometimes it doesn't give you that information. Regardless, palm sugar is a nutrient-rich, low-glycemic sugar that looks, tastes, dissolves, and melts almost exactly like sugar, but it's unrefined, which allows it to retain its unique taste, naturally occurring deep brown color, and host of vitamins and nutrients, including potassium, zinc, iron, and vitamins B_1, B_2, B_3, and B_6. That's rare for sweeteners, most of which are highly refined.

Palm sugar, also known as jaggery, is produced in parts of Africa as well as Asia. The production is similar to that of maple sugar: A tree is tapped and the sap is collected before being boiled down to crystallize into sugar. You'll often see palm sugar in funny little shapes, like swirly domes or blocks, but sometimes you'll also see it "granulated," much like regular table sugar. Palm sugar is perhaps most prominent in Southeast Asian cooking, but it's becoming more and more popular in Western cooking, often replacing brown sugar, delivering richer caramel and butterscotch notes, minus the tinny flavor of the brown sugar.

We became a lot more familiar with palm sugar after Laura and Ben visited Bali. While there, they discovered a family-run farm, Big Tree Farms, that, in addition to being the world's largest supplier of organic coconut palm sweeteners to the international market, also grows more than eighty different crops, ranging from Chioggia beets, vanilla beans, and passion fruit; harvests sea salt; and cultivates cacao plants.

We loved this sugar, with its deep caramel notes, and we loved the farm's commitment to the environment, so we decided to make ice cream with it. Our Heritage Palm Sugar Ice Cream (page 120) is not unlike caramel ice cream, except with deeper butterscotch notes.

HERITAGE PALM SUGAR ICE CREAM

Ben and I discovered palm sugar while on a trip to Bali and were instantly smitten with its rich caramel flavor. The ice cream couldn't be simpler to make: basic ice cream custard flavored only with palm sugar and a touch of coconut oil. We like to think of it as a tropical cousin to our Salted Caramel Ice Cream (page 127), only with earthier, maltier notes. Palm sugar is made by boiling down sap from coconut palm trees, and also happens to be low on the glucose index, making it a better option for those seeking foods with less sugar.

MAKES ABOUT 1 QUART

2 cups heavy cream

1 cup whole milk

¾ cup plus 2 tablespoons
(150 grams) unrefined
palm sugar

2 teaspoons extra-virgin
coconut oil

¼ teaspoon (1 gram) kosher
salt

6 large egg yolks

1. Pour the cream and milk into a double boiler or a heatproof bowl set over a saucepan of gently simmering water (the bottom of the bowl should not touch the water). Whisk in ½ cup plus 2 tablespoons (about 110 grams) of the palm sugar, the coconut oil, and the salt and stir until the sugar and salt have dissolved. Warm the mixture until you see steam rising from the top.

2. Meanwhile, prepare an ice bath in a large bowl and set another bowl over it. Set aside.

3. In a medium bowl, with a kitchen towel underneath it to prevent slipping, whisk together the egg yolks with the remaining ¼ cup (about 43 grams) palm sugar until uniform. While whisking, add a splash of the hot dairy mixture to the yolks. Continue to add the dairy mixture, whisking it in bit by bit, until you've added about half. Add the yolk mixture to the remaining dairy mixture in the double boiler. Set the heat under the double boiler to medium and cook the custard, stirring continuously with a wooden spoon and reducing the heat to medium-low as necessary, until steam begins to rise from the surface and the custard thickens enough to coat the back of the spoon. Hold the spoon horizontally and run your finger through the custard. If the trail left by your finger stays separated, the custard is ready to be cooled.

4. Strain the custard into the bowl sitting over the prepared ice bath and stir for 3 to 5 minutes, or until the custard has cooled. Transfer the custard to a quart-size container, cover, and refrigerate for at least 4 hours or, preferably, overnight.

5. Pour the chilled custard into an ice cream maker and freeze according to the manufacturer's instructions. Place the container in which you refrigerated the custard in the freezer so you can use it to store the finished ice cream. Churn the ice cream until the texture resembles "soft serve." Transfer the ice cream to the chilled storage container and freeze until hardened to your desired consistency. Alternatively, you can serve it immediately—it will be the consistency of gelato. The ice cream will keep, frozen, for up to 7 days.

BUTTERSCOTCH AND BROWNIES ICE CREAM

When we first made this ice cream, we worried that the combination of butterscotch ice cream and brownies might be too sweet for our palates. But we had nothing to be worried about—rich butterscotch is perfectly offset by the bittersweet chocolate brownies.

For brownies, we went to our favorite recipe, inspired by the queen of all things chocolate—Alice Medrich.

MAKES ABOUT 1 QUART

3½ tablespoons (about 50 grams) unsalted butter

1 cup (227 grams) dark brown sugar

2 cups heavy cream

1½ cups whole milk

½ plump vanilla bean, split lengthwise and seeds scraped out

¼ teaspoon (1 gram) kosher salt

8 large egg yolks

½ to ⅔ cup diced Cocoa Brownies (page 191)

1. In a medium skillet or a saucepan, melt the butter over medium heat. Add the brown sugar and stir until well moistened. Bring to a very gentle boil and cook for 5 minutes. Add 1 cup of the cream and stir until the butterscotch becomes uniform; remove from the heat and set aside.

2. Pour the remaining 1 cup cream and the milk into a double boiler or a heatproof bowl set over a saucepan of simmering water (the bottom of the bowl should not touch the water). Add the butterscotch, vanilla bean seeds and pod, and salt, and stir until combined. Warm the mixture until you see steam rising from the top. Remove from the heat and remove the vanilla bean (see page 34 for ideas on what to do with it).

3. Meanwhile, prepare an ice bath in a large bowl and set another bowl over it. Set aside.

4. In a medium bowl, with a kitchen towel underneath it to prevent slipping, whisk together the egg yolks. While whisking, add a splash of the hot dairy mixture to the yolks. Continue to add the dairy mixture, whisking it in bit by bit, until you've added about half. Add the yolk mixture to the remaining dairy mixture in the double boiler. Set the heat under the double boiler to medium and cook the custard, stirring continuously with a wooden spoon and reducing the heat to medium-low as necessary, until steam begins to rise from the surface and the custard thickens enough to coat the back of the spoon. Hold the spoon horizontally and run your finger through the custard. If the trail left by your finger stays separated, the custard is ready to be cooled.

5. Strain the custard into the bowl sitting over the prepared ice bath and stir for 3 to 5 minutes, or until the custard has cooled. Transfer the custard to a quart-size container, cover, and refrigerate for at least 4 hours or, preferably, overnight.

6. Pour the chilled custard into an ice cream maker and freeze according to the manufacturer's instructions. Place the container in which you refrigerated the custard in the freezer so you can use it to store the finished ice cream. Churn the ice cream until the texture resembles "soft serve." Fold in the brownie pieces, transfer to the chilled storage container, and freeze until hardened to your desired consistency. Alternatively, you can serve it immediately—it will be the consistency of gelato. The ice cream will keep, frozen, for up to 7 days.

ALMOND BUTTER AND JELLY ICE CREAM

When Ben and Pete were kids, their typically American lunch boxes often contained peanut butter and jelly sandwiches—and they couldn't get enough of them. While they still love a good PB&J, now that they're older, they're finding themselves reaching for almond butter and jelly even more often. Almonds have a more delicate flavor than peanuts, and so the sandwiches feel a bit more sophisticated. Eager to weave their love of almond butter into ice cream, they thought it'd be great to do an ice cream riff on the sandwich. After some trial and error, they learned that tart jelly works better than sweet, so stick with something like red currant or lingonberry, or anything with some pucker.

MAKES ABOUT 1 QUART

SPECIAL EQUIPMENT
Immersion blender

2 cups heavy cream

1½ cups whole milk

¾ cup (150 grams) sugar

¼ teaspoon (1 gram) kosher salt

6 large egg yolks

6 tablespoons (120 grams) smooth unsalted almond butter

½ cup tart jelly, such as lingonberry, red currant, sour cherry

1. Pour the cream and milk into a double boiler or a heatproof bowl set over a saucepan of gently simmering water (the bottom of the bowl should not touch the water). Whisk in ½ cup (100 grams) of the sugar and the salt and stir until they have dissolved. Warm the mixture until you see steam rising from the top.

2. Meanwhile, prepare an ice bath in a large bowl. Set aside.

3. In a medium bowl, with a kitchen towel underneath it to prevent slipping, whisk together the egg yolks with the remaining ¼ cup (50 grams) sugar until uniform. While whisking, add a splash of the hot dairy mixture to the yolks. Continue to add the dairy mixture, whisking it in bit by bit, until you've added about half. Add the yolk mixture to the remaining dairy mixture in the double boiler. Set the heat under the double boiler to medium and cook the custard, stirring continuously with a wooden spoon and reducing the heat to medium-low as necessary, until steam begins to rise from the surface and the custard thickens enough to coat the back of the spoon. Hold the spoon horizontally and run your finger through the custard. If the trail left by your finger stays separated, the custard is ready to be cooled.

4. Strain the custard into a bowl and add the almond butter. Using an immersion blender, buzz the custard until emulsified. Set the bowl over the prepared ice bath and stir for 3 to 5 minutes, or until the custard has cooled. Transfer the custard to a quart-size container, cover, and refrigerate for at least 4 hours or, preferably, overnight.

5. Pour the chilled custard into an ice cream maker and freeze according to the manufacturer's instructions. Place the container in which you refrigerated the custard in the freezer so you can use it to store the finished ice cream. Churn the ice cream until the texture resembles "soft serve." In the last minute of churning, fold in the jelly until swirled in or incorporated, depending on your preference. Transfer the ice cream to the chilled storage container and freeze until hardened to your desired consistency. Alternatively, you can serve it immediately—it will be the consistency of gelato. The ice cream will keep, frozen, for up to 7 days.

SALTED CARAMEL ICE CREAM

Here's a funny thing about salt: Used wisely and judiciously, it highlights flavors and makes them sing. Dessert without even a pinch of salt seems flatter, less lively, and food cooked without salt is bland and barely edible. Somewhere along the line, perhaps because of high sodium levels in processed foods, salt became public enemy number one. But if you cook and eat whole foods, salt isn't something to be afraid of. A little bit will make your food shine brighter.

With salted caramel ice cream, the salt takes on a starring role. Salted caramel is nothing new—a classic flavor from the Brittany region in France. Still, despite its name, most of the time when we try salted caramel ice cream, we find ourselves wondering, *Where's the salt?* And so, in making our Salted Caramel Ice Cream, we wanted you to taste the contrast between the salty and the sweet; we think it makes for one of the most alluring flavors. If you're worried about making your ice cream too salty, start with half the suggested amount and work your way up, tasting as you go.

MAKES ABOUT 1 QUART

¾ cup (150 grams) sugar

2 cups heavy cream

1 teaspoon flaky sea salt, such as Maldon

1 cup whole milk

½ vanilla bean, split lengthwise and seeds scraped out

8 large egg yolks

1. Place the sugar in a deep, heavy saucepan over medium heat. Stir continuously and break up any lumps of sugar—this will help the sugar caramelize evenly. Bring to a simmer over medium heat, stirring with a spatula to dissolve the sugar, then simmer, without stirring, until the caramel turns the color of a copper penny (or an Irish setter), about 4 minutes. If, while the caramel cooks, any sugar crystallizes on the sides of the pan, brush down the sides with a clean, wet pastry brush. Reduce the heat to low, and slowly add ½ cup of the cream (the caramel will rise and bubble and might spit, so be careful). Stir until the cream is well incorporated into the caramel. Remove from the heat and stir in the salt. Should the caramel seize and harden, return the mixture to the heat and stir until it softens. Remove from the heat and set aside.

2. Prepare an ice bath in a large bowl and set another bowl over it. Set aside.

3. Pour the milk and remaining 1½ cups cream into a double boiler or a heatproof bowl set over a saucepan of simmering water (the bottom of the bowl should not touch the water). Add the vanilla bean seeds and pod and warm the mixture until you see steam rising from the top.

4. Meanwhile, in a medium bowl, with a kitchen towel underneath it to prevent slipping, whisk together the egg yolks until uniform. While whisking, add a splash of the hot dairy mixture to the yolks. Continue to add the dairy mixture, whisking it in bit by bit, until you've added about half. Add the yolk mixture to the remaining dairy mixture in the double boiler, and stir in the caramel. Set the heat under the double boiler to medium and cook the custard, stirring continuously with a wooden spoon and reducing the heat to medium-low as necessary, until steam begins to rise from the surface and the custard thickens enough to coat the back of the

spoon. Hold the spoon horizontally and run your finger through the custard. If the trail left by your finger stays separated, the custard is ready to be cooled.

5. Strain the custard into the bowl sitting over the prepared ice bath and stir for 3 to 5 minutes, or until the custard has cooled. Transfer the custard to a quart-size container, cover, and refrigerate for at least 4 hours or, preferably, overnight.

6. Pour the chilled custard into an ice cream maker, add the salted caramel, and freeze according to the manufacturer's instructions. Place the container in which you refrigerated the custard in the freezer so you can use it to store the finished ice cream. Churn the ice cream until the texture resembles "soft serve." Transfer the ice cream to the chilled storage container and freeze until hardened to your desired consistency. Alternatively, you can serve it immediately—it will be the consistency of gelato. The ice cream will keep, frozen, for up to 7 days.

ben's note *You'll notice that some ice creams yield a perfect quart, while others, such as this one, come up a bit short. In the case of Salted Caramel Ice Cream, there's quite a bit of evaporation as you make the caramel, hence the smaller yield. Depending on the time of year and humidity levels, evaporation will vary, but you will likely always get somewhat less than 1 quart of ice cream for the yield here.*

SALTED PEANUT BUTTER ICE CREAM
WITH CHOCOLATE-COVERED PRETZELS

We can't get enough of this ice cream. Chocolate and peanut butter are perhaps one of the universe's greatest food pairings, but throw in salty pretzels and you have the dessert trifecta. If you don't want to dip pretzels into chocolate, by all means, find premade chocolate-covered pretzels that you like and go with those.

MAKES ABOUT 1 QUART

SPECIAL EQUIPMENT

Immersion blender

FOR THE CHOCOLATE-COVERED PRETZELS

80 grams (3 ounces) dark chocolate (72% cacao), preferably Michel Cluizel (see Sources, page 218)

½ cup thin pretzels, broken into ½-inch pieces

½ teaspoon flaky sea salt, such as Maldon, plus more to taste

FOR THE PEANUT BUTTER ICE CREAM

1½ cups heavy cream

1½ cups whole milk

½ cup plus 2 tablespoons (125 grams) sugar

½ teaspoon (2 grams) kosher salt

6 large egg yolks

3 tablespoons (54 grams) smooth natural peanut butter

1. To make the chocolate-covered pretzels, line a baking sheet with parchment paper. Place the chocolate in a double boiler or a heat-proof bowl set over a saucepan of gently simmering water (the bottom of the bowl should not touch the water). When the chocolate has melted completely, add the pretzel pieces and stir until all the pieces are generously coated with chocolate. Using a slotted spoon, transfer the chocolate-covered pretzels to the prepared baking sheet, making sure to keep each piece separate; sprinkle with flaky sea salt. Refrigerate, uncovered, until fully set and cold (see Ben's Note). For a thicker coating of chocolate, repeat this process up to 2 more times.

2. To make the peanut butter ice cream, pour the cream and milk into a double boiler or a heatproof bowl set over a saucepan of gently simmering water (the bottom of the bowl should not touch the water). Whisk in ½ cup (100 grams) of the sugar and the salt and stir until they have dissolved. Warm the mixture until you see steam rising from the top.

3. Meanwhile, prepare an ice bath in a large bowl. Set aside.

4. In a medium bowl, with a kitchen towel underneath it to prevent slipping, whisk together the egg yolks with the remaining 2 table-spoons (25 grams) sugar until uniform. While whisking, add a splash of the hot dairy mixture to the yolks. Continue to add the dairy mixture, whisking it in bit by bit, until you've added about half. Add the yolk mixture to the remaining dairy mixture in the double boiler. Set the heat under the double boiler to medium and cook the custard, stirring continuously with a wooden spoon and reducing the heat to medium-low as necessary, until steam begins to rise from the surface and the custard thickens enough to coat the back of the spoon. Hold the spoon horizontally and run your finger through the custard. If the trail left by your finger stays separated, the custard is ready to be cooled.

5. Strain the custard into a bowl and stir in the peanut butter. Using an immersion blender, buzz the custard until emulsified. Place the bowl over the prepared ice bath and stir for 3 to 5 minutes, or

until the custard has cooled. Transfer the custard to a quart-size container, cover, and refrigerate for at least 4 hours or, preferably, overnight.

6. Pour the chilled custard into an ice cream maker and freeze according to the manufacturer's instructions. Place the container in which you refrigerated the custard in the freezer so you can use it to store the finished ice cream. Churn the ice cream until the texture resembles "soft serve." Using a spatula, fold in the chocolate-covered pretzels until incorporated. Transfer the ice cream to the chilled storage container and freeze until hardened to your desired consistency. Alternatively, you can serve it immediately—it will be the consistency of gelato. The ice cream will keep, frozen, for up to 7 days.

ben's note For commercial batches, we double-dip our pretzels in chocolate in order to give them a thicker chocolate shell and keep the pretzels crunchy longer. We don't think it's necessary for a home batch, and it might just be an extra step for you. Still, if you feel like you want to re-create the ice cream shop experience, by all means, double-dip the pretzels before folding them into the ice cream.

CEYLON CINNAMON ICE CREAM

Ben and Pete first came across cinnamon ice cream in a little beach town in Mexico while on vacation. They were in an arid region, far from any land suitable for dairy farming, so the ice cream was made with powdered milk and UHT boxed cream—and still, it was delicious! While you might not think of a spice-flavored ice cream as something refreshing in the height of summer—maybe you prefer Strawberry Ice Cream (page 61) or Lemon Sorbet (page 168)—but perhaps because of its woodsy, floral notes, cinnamon ice cream is cooling and rejuvenating on a sweltering day. I was skeptical at first, until I tried it—and it's true.

In Mexico, they mostly grow the Ceylon variety of cinnamon, which has a milder and more floral flavor than its Vietnamese or Chinese counterpart—it's considered to be true cinnamon rather than its cousin, cassia, which is what we know in the United States as cinnamon. On hot summer days, Ben will frequently drop in on our Greenpoint store and get a scoop of cinnamon and a scoop of Chocolate Ice Cream (page 17) with Hot Fudge Sauce (page 183), cocoa nibs, and a pinch of New Mexican Hatch chile powder—it's bliss.

MAKES ABOUT 1 QUART

1½ cups heavy cream

1½ cups whole milk

8 3-inch cinnamon quills (about 20 grams), crushed

¾ cup (150 grams) sugar

¼ teaspoon (1 gram) kosher salt

6 large egg yolks

1 tablespoon (4 grams) ground cinnamon, preferably from Ceylon

1. Pour the cream and milk into a double boiler or a heatproof bowl set over a saucepan of gently simmering water (the bottom of the bowl should not touch the water). Add the cinnamon quills, whisk in ½ cup (100 grams) of the sugar and the salt, and stir until the sugar and salt have dissolved. Warm the mixture until you see steam rising from the top. Remove from the heat and strain the mixture into a bowl to remove the cinnamon quills. Return the dairy mixture to the double boiler.

2. Meanwhile, prepare an ice bath in a large bowl and set another bowl over it. Set aside.

3. In a medium bowl, with a kitchen towel underneath it to prevent slipping, whisk together the egg yolks with the remaining ¼ cup (50 grams) sugar until uniform. While whisking, add a splash of the hot dairy mixture to the yolks. Continue to add the dairy mixture, whisking it in bit by bit, until you've added about half. Add the yolk mixture to the remaining dairy mixture in the double boiler. Set the heat under the double boiler to medium and cook the custard, stirring continuously with a wooden spoon and reducing the heat to medium-low as necessary, until steam begins to rise from the surface and the custard thickens enough to coat the back of the spoon. Hold the spoon horizontally and run your finger through the custard. If the trail left by your finger stays separated, the custard is ready to be cooled.

4. Strain the custard into the bowl sitting over the prepared ice bath. Whisk in the ground cinnamon and stir for 3 to 5 minutes, or until the custard has cooled. Transfer the custard to a quart-size container, cover, and refrigerate for at least 4 hours or, preferably, overnight.

5. Pour the chilled custard into an ice cream maker and freeze according to the manufacturer's instructions. Place the container in which you refrigerated the custard in the freezer so you can use it to store the finished ice cream. Churn the ice cream until the texture resembles "soft serve." Transfer the ice cream to the chilled storage container and freeze until hardened to your desired consistency. Alternatively, you can serve it immediately—it will be the consistency of gelato. The ice cream will keep, frozen, for up to 7 days.

ben's note If you can, steep the cinnamon quills in the dairy mixture (the cream and milk) overnight in the fridge—you'll get an even deeper flavor.

CEYLON CINNAMON

You might be surprised to learn that in all these years of eating cinnamon toast, you weren't actually eating cinnamon. Instead, you were eating cassia, a plant often mistaken for and, in the United States, often sold as cinnamon. How's that for learning something new?

Ceylon cinnamon and cassia are two of the oldest spices that we know, for certain, were used for many centuries. Both are mentioned early on in the Bible, and both have a long history of religious, ritualistic, and culinary significance. The former, also known as "true cinnamon," is native to Sri Lanka and is actually not the predominant spice sold as cinnamon in the United States. According to a U.S. law, the word *cinnamon* may be used interchangeably for both true cinnamon and cassia. It should not be surprising, then, that cassia, which is significantly cheaper than cinnamon, is the spice predominantly imported into the United States. Geographically speaking, cassia is grown primarily in Myanmar, China, and Vietnam; is a little darker in color when compared with Ceylon cinnamon; and has a stronger, less-nuanced aroma. Ceylon cinnamon is also known for its softer, flakier quill, whereas cassia bark is quite hard, similar to what you think of when you imagine a cinnamon stick.

Aside from cinnamon's long and illustrious history (it was a much-coveted and fought-over spice from the 1500s to the 1800s), there are some other notable differences between true cinnamon and cassia, with perhaps none more important than their nutritional content. A critical difference between Ceylon cinnamon and cassia is their coumarin content. Coumarin is a naturally occurring toxin that, in high doses, can be hazardous to the liver. Unlike Ceylon cinnamon, which contains barely traceable amounts of coumarin, cassia has quite a bit of it, and it is cassia that we most frequently use in our day-to-day cooking. Now, if you use cinnamon only occasionally, this won't make much difference to you. However, if you make daily smoothies with a healthy heap of cinnamon (to lower your blood sugar or for its antiaging properties), you may want to seek out the Ceylon kind from a spice seller you trust.

We, of course, love Ceylon cinnamon for its delicate, floral-tasting notes, which make it absolutely perfect for an elegant ice cream flavor. To make our Cinnamon Ice Cream (page 133), we crush Ceylon cinnamon quills and steep them in the custard for at least 4 hours, and preferably overnight. We also add ground cinnamon for a more defined flavor, but we err on the side of moderation, as it's quite easy to go from flavorful to chalky when using ground cinnamon.

SICHUAN PEPPERCORN WITH CHERRY COMPOTE ICE CREAM

This is a great seasonal flavor to highlight some of our greenmarkets' finest offerings—cherries. It may seem strange to add peppercorns to ice cream, but the flavors (cherry and pepper) pair exceptionally well, particularly the fragrant, slightly floral Sichuan peppercorns we use to infuse the base. At the end of churning, we pair the ice cream with sweet cherry compote. The bite of the peppercorns cuts through the sugar, and gives the ice cream an unexpected and grown-up taste. When working with fruit, keep in mind that both sugar and alcohol deter ice crystallization. You'll notice we add sugar and alcohol to some of our compotes and macerations. Without these, as ice cream freezes, the fruit, which is mostly water, would become hard and icy.

MAKES ABOUT 1 QUART

FOR THE CHERRY COMPOTE

2 cups (350 grams) cherries, preferably sour cherries, pitted and halved

1 cup (200 grams) sugar

Pinch of kosher salt

FOR THE SICHUAN PEPPERCORN ICE CREAM

2 cups heavy cream

1¼ cups whole milk

½ cup plus 2 tablespoons (125 grams) sugar

2 tablespoons (8 grams) Sichuan peppercorns, cracked

¼ teaspoon (1 gram) kosher salt

6 large egg yolks

1. To make the cherry compote, in a medium saucepan, combine the cherries, sugar, and salt and cook over medium heat until the sugar has dissolved and the juices released by the cherries come to a simmer. Skim any foam that forms on the surface; reduce the heat to low and simmer gently until the syrup thickens and the fruit softens and slumps, about 30 minutes. Transfer the compote to a jar and set aside. The compote can be made up to 1 week in advance and stored in the refrigerator; you will need ¼ cup for this recipe.

2. To make the Sichuan peppercorn ice cream, pour the cream and milk into a double boiler or a heatproof bowl set over a saucepan of gently simmering water (the bottom of the bowl should not touch the water). Whisk in ½ cup (100 grams) of the sugar, the peppercorns, and the salt and stir until the sugar and salt have dissolved. Warm the mixture until you see steam rising from the top. Remove from the heat, cover, and let the mixture infuse for 15 minutes. Strain the mixture into a bowl; discard the peppercorns in the strainer. Return the dairy mixture to the double boiler and warm until steam starts to rise again.

3. Meanwhile, prepare an ice bath in a large bowl and set another bowl over it. Set aside.

4. In a medium bowl, with a kitchen towel underneath it to prevent slipping, whisk together the egg yolks with the remaining 2 tablespoons (25 grams) sugar until uniform. While whisking, add a splash of the hot dairy mixture to the yolks. Continue to add the dairy mixture, whisking it in bit by bit, until you've added about half. Add the yolk mixture to the remaining dairy mixture in the double boiler. Set the heat under the double boiler to medium and cook the custard, stirring continuously with a wooden spoon and reducing the heat to medium-low as necessary, until steam begins to rise from the surface and the custard thickens enough

The peppercorns will absorb some liquid, which is why you are adding a bit more milk to compensate.

to coat the back of the spoon. Hold the spoon horizontally and run your finger through the custard. If the trail left by your finger stays separated, the custard is ready to be cooled.

5. Strain the custard into the bowl sitting over the prepared ice bath and stir for 3 to 5 minutes, or until the custard has cooled. Transfer the custard to a quart-size container, cover, and refrigerate for at least 4 hours or, preferably, overnight.

6. Pour the chilled custard into an ice cream maker and freeze according to the manufacturer's instructions. Place the container in which you refrigerated the custard in the freezer so you can use it to store the finished ice cream. Churn the ice cream until the texture resembles "soft serve." Using a spatula, fold in $1/4$ cup of the cherry compote, along with some of its syrup, until incorporated. Transfer the ice cream to the chilled storage container and freeze until hardened to your desired consistency. Alternatively, you can serve it immediately—it will be the consistency of gelato. Feel free to top your ice cream with additional cherry compote. The ice cream will keep, frozen, for up to 7 days.

MASALA CHAI WITH BLACK PEPPERCORNS ICE CREAM

While there are countless variations of masala chai, a generously sweetened Indian spice-infused black tea made with milk and water, we prefer ones where cardamom is the dominant flavor. It also translates well into ice cream; it's easy for chai to taste amazing hot, yet overwhelmingly sweet as a creamy dessert. Something about the cardamom version, however, keeps the ice cream restrained and balanced. When we first tried it, it tasted just like masala chai, but frozen. As everyone's palate is different, we recommend you play around with masala chai ingredients to find your favorite combination.

MAKES ABOUT 1 QUART

2 cups heavy cream

1½ cups whole milk

½ cup plus 2 tablespoons (125 grams) sugar

2 tablespoons (10 grams) loose black tea, preferably Assam

2 tablespoons (12 grams) green cardamom pods, cracked

3 whole cloves

1 3-inch cinnamon stick

½ teaspoon (2 grams) kosher salt

¼ teaspoon ground ginger

8 large egg yolks

1 teaspoon freshly cracked black peppercorns

1. Pour the cream and milk into a double boiler or a heatproof bowl set over a saucepan of gently simmering water (the bottom of the bowl should not touch the water). Whisk in ½ cup (100 grams) of the sugar, the tea, cardamom, cloves, cinnamon stick, salt, and ginger, and stir until the sugar has dissolved. Warm the mixture until you see steam rising from the top. Remove from the heat, cover, and let the mixture steep for 15 minutes. Strain the mixture into a bowl, pressing on the solids; discard the tea leaves and spices in the strainer. Return the dairy mixture to the double boiler.

2. Meanwhile, prepare an ice bath in a large bowl and set another bowl over it. Set aside.

3. In a medium bowl, with a kitchen towel underneath it to prevent slipping, whisk together the egg yolks with the remaining 2 tablespoons (25 grams) sugar until uniform. While whisking, add a splash of the hot dairy mixture to the yolks. Continue to add the dairy mixture, whisking it in bit by bit, until you've added about half. Add the yolk mixture to the remaining dairy mixture in the double boiler. Set the heat under the double boiler to medium and cook the custard, stirring continuously with a wooden spoon and reducing the heat to medium-low as necessary, until steam begins to rise from the surface and the custard thickens enough to coat the back of the spoon. Hold the spoon horizontally and run your finger through the custard. If the trail left by your finger stays separated, the custard is ready to be cooled.

4. Strain the custard into the bowl sitting over the prepared ice bath and stir for 3 to 5 minutes, or until the custard has cooled; stir in the cracked peppercorns. Transfer the custard to a quart-size container, cover, and refrigerate for at least 4 hours or, preferably, overnight.

5. Pour the chilled custard into an ice cream maker and freeze according to the manufacturer's instructions. Place the container in which you refrigerated the custard in the freezer so you can use it to store the finished ice cream. Churn the ice cream until the texture resembles "soft serve." Transfer the ice cream to the chilled storage container and freeze until hardened to your desired consistency. Alternatively, you can serve it immediately—it will be the consistency of gelato. The ice cream will keep, frozen, for up to 7 days.

CURRIED NUTS WITH
SALTED CARAMEL SWIRL ICE CREAM

This flavor is the result of a collaboration between our ice cream company and Selamat Pagi, our Balinese restaurant in Greenpoint. Our ice cream headquarters are in the back of the restaurant, and one day we were snacking on some vanilla ice cream and saw a bowl of Selamat's curried nuts sitting around. On a whim, we threw the nuts into the ice cream and took a spoonful. And immediately, we knew this had to become its own special flavor.

We serve the spiced, caramelized nuts at the restaurant as a bar snack; they are dangerously addictive and go perfectly with a cold lager. But, as you can see below, the ingredient list for the nuts alone goes on and on. In fact, when *Bon Appétit* magazine came to us asking to feature this ice cream in their August 2014 issue, they were surprised to get such a long recipe. We told them the same thing we're telling you now: That time and effort? Totally worth it.

MAKES ABOUT 1 QUART

FOR THE ICE CREAM BASE

2 cups heavy cream

1 cup whole milk

½ cup plus 2 tablespoons (125 grams) granulated sugar

¼ teaspoon (1 gram) kosher salt

8 large egg yolks

FOR THE CURRIED NUTS

6 tablespoons (45 grams) unrefined palm sugar

½ teaspoon (2 grams) brown rice syrup

2 teaspoons (5 grams) whole coriander seeds

2 teaspoons (2 grams) whole black peppercorns, or preferably long pepper, if you can find it

5 teaspoons (20 grams) kosher salt

(continued on next page)

1. To make the ice cream, pour the cream and milk into a double boiler or a heatproof bowl set over a saucepan of gently simmering water (the bottom of the bowl should not touch the water). Whisk in ½ cup (100 grams) of the granulated sugar and the salt and stir until they have dissolved. Warm the mixture until you see steam rising from the top.

2. Meanwhile, prepare an ice bath in a large bowl and set another bowl over it. Set aside.

3. In a medium bowl, with a kitchen towel underneath it to prevent slipping, whisk together the egg yolks with the remaining 2 tablespoons (25 grams) granulated sugar until uniform. While whisking, add a splash of the hot dairy mixture to the yolks. Continue to add the dairy mixture, whisking it in bit by bit, until you've added about half. Add the yolk mixture to the remaining dairy mixture in the double boiler. Set the heat under the double boiler to medium and cook the custard, stirring continuously with a wooden spoon and reducing the heat to medium-low as necessary, until steam begins to rise from the surface and the custard thickens enough to coat the back of the spoon. Hold the spoon horizontally and run your finger through the custard. If the trail left by your finger stays separated, the custard is ready to be cooled.

4. Strain the custard into the bowl sitting over the prepared ice bath and stir for 3 to 5 minutes, or until the custard has cooled. Transfer the custard to a quart-size container, cover, and refrigerate for at least 4 hours or, preferably, overnight.

5. To make the curried nuts, preheat the oven to 350°F; position a rack in the middle. Line a rimmed baking sheet with parchment paper.

(continued)

2½ teaspoons (5 grams)
ground ginger

2½ teaspoons (5 grams)
ground cinnamon

2½ teaspoons (5 grams)
ground turmeric

2 teaspoons (4 grams)
cayenne pepper

1 cup (150 grams) unsalted
raw peanuts

⅓ cup (40 grams) slivered
unsalted raw almonds

¼ cup (32 grams) chopped
unsalted raw walnuts

¼ cup (32 grams) chopped
unsalted raw pecans

¼ cup (40 grams) unsalted
raw pepitas

¼ cup (40 grams) unsalted
raw sunflower seeds

**FOR THE SALTED
CARAMEL**

1 cup (200 grams)
granulated sugar

¾ cup heavy cream

1¼ teaspoons (1 gram) flaky
sea salt, such as Maldon

6. In a small saucepan, combine the palm sugar with 1 tablespoon (15 grams) water and stir over low heat until the sugar has dissolved. Stir in the brown rice syrup and set the simple syrup aside.

7. In a small, dry skillet, combine the coriander and black pepper and toast over low heat until fragrant, 3 to 5 minutes. Remove from the heat and immediately transfer to a spice grinder or a mortar and pestle; finely grind the spices and place in a small bowl. Add the salt, ginger, cinnamon, turmeric, and cayenne and whisk thoroughly to combine. Set the spice blend aside.

8. In large skillet, combine the peanuts, almonds, walnuts, and pecans and toast over medium heat, stirring or tossing continuously to ensure even toasting, until fragrant, 5 to 7 minutes. (The toasting time will depend on how powerful your burner is, so always navigate this part by your nose, rather than by the cooking time.)

9. Stir the spice mixture into the toasted nuts, and then add the pepitas and sunflower seeds; stir to combine. Add the simple syrup and stir to evenly distribute.

10. Spread the nut mixture on the prepared baking sheet and bake for about 10 minutes, or until the nuts are fragrant. Transfer the baking sheet to a wire rack and let cool completely before using in ice cream or enjoying as a snack.

11. To make the salted caramel, place the granulated sugar in a deep, heavy saucepan. Stir continuously and break up the lumps—this will help the sugar caramelize evenly. Bring to a simmer over medium heat, stirring with a spatula to dissolve the sugar, then simmer, without stirring, until the caramel turns the color of a copper penny (or an Irish setter), about 4 minutes. If, while the caramel cooks, any sugar crystallizes on the sides of the pan, brush the sides down with a clean, wet pastry brush. Reduce the heat to low, and slowly add the heavy cream (the caramel will rise and bubble and might spit, so be careful); stir until the heavy cream is incorporated. Remove from the heat and stir in the salt. Should the caramel seize and harden, return the mixture to the heat and stir until it softens. Remove from the heat and set aside.

12. To assemble the ice cream, pour the chilled custard into an ice cream maker and freeze according to the manufacturer's instructions. Place the container in which you refrigerated the custard in the freezer so you can use it to store the finished ice cream. Churn the ice cream until the texture resembles "soft

serve." Using a spatula, fold in ²/₃ cup of the curried nuts and ¹/₂ cup of the caramel so both ingredients are well incorporated. Transfer the ice cream to the chilled storage container and freeze until hardened to your desired consistency. Alternatively, you can serve it immediately—it will be the consistency of gelato. The ice cream will keep, frozen, for up to 7 days. You can use the remaining curried nuts and salted caramel as toppings, or save them for another batch of ice cream. The nuts will keep in an airtight container at room temperature for about 1 week; the salted caramel will keep in an airtight container in the refrigerator for about 1 week.

ben's note *This batch makes spiced nuts that are aggressively salty and—upon first taste—may seem a bit overseasoned. However, when you combine the nuts with the sweet base and salted caramel, the nuts offer some counterbalance. If, however, you still find the salt to be a bit much, simply scale it back to your perfect amount.*

VEGAN PEANUT BUTTER AND
CHOCOLATE CHIP ICE CREAM, PAGE 147

two

VEGAN ICE CREAM

We've always wanted to make vegan ice cream, and knew that one day we would, but it took us some time to figure out a way to make our vegan ice cream taste as good as our regular stuff. For the first few years at Van Leeuwen, we were focused on perfecting our custard-based ice creams; we wanted to get those formulas right before expanding our product offerings. At the same time, many of our patrons and would-be patrons had been clamoring for vegan and dairy-free options since the day we launched.

In our personal lives, we make a conscious attempt to eat less meat to decrease our impact on the environment and reduce animal suffering; I only eat fish, and Ben and Pete have made a choice to cut out meat from their diets. It is generally agreed that eating a primarily plant-based diet is gentler on the environment. While we're not suggesting you adopt a vegan lifestyle (did you see our last chapter on dairy-based ice cream?), we do like having the option of ice cream that tastes just as good as one containing dairy or egg yolks—but actually doesn't.

When we first began experimenting with a vegan ice cream base, we started with coconut milk, cocoa butter, sugar, and guar gum. It was the first and only time we used gums in anything, because we couldn't get the right texture without a stabilizer. And though our patrons loved it and we were selling a lot of it,

we weren't happy. We had always prided ourselves on not using gums, and we felt we had to find a way around that.

So, we went back to the drawing board, and after playing around with homemade nut milks—with cashew milk coming out a clear winner!—we finally got it. The result is smooth and rich vegan ice cream—no gums needed. We couldn't believe there was no cream or egg yolks!

If you're wondering why cashew milk was a winner, we have an explanation: There's no straining needed for cashew milk, which made large-scale production logistics a great deal easier. Imagine a giant muslin bag of almond pulp that needs to be squeezed out. With cashew milk, we just needed a high-powered blender like a Vitamix. If you're a home cook, this means you don't need to go out and buy cheesecloth—and that, in our book, makes life just a little easier. You can definitely blend your cashews using a regular standing blender but, depending on its make and motor power, you may need to strain the resulting cashew milk to get the perfect, smooth consistency.

We also liked cashew milk because blending the cashews into water (and not having to strain the cashew milk) resulted in a thicker product, which gave us thicker, more luscious ice cream. And cashews, in our opinion, are a bit more neutral-tasting than almonds, which means a more neutral base, ready to take on flavors without a funny aftertaste.

Using cashew milk allowed us to pull back on the coconut milk, which helped to create a neutral base idea for all flavors and not just those that blend well with coconut. This is why, when you taste our vegan ice cream, you might note that it doesn't have that "vegan" taste so many vegan ice creams have.

When we make our cashew milk, we blend it with just enough water to get it to about 12 percent fat. It's perfect for ice cream making, though if you want to make some for your morning cereal, you may want to add more water to make it looser.

The coconut milk that we use (Native Forest brand is our favorite) has between 14 and 15 percent fat and needs to be shaken well, as it contains no emulsifiers and is prone to separation. In general, it's a good idea to give your coconut milk a good shake before use.

We then combine the two milks, and to bring our fat percentage closer to that of regular ice cream, which is about 22 percent, we add cocoa butter and extra-virgin coconut oil.

As far as sweetener goes, we decided to stick with organic sugar. We contemplated using agave syrup, but after learning how processed it is, and how much fructose (the re-

ally bad sugar) it contained, we decided that regular sugar was actually, if you can believe it, a slightly healthier alternative. Still, sugar is a treat, and we're well aware that too much sugar is not good for you.

There are two pieces of equipment you will absolutely need to make our vegan ice creams. The first is an immersion blender, which we found to be indispensable in every recipe, as it really helped with emulsification of our ice cream base. Immersion blenders are inexpensive and take up almost no space in your kitchen—so it's a smart move for any kitchen, big or small.

The second piece of equipment that you'll most definitely need is a kitchen scale. We were initially tempted to put weights first and volume measurements second in this chapter only, in order to stress the importance of weights over volume when making vegan ice cream. Volume measurements can be deceptive and vegan ice cream formulas are sensitive to minute changes in fat, moisture, and liquid. In the end, we stuck to the original format of volume first, weight following—however, we can't stress enough that, in this chapter, grams are king. Besides, once you start weighing your ingredients, you'll find it's so much faster and easier than measuring by volume that you may never go back to your cups and spoons!

note When making vegan ice cream, it's important to blend continuously when adding the sugar to the fat. If you don't, depending on the temperatures of the room and the cashew/coconut mix, the oil could solidify immediately, resulting in a grainy ice cream with gobs of fat. If that ever happens to you, it can be fixed by reheating the entire mixture and reblending once it's warm.

VEGAN PEANUT BUTTER AND CHOCOLATE CHIP ICE CREAM

If you're on the fence about vegan ice creams (don't worry, we were also skeptical for a while), may we suggest this as the first flavor you try? It tastes just like frozen chocolate peanut butter cups, and we've yet to meet anyone who doesn't like those!

MAKES ABOUT 1 QUART

SPECIAL EQUIPMENT
Immersion blender

1 cup plus 2 tablespoons (242 grams) coconut milk (see opposite)

1 cup (212 grams) Cashew Milk (page 180)

1 cup (200 grams) granulated sugar

¼ cup (40 grams) cocoa butter

2 tablespoons plus 2 teaspoons (40 grams) extra-virgin coconut oil

½ teaspoon (2 grams) kosher salt

2 tablespoons plus 2 teaspoons (46 grams) smooth all-natural peanut butter (see Ben's Note)

3 tablespoons (32 grams) unrefined peanut oil

22 grams finely chopped bittersweet (72% cacao) chocolate

1. Pour the coconut and cashew milks into a tall (2-quart or larger) container and set aside. In a small saucepan, combine the sugar and 2 tablespoons and 2 teaspoons (40 grams) water and stir over low heat until the sugar has melted. Stir in the cocoa butter and coconut oil until melted. Stir in the salt until dissolved.

2. Gently pour the sugar mixture into the coconut milk mixture. Using an immersion blender, buzz the liquids together until emulsified. Add the peanut butter and peanut oil and use the immersion blender to buzz the mixture until emulsified. Cover and refrigerate the ice cream base until chilled, 1 to 2 hours. Do not refrigerate overnight. (If you must refrigerate overnight, "loosen" the solidified ice cream base by placing the container in a bowl with some warm water until it becomes more liquid.)

3. Pour the chilled ice cream base into an ice cream maker and freeze according to the manufacturer's instructions. Place the container in which you refrigerated the custard in the freezer so you can use it to store the finished ice cream. Churn the ice cream until the texture resembles "soft serve." In the last minute of churning, add the chocolate chips and churn until incorporated. Transfer the ice cream to the chilled storage container and freeze until hardened to your desired consistency. Alternatively, you can serve it immediately—it will be the consistency of gelato. The ice cream will keep, frozen, for up to 7 days.

ben's note Many peanut butter brands claim to be all natural, but the best one for this recipe, and the only true "all-natural" peanut butter, is the one that contains only one ingredient—peanuts. I recommend one without salt, too, since it works better in this recipe.

VEGAN SALTED CARAMEL ICE CREAM

For our vegan ice cream launch, we were looking to introduce seven flavors. We had six done and ready to go but wanted to complete our launch with a lucky seventh offering. On a lark, at the eleventh hour, we made salted caramel vegan ice cream and, just like that, we had our seventh flavor.

MAKES ABOUT 1 QUART

SPECIAL EQUIPMENT
Immersion blender

1 cup (212 grams) coconut milk, well shaken (see page 146)

1 cup (212 grams) Cashew Milk (page 180)

¾ cup plus 2 tablespoons (175 grams) granulated sugar

¼ cup (60 grams) extra-virgin coconut oil

6 tablespoons (60 grams) cocoa butter

1 teaspoon flaky sea salt, such as Maldon

1. Pour the coconut and cashew milks into a tall (2-quart or larger) container and set aside.

2. Spread the sugar in an even layer over the bottom of a clean, heavy-duty saucepan or deep skillet; oil and grease are caramel's mortal enemies—so make sure the skillet is clean! Heat the sugar over medium heat, keeping an eye on it. Sometimes it'll start burning in a spot beneath the surface, where you can't see it; this happens especially if the sugar layer is pretty deep. You should see it start to liquefy at the edges first, with perhaps some random blobs in the middle. Once you spot browning at the edges, shift the sugar toward the center to prevent any burnt spots. If the caramel looks grainy, don't worry; reduce the heat to low and stir gently and infrequently; stirring often can cause your sugar to lump and cluster instead of melting evenly. (If this happens, don't worry; just continue to use gentle heat, stirring as little as possible, to let the caramel form and the sugar melt.) If any chunks remain, they will most likely dissolve on their own and any stubborn chunks refusing to melt can be strained out later (see Ben's Note). Cook the caramel until it's a rich brown color—the color of an Irish setter. Reduce the heat to low; add half of the coconut oil and stir, being careful, as caramel can spit and sputter. Stir in the remaining coconut oil until melted; stir in the cocoa butter until melted. Stir in the salt until dissolved.

3. Transfer the caramel to the container with the milks and, using an immersion blender, emulsify the liquid until uniform. Cover and refrigerate the ice cream base until chilled, 1 to 2 hours. Do not refrigerate overnight. (If you must refrigerate overnight, "loosen" the solidified ice cream base by placing the container in a bowl with some warm water until it becomes more liquid.)

4. Pour the ice cream base into an ice cream maker and freeze according to the manufacturer's instructions. Place the container in which you refrigerated the custard in the freezer so you can use it to store the finished ice cream. Churn the ice cream until the texture resembles "soft serve." Transfer the ice cream to the

chilled storage container and freeze until hardened to your desired consistency. Alternatively, you can serve it immediately—it will be the consistency of gelato. The ice cream will keep, frozen, for up to 7 days.

ben's note Sometimes caramel can "seize"—harden—and it can feel like a massive kitchen failure. But not all is lost! In most cases, you can rescue it, at least where this ice cream is concerned. Should this happen to you, return the whole mess to the saucepan, and over medium-low heat, stir the caramel until all the pieces have melted and the caramel is liquid again. Should any small loose, stubborn pieces remain, just discard them and proceed with the recipe as usual.

VEGAN MINT CHIP ICE CREAM

Mint chip ice cream is a crowd-pleaser that continuously hovers at the top of ice cream charts. When we set out to make vegan ice creams, we knew mint chip had to be one of the flavors—there was just no question about it. From experimenting with our regular Mint Chip Ice Cream (page 33), we learned that the trick to getting good mint flavor is quality mint extract. A proper mint extract—we prefer the organic kind—will not taste like mouthwash but, instead, will remind you of delicate mint leaves and the flavor they hold. In order to have the oil perfectly emulsified into the mixture, you need to use an immersion blender.

MAKES ABOUT 1 QUART

SPECIAL EQUIPMENT
Immersion blender

1 cup (212 grams) coconut milk, well shaken (see page 146)

1 cup (212 grams) Cashew Milk (see page 180)

¾ cup (150 grams) granulated sugar

6 tablespoons (60 grams) cocoa butter

¼ cup (60 grams) extra-virgin coconut oil

½ teaspoon (2 grams) kosher salt

1 teaspoon mint extract (see headnote)

22 grams finely chopped bittersweet (72% cacao) chocolate

1. Pour the coconut and cashew milks into a tall (2-quart or larger) container and set aside. In a small saucepan, combine the sugar and 4 teaspoons (20 grams) water and stir over low heat until the sugar has melted. Stir in the cocoa butter and coconut oil until melted. Stir in the salt until dissolved.

2. Gently pour the sugar mixture into the coconut milk mixture. Using an immersion blender, buzz the liquids together until emulsified. Cover and refrigerate the ice cream base until chilled, 1 to 2 hours. Do not refrigerate overnight. (If you must refrigerate overnight, "loosen" the solidified ice cream base by placing the container in a bowl with some warm water until it becomes more liquid.)

3. Add the mint extract to the chilled ice cream base and use an immersion blender to buzz the mixture until uniform. Pour the ice cream base into an ice cream maker and freeze according to the manufacturer's instructions. Place the container in which you refrigerated the ice cream base in the freezer, so you can use it to store the finished ice cream. Churn the ice cream until the texture resembles "soft serve." In the last minute of churning, fold in the chocolate chips and churn until incorporated. Transfer the ice cream to the chilled storage container and freeze until hardened to your desired consistency. Alternatively, you can serve it immediately—it will be the consistency of gelato. The ice cream will keep, frozen, for up to 7 days.

VEGAN COCONUT ICE CREAM

Making this flavor was a no-brainer for us: We were using coconut milk, so why not make a coconut vegan ice cream to celebrate its flavor? The resulting ice cream makes us think of the tropics, especially when we top it with sliced mango. It's also wonderful drizzled with Bitter Vegan Chocolate Syrup (page 184).

MAKES ABOUT 1 QUART

SPECIAL EQUIPMENT
Immersion blender

2 cups (424 grams) coconut milk (see page 146)

1 cup (212 grams) Cashew Milk (page 180)

1¼ cups (250 grams) granulated sugar

3 tablespoons (30 grams) cocoa butter

½ cup plus 2 tablespoons (150 grams) extra-virgin coconut oil

1 teaspoon (4 grams) kosher salt

2 tablespoons (12 grams) sweetened shredded coconut

1. Pour the coconut and cashew milks into a tall (2-quart or larger) container and set aside. In a small saucepan, combine the sugar and ¼ cup (60 grams) water and stir over low heat until the sugar has melted. Stir in the cocoa butter and coconut oil until melted. Stir in the salt until dissolved.

2. Gently pour the sugar mixture into the coconut milk mixture. Using an immersion blender, buzz the liquids together until emulsified. Cover and refrigerate the ice cream base until chilled, 1 to 2 hours. Do not refrigerate overnight. (If you must refrigerate overnight, "loosen" the solidified ice cream base by placing the container in a bowl with some warm water until it becomes more liquid.)

3. Pour the chilled ice cream base into an ice cream maker and freeze according to the manufacturer's instructions. Place the container in which you refrigerated the custard in the freezer so you can use it to store the finished ice cream. Churn the ice cream until the texture resembles "soft serve." In the last minute of churning, add the shredded coconut and churn until incorporated. Transfer the ice cream to the chilled storage container and freeze until hardened to your desired consistency. Alternatively, you can serve it immediately—it will be the consistency of gelato. The ice cream will keep, frozen, for up to 7 days.

VEGAN CHOCOLATE ICE CREAM

You might think of chocolate as a strong flavor that will overpower the taste of coconut. However, perhaps because the two are complementary flavors, you taste both in this recipe, but in such a way that it still remains very much a chocolate ice cream. It's rich and luxurious and has been, unsurprisingly, wildly popular since its launch. Because it contains cocoa solids in addition to the coconut and cashew milks, it's a little higher in fat than some other vegan ice cream flavors and thus tastes a little fuller.

MAKES ABOUT 1 QUART

SPECIAL EQUIPMENT
Immersion blender

1 cup (212 grams) coconut milk (see page 146)

1 cup (212 grams) Cashew Milk (page 180)

½ cup plus 2 tablespoons (125 grams) granulated sugar

¼ cup (40 grams) cocoa butter

2 tablespoons plus 2 teaspoons (40 grams) extra-virgin coconut oil

40 grams unsweetened chocolate (99% cacao), preferably Michel Cluizel (see Sources, page 218)

2 tablespoons plus 2 teaspoons (16 grams) unsweetened cocoa powder

½ teaspoon (2 grams) kosher salt

1. Pour the coconut and cashew milks into a tall (2-quart or larger) container and set aside. In a small saucepan, combine the sugar and 2 tablespoons plus 2 teaspoons (40 grams) water and stir over low heat until the sugar has dissolved. Stir in the cocoa butter, coconut oil, chocolate, and cocoa powder until melted and uniform. Stir in the salt until dissolved.

2. Gently pour the sugar mixture into the coconut milk mixture. Using an immersion blender, buzz the liquids together until emulsified. Cover and refrigerate the ice cream base until chilled, 1 to 2 hours. Do not refrigerate overnight. (If you must refrigerate overnight, "loosen" the solidified ice cream base by placing the container in a bowl with some warm water until it becomes more liquid.)

3. Pour the chilled ice cream base into an ice cream maker and freeze according to the manufacturer's instructions. Place the container in which you refrigerated the custard in the freezer so you can use it to store the finished ice cream. Churn the ice cream until the texture resembles "soft serve." Transfer the ice cream to the chilled storage container and freeze until hardened to your desired consistency. Alternatively, you can serve it immediately—it will be the consistency of gelato. The ice cream will keep, frozen, for up to 7 days.

VEGAN CHOCOLATE, OPPOSITE, AND VEGAN COFFEE ICE CREAM, PAGE 161

CHOCOLATE

Chocolate, as the mostly confectionary product we know today, has come a long way in its historic lineage that encompasses at least three millennia of cultivation. Until a few hundred years ago, chocolate was prepared as a drink, most often for religious and spiritual rituals. Today, chocolate, which comes from the seeds of a cacao plant, and, as we know it, was originally native to Mexico and Central America, is a global commodity, beloved by the almost everyone. (There *are* a few chocolate haters out there, which means more chocolate for the rest of us!)

Christopher Columbus is generally credited with bringing cacao beans to Europe and introducing them to the Spanish royal court. But the appeal of the funny little bean with its bitter taste was lost on the Spaniards. It wasn't until Spanish friars introduced chocolate as a sweetened beverage that cacao beans became a hot, in-demand item. The new sweetened concoction was an instant hit; it was as if chocolate and sugar were destined to be together. That magical combination sealed chocolate's fate, and after that, Spain, as well as the rest of Europe, couldn't get enough of it.

Despite the plant's origins in Mesoamerica, most of today's cacao is grown in western Africa, particularly in Côte d'Ivoire. The beans are harvested, fermented, dried, cleaned, and roasted—a seemingly straightforward process that is anything but. Instead, it's a laborious endeavor that takes months of meticulous manual labor. This might explain why quality chocolate is still, to this day, very much a luxury product.

There are four main types of chocolate: unsweetened, dark, milk, and white—with most of the chocolate we consume today being sweetened. Despite industrial processes, chocolate remains an expensive ingredient, and facing growing demand, many producers decrease production costs by reducing cocoa solids or by swapping out cocoa butter for another fat.

Since we're talking all things chocolate, we'd be remiss if we didn't mention the process of conching, a procedure that makes chocolate taste smoother and more luscious on the palate by breaking the cocoa and sugar particles up so that they are smaller than the tongue can detect. A conche is essentially a container filled with metal beads that act as grinders. The longer the conching takes, the smoother the final mouthfeel and the better the quality of the chocolate. High-quality chocolate is conched for about seventy-two hours, while the lesser grades are conched for four to six hours.

As you probably guessed, we at Van Leeuwen love our chocolate, and we took the time to find a chocolate we could love without reservations. In the end, we selected Michel Cluizel as our chocolate supplier. We made our decision after tasting products from many top chocolate producers; Michel Cluizel was the most extraordinary chocolate that we had ever tasted.

This small, family-run French company processes their cocoa without the use of soy lecithin, an emulsifier that can sometimes leave a waxy feeling in your mouth. Since 1997, Michel Cluizel has worked to develop enduring relationships with renowned growers. We loved that all Michel Cluizel's chocolate was single plantation—meaning the cocoa beans for a particular bar or kind of chocolate are grown on one plantation (very rare!)—and not just single origin, meaning the geographic origin of the cocoa beans (Madagascar, for instance) is the same. Single-origin chocolate usually has cocoa beans from several different plantations, muddling their individual flavors, while single-plantation chocolate has very distinct terroir notes.

All this showed us that Michel Cluizel meticulously did their research on plantations, found the best in class, and made an exclusive commitment to source from those places. We also loved that their practices went even further than Fair Trade; they pay several times the commodity rate, far beyond that of Fair Trade stipulations. A few years ago, Pete took a trip to the Dominican Republic to look at one of Michel Cluizel's plantations and their farming and processing practices, and he came back blown away by the company's commitment to quality as well as its awareness of how its practices affect the community.

Michel Cluizel also takes time to process their cocoa beans post-harvest, air-drying the beans after fermentation. Most cocoa processors use an oven to dry the beans, as it greatly expedites the processing time, but this can result in a slightly burnt taste, diminishing the nuances in the intricate flavor components of the chocolate. Michel Cluizel insists that all of their plantations air-dry the beans; in wet climates like that of São Tomé, an island off western Africa, this can mean building special drying housing and having to wait for days. But, as with all great artisanal producers, quality cannot be sacrificed.

Unlike most cocoa processors, Michel Cluizel grinds *whole* vanilla beans into their mills along with the cocoa beans. This is a far superior practice than using an extract—a practice used by most chocolatiers, and one you can readily taste. The actual beans give the chocolate a more pure, less diluted flavor than extract, which is usually alcohol based.

VEGAN ROASTED BANANA ICE CREAM

Some of our vegan flavors came together in a flash; others, like this vegan roasted banana flavor, took some time to get just right. The trick, as we learned, was to get just the right fat percentage without sacrificing texture or flavor. Don't skip the roasting of the banana—not only does roasting help with moisture evaporation but it also brings out the banana's rich caramel notes, making this ice cream truly memorable.

MAKES ABOUT 1 QUART

SPECIAL EQUIPMENT
Immersion blender

1 cup plus 2 tablespoons (242 grams) coconut milk (see page 146)

1 cup (212 grams) Cashew Milk (page 180)

¾ cup plus 2 tablespoons (175 grams) granulated sugar

½ cup (80 grams) cocoa butter

¼ cup plus 2 teaspoons (70 grams) extra-virgin coconut oil

1 teaspoon (4 grams) kosher salt

1 recipe Roasted Bananas (about 160 grams; see page 67)

½ cup (64 grams) chopped walnuts

1. Pour the coconut and cashew milks into a tall (2-quart or larger) container and set aside. In a small saucepan, combine the sugar and ¼ cup (60 grams) water and stir over low heat until the sugar has melted. Stir in the cocoa butter and coconut oil until melted. Stir in the salt until dissolved.

2. Gently pour the sugar mixture into the coconut milk mixture. Using an immersion blender, buzz the liquids together until emulsified. Add the roasted bananas and use the immersion blender to buzz the mixture until emulsified. Cover and refrigerate the ice cream base until chilled, 1 to 2 hours. Do not refrigerate overnight. (If you must refrigerate overnight, "loosen" the solidified ice cream base by placing the container in a bowl with some warm water until it becomes more liquid.)

3. Pour the chilled ice cream base into an ice cream maker and freeze according to the manufacturer's instructions. Place the container in which you refrigerated the custard in the freezer so you can use it to store the finished ice cream. Churn the ice cream until the texture resembles "soft serve."

4. While the ice cream churns, preheat the oven to 300°F; position a rack in the middle. Spread the walnuts on a rimmed baking sheet and toast in the oven for about 5 minutes, or until fragrant; transfer the nuts to a bowl to cool. In the last minute of churning, add the toasted walnuts and churn until incorporated. Transfer the ice cream to the chilled storage container and freeze until hardened to your desired consistency. Alternatively, you can serve it immediately—it will be the consistency of gelato. The ice cream will keep, frozen, for up to 7 days.

VEGAN PISTACHIO ICE CREAM

Nuts are such an essential part of making vegan ice cream (our base is heavy on homemade Cashew Milk, page 180), that this recipe was a no-brainer. We use the same pistachio paste we rely on in our regular Pistachio Ice Cream (page 85), letting its nutty flavor shine through. It took us a while to perfect the vegan version, but it was worth every batch that came up short.

MAKES ABOUT 1 QUART

SPECIAL EQUIPMENT
Immersion blender

1 cup plus 2 tablespoons
(242 grams) coconut milk
(see page 146)

1 cup plus 2 tablespoons
(242 grams) Cashew Milk
(page 180)

¾ cup plus 2 tablespoons
(175 grams) granulated
sugar

3 tablespoons (30 grams)
cocoa butter

¼ cup plus 2 teaspoons
(70 grams) extra-virgin
coconut oil

½ teaspoon (2 grams)
kosher salt

3 tablespoons (37 grams)
pistachio paste (see
Sources, page 218)

1. Pour the coconut and cashew milks into a tall (2-quart or larger) container and set aside. In a small saucepan, combine the sugar and 3 tablespoons plus 1 teaspoon (50 grams) water and stir over low heat until the sugar has melted. Stir in the cocoa butter and coconut oil until melted. Stir in the salt until dissolved.

2. Gently pour the sugar mixture into the coconut milk mixture. Using an immersion blender, buzz the liquids together until emulsified. Add the pistachio paste and use the immersion blender to buzz the mixture until emulsified. Cover and refrigerate the ice cream base until chilled, 1 to 2 hours. Do not refrigerate overnight. (If you must refrigerate overnight, "loosen" the solidified ice cream base by placing the container in a bowl with some warm water until it becomes more liquid.)

3. Pour the chilled ice cream base into an ice cream maker and freeze according to the manufacturer's instructions. Place the container in which you refrigerated the custard in the freezer so you can use it to store the finished ice cream. Churn the ice cream until the texture resembles "soft serve." Transfer the ice cream to the chilled storage container and freeze until hardened to your desired consistency. Alternatively, you can serve it immediately—it will be the consistency of gelato. The ice cream will keep, frozen, for up to 7 days.

PISTACHIOS

Pistachios, members of the cashew family, are a hardy plant capable of surviving in harsh soil conditions. They fare much better in drier soil; long, hot, dry summers are essential for the proper ripening of the fruit.

Pistachios are some of the oldest nuts we know. They have a long culinary history; they were written about by Pliny the Elder and are mentioned in the Bible.

On the slopes of Mount Etna in Sicily, multigenerational Italian growers harvest the finest pistachios on earth. These pistachios account for less than 1 percent of the world's production of the nut. They have a rich green color and a deep, unique flavor drawn from Mount Etna's volcanic soil.

The International Slow Food Institute has certified these pistachios, but no other. This variety of pistachio grows on the rugged lands of Bronte and nowhere else in Europe. It is only here that the pistachios acquire such a brilliant emerald green color and such an intense, resinous, and full fragrance.

Bronte is perched on the steep roads between the Etna volcano and the Park of Nebrodi, one of the largest parks in Sicily—it's a beautiful landscape! Bronte's livelihood depends on pistachios: The people of Bronte grow them, sell them, and turn them into sweets, creams, and sauces. The trees are not fertilized, nor are they watered, in part because there is very little water in that area, and also because the pistachio trees are robust and can survive an arid climate. The trees require minimal attention and are pruned only a couple of times to remove the dead branches and the shoots in the "fallow" years (the pistachio tree produces its nuts one year and rests the following year). It is during the resting period that the farmers remove the few buds that may sprout on the branches; and the plant gets to store all its energy and explode with fruit during the following season. Allowing the trees to rest every other year ensures that the flavor of the resulting pistachios has a depth unmatched by other varieties. Etna's volcanic, mineral-rich soil ensures its unparalleled taste.

After a two-year wait, the harvest is an exciting and busy time. Between the end of August and the beginning of September, the town empties and everyone gathers in the *loci* (the local name for the pistachio orchards): women, children—even the elderly! The operation is almost acrobatic. Balancing on blocks of lava, people hold on to the branches with one hand, and with the other pick the pistachio nuts, one by one, dropping them into a canvas bag tied around their necks. In a day's work, they manage to pick 20 kilos of pistachios at the most. On flat lands, a sheet can be spread out under the tree to make it easier to gather the nuts. The price of the pistachios from Bronte dwarfs that of the less tasty nuts from Iran, Turkey, and the United States. For this reason, leading confectionary and cold cuts producers in Italy—who originally purchased their pistachios from Sicily—no longer use these premium pistachios, opting for a cheaper alternative. We, however, feel these pistachios make a real difference in our ice cream.

VEGAN COLD-BREWED EARL GREY TEA ICE CREAM

At Van Leeuwen, we are big fans of social media—not only is it great for getting your message out, but it also connects you with amazing people and brings you closer to your audience. And it's thanks to social media that we now serve our vegan Earl Grey flavor. It started with one of our Instagram followers who kept asking us, time after time, when we'd have this flavor available as a vegan version. We're so glad we listened to her—it's absolutely delicious!

MAKES ABOUT 1½ PINTS

SPECIAL EQUIPMENT
Immersion blender

1 cup (212 grams) coconut milk (see page 146)

1 cup (212 grams) Cashew Milk (page 180)

¾ cup (150 grams) granulated sugar

6 tablespoons (30 grams) loose Earl Grey tea (see Sources, page 218)

6 tablespoons (60 grams) cocoa butter

¼ cup (60 grams) extra-virgin coconut oil

½ teaspoon (2 grams) kosher salt

1. Pour the coconut milk, cashew milk, sugar, tea, and 2 tablespoons (30 grams) water into a tall (2-quart or larger) container. Stir to combine; cover and refrigerate for 12 to 24 hours. Stir the liquid, then strain it into a large bowl, pressing on the solids; discard the tea leaves in the strainer. Return the liquid to the container and set aside.

2. In a small saucepan, melt the cocoa butter and coconut oil together over low heat until combined. Stir in the salt and remove from the heat.

3. Gently pour the cocoa butter mixture into the coconut milk mixture. Using an immersion blender, buzz the liquids together until emulsified. Cover and refrigerate the ice cream base until chilled, 1 to 2 hours. Do not refrigerate overnight. (If you must refrigerate overnight, "loosen" the solidified ice cream base by placing the container in a bowl with some warm water until it becomes more liquid.)

4. Pour the chilled ice cream base into an ice cream maker and freeze according to the manufacturer's instructions. Place the container in which you refrigerated the custard in the freezer so you can use it to store the finished ice cream. Churn the ice cream until the texture resembles "soft serve." Transfer the ice cream to the chilled storage container and freeze until hardened to your desired consistency. Alternatively, you can serve it immediately—it will be the consistency of gelato. The ice cream will keep, frozen, for up to 7 days.

VEGAN COFFEE ICE CREAM

This coffee vegan ice cream tastes so much like ice cream made with dairy and egg yolks, we're still a bit in disbelief. We like to add cocoa nibs at the end for some crunch and texture.

MAKES ABOUT 1 QUART

SPECIAL EQUIPMENT
Immersion blender

¾ cup (160 grams) coconut milk (see page 146)

¾ cup (160 grams) Cashew Milk (see page 180)

½ cup plus 1 teaspoon (104 grams) granulated sugar

5 tablespoons (50 grams) cocoa butter

3 tablespoons plus 1 teaspoon (50 grams) extra-virgin coconut oil

2 tablespoons (7 grams) freeze-dried coffee

½ tablespoon (3 grams) unsweetened cocoa powder

3 tablespoons (22 grams) unrefined palm sugar

½ teaspoon (2 grams) kosher salt

2 tablespoons (10 grams) cocoa nibs (optional)

1. Pour the coconut and cashew milks into a tall (2-quart or larger) container and set aside. In a small saucepan, combine the granulated sugar and 2 tablespoons (30 grams) water and stir over low heat until the sugar has melted. Stir in the cocoa butter and coconut oil until melted. Stir in the coffee, cocoa powder, palm sugar, and salt until dissolved.

2. Gently pour the sugar mixture into the coconut milk mixture. Using an immersion blender, buzz the liquids together until emulsified. Cover and refrigerate the ice cream base until chilled, 1 to 2 hours. Do not refrigerate overnight. (If you must refrigerate overnight, "loosen" the solidified ice cream base by placing the container in a bowl with some warm water until it becomes more liquid.)

3. Pour the chilled ice cream base into an ice cream maker and freeze according to the manufacturer's instructions. Place the container in which you refrigerated the custard in the freezer so you can use it to store the finished ice cream. Churn the ice cream until the texture resembles "soft serve." In the last minute of churning, add the cocoa nibs, if using, and churn until incorporated. Transfer the ice cream to the chilled storage container and freeze until hardened to your desired consistency. Alternatively, you can serve it immediately—it will be the consistency of gelato. The ice cream will keep, frozen, for up to 7 days.

CLOCKWISE FROM TOP LEFT:
GIANDUJA ICE CREAM, PAGE 22; MANGO SORBET,
PAGE 170; LAVENDER AND HONEY ICE CREAM,
PAGE 114; RASPBERRY SORBET, PAGE 170

three

SORBET, FROZEN YOGURT, AND GRANITA

As much as we love ice cream, sometimes, especially after a hearty meal, we find ourselves a bit too full for a rich dessert—that's where sorbet comes in. Sorbet, with its clean flavor and light texture, can be a great palate cleanser.

The best sorbets, unsurprisingly, are made with ripe fruit at the peak of its season. We prefer fruit from the greenmarket—it is always higher in quality than anything we find at the grocery store. The stuff sold in the frozen aisle of your supermarket will pale in comparison to in-season market fruit and, subsequently, what will emerge out of your ice cream maker.

Keep in mind that your sorbet results will vary from batch to batch. First, fruit itself varies in sweetness and moisture content. Additional factors that affect moisture level include where the fruit was grown, the climate during the growth season as well as right before harvesting, and time of year of the harvest itself. Supermarket strawberries will be very different from heirloom farmers' market varieties, and those at the farmers' market will vary from farmer to farmer depending on strains, climate, and so on. Likewise, strawberries picked in June will be different from those that become ripe in August.

Because we think of sorbets as a celebration of fruit, we like to keep our sorbets simple: fruit, sugar, maybe a little acid to brighten things up—and that's pretty much it. We tend to favor tart flavors, so we've stuck with our favorites, but sorbet can be made with just about any fruit you like.

While you can definitely play around with sugar amounts, don't scale sugar up or down too much if you want the sorbet to remain scoopable. It's always a good idea to let sorbets sit on your counter for about five minutes before scooping. Since they're mostly sugar and fruit (and fruit contains a lot of water), sorbets can freeze harder than ice creams and some, like Lemon (page 168), might even feel icy right out of the freezer.

We also love a good frozen yogurt, but perhaps we're a bit boring in that we like the most basic, simplest kind. If you want to spruce yours up, you can always include a chocolate swirl (see page 183), rhubarb compote (see page 72), or any add-ins you might like.

Finally, because we love granitas, we share our two favorites, Watermelon (page 175) and Espresso (page 176)—they're our go-to frozen desserts when we're on vacation and away from our beloved ice cream machines. Unsurprisingly, rental home kitchens don't come equipped with an ice cream machine (or much in the way of kitchen equipment), and it's wonderful to have a low-tech option that's delicious and easy to throw together.

CHOCOLATE SORBET

This is a rich-tasting sorbet thanks to the fat solids from the cocoa butter. It's pretty much the closest manifestation of dark chocolate in frozen form that we can think of. If you like dark chocolate, you will absolutely love this. And if you're suspicious of sorbet because you think it's too icy or wimpy in flavor, we think you ought to give chocolate sorbet a try—you'll be impressed by how thick and fudgy it is. Chocolate ice cream fans, beware—this might give ice cream a run for its money.

MAKES ABOUT 1 QUART

1¼ cups plus 2 tablespoons (274 grams) sugar

4½ ounces (127 grams) unsweetened chocolate (99% cacao), preferably Michel Cluizel (see Sources, page 218)

¾ cup (60 grams) unsweetened natural cocoa powder

½ teaspoon (2 grams) kosher salt

1. In a medium saucepan, combine the sugar and 2 cups water and stir over low heat until the sugar is fully coated. Stir in the chocolate, cocoa powder, and salt until combined. Cook, stirring until the liquid is uniform, the chocolate has melted, and the sugar and cocoa powder have dissolved completely. Transfer the sorbet base to a quart-size container, cover, and refrigerate until fully cold, about 3 hours.

2. Pour the chilled sorbet base into an ice cream maker and freeze according to the manufacturer's instructions. Place the container in which you refrigerated the sorbet base in the freezer so you can use it to store the finished sorbet. Churn the sorbet until it resembles Italian ice. Transfer the sorbet to the chilled storage container and freeze until hardened to your desired consistency. The sorbet will keep, frozen, for up to 7 days.

CHOCOLATE SORBET (OPPOSITE) AND COCONUT ICE CREAM, PAGE 106

CANTALOUPE SORBET

Ripe cantaloupe is one of the most seductive fruits of the summer: Fragrant and honey-sweet, its perfumed aroma saturates the air around it. When it's good, it's irresistible. Aside from popping pieces of it straight from the fridge, we love to transform cantaloupe into sorbet. Wait until it's melon season, and then make this wonderful dessert.

MAKES ABOUT 1 QUART

1 2-pound cantaloupe

½ cup (100 grams) sugar

1½ teaspoons fresh lime juice

1 teaspoon finely grated lime zest

Pinch of kosher salt

1. Place the cantaloupe, sugar, lime juice, lime zest, and salt in a blender and puree until smooth. Transfer the sorbet base to a quart-size container, cover, and refrigerate until fully cold, about 3 hours.
2. Pour the chilled sorbet base into an ice cream maker and freeze according to the manufacturer's instructions. Place the container in which you refrigerated the sorbet base in the freezer, so you can use it to store the finished sorbet. Churn the sorbet until it resembles Italian ice. Transfer the sorbet to the chilled storage container and freeze until hardened to your desired consistency. The sorbet will keep, frozen, for up to 7 days.

GRAPEFRUIT SORBET

Grapefruit is that citrus fruit that splits people down the middle: There are as many lovers as there are haters, and we are firmly in the lovers' camp. We love grapefruit's lower sugar, its bracing acidity—we even love its subtle bitterness. While grapefruit is best in the dead of winter, we like to make this sorbet year-round, especially in the summer when it's most refreshing. Because we hate to waste ingredients, we like to candy the grapefruit peel for the grapefruit version of *orangettes*. It makes an excellent sorbet topping, and everyone loves getting candied citrus peels as a gift.

MAKES ABOUT 1 QUART

FOR THE SORBET

8 medium grapefruits,
    preferably organic

½ cup (100 grams) sugar

**FOR THE CANDIED
GRAPEFRUIT PEELS**

2 cups (400 grams) sugar,
    plus more for tossing

> **ben's note** *You are more than welcome to candy all of the grapefruit peels; just be sure to adjust the proportions accordingly. Everyone loves these and you can package them up in cellophane bags and give them out as gifts. And, because a little chocolate has never hurt anyone, you can also dip the candied peels into melted dark chocolate and allow it to harden before packaging.*

1. To make the sorbet, halve and juice the grapefruits into a quart-size container, reserving 8 of the empty halves (see Ben's Note). You should have about 4 cups grapefruit juice. In a saucepan, combine the sugar with about ½ cup of the grapefruit juice and stir over medium heat until the sugar has fully dissolved. Remove from the heat and add the syrup to the container with the remaining grapefruit juice. Cover and refrigerate the sorbet base until fully chilled.

2. To make the candied grapefruit peels, using your fingers, remove the fleshy remains of the grapefruits from the peels; cut the peels into ⅜-inch-wide strips, leaving about ⅛ inch of the white pith attached. Place the peels in a medium saucepan and add cold water to cover. Bring the water to a boil, then drain. Repeat twice.

3. After the third draining, return the peels to the saucepan and add the sugar and 1 cup water. Bring to a boil; reduce the heat to low, cover, and simmer until the peels are translucent, 35 to 40 minutes. Drain and transfer the peels to a wire rack to dry, 2 to 4 hours. Transfer the peels to a bowl and toss with more sugar until coated. Return the peels to the wire rack and let dry for at least 10 hours before eating.

4. Pour the chilled sorbet base into an ice cream maker and freeze according to the manufacturer's instructions. Place the container in which you refrigerated the sorbet base in the freezer, so you can use it to store the finished sorbet. Churn the sorbet until the texture resembles Italian ice. Transfer the sorbet to the chilled storage container and freeze until hardened to your desired consistency. Alternatively, you can serve it immediately—it will be the consistency of gelato. Top the sorbet with the candied grapefruit peels. The sorbet will keep, frozen, for up to 7 days. The grapefruit peels will keep in an airtight container for up to a few months.

LEMON SORBET

In our book, lemon sorbet claims the prize for "Most Refreshing on the Hottest Day of Summer." And yet, more often than not, store-bought lemon sorbet is strangely disappointing, with a fake lemon flavor and dish-soap overtones. We think that a homemade version beats those other ones hands down, and might be just the thing you're looking for when you desperately need to cool off. Because this sorbet uses some zest from the lemons, we recommend using organic lemons not sprayed with pesticides, which remain on the skin of lemons even after you wash them.

MAKES ABOUT 1 QUART

FOR THE BASIC SIMPLE SYRUP

2 cups (400 grams) sugar

FOR THE LEMON SORBET

2 cups fresh lemon juice (from 8 to 10 lemons), strained

1 tablespoon finely grated lemon zest

1. To make the basic simple syrup, in a small saucepan, combine the sugar and 2 cups water and bring to a boil; reduce the heat to low and simmer until the sugar has dissolved, 3 minutes. Remove from the heat and let cool completely. You should have about 3 cups simple syrup. You will need 2 cups for this recipe; use whatever remains for iced tea, iced coffee, lemonade, or cocktails. The syrup can be refrigerated in a clean, sealed jar for up to 1 month.

2. To make the lemon sorbet, combine the lemon juice, lemon zest, and 2 cups of the simple syrup in a quart-size container. Cover and refrigerate the sorbet base until fully cold, about 3 hours.

3. Pour the chilled sorbet base into an ice cream maker and freeze according to the manufacturer's instructions. Place the container in which you refrigerated the sorbet base in the freezer, so you can use it to store the finished sorbet. Churn the sorbet until it resembles Italian ice. Transfer the sorbet to the chilled storage container and freeze until hardened to your desired consistency. The sorbet will keep, frozen, for up to 7 days.

PASSION FRUIT SORBET

As you probably already guessed, we go weak in the knees when it comes to a good, tangy sorbet, and this one will really make you pucker. Passion fruit puree, which can be found online and in specialty stores, makes this sorbet pretty easy to make, and gives it that unique, tropical flavor. Since I grew up with a passion fruit vine in my parents' garden (talk about taking passion fruit for granted back then!), it always makes me think fondly of Australia and of my family.

MAKES ABOUT 1 QUART

FOR THE CONCENTRATED SIMPLE SYRUP

2 cups (400 grams) sugar

FOR THE PASSION FRUIT SORBET

3 cups passion fruit puree
(see Sources, page 218)

1. To make the concentrated simple syrup, in a small saucepan, combine the sugar and 1 cup water and bring to a boil; reduce the heat to low and simmer until the sugar has dissolved, 3 minutes. Remove from the heat and let cool completely. You should have about 2½ cups concentrated syrup. You will need 1 cup for this recipe; use whatever remains for iced tea, iced coffee, lemonade, or cocktails. Because the syrup is twice as concentrated as our Basic Simple Syrup (see opposite), be sure to adjust the proportions accordingly. The syrup can be refrigerated in a clean, sealed jar for up to 1 month.

2. To make the passion fruit sorbet, combine the passion fruit puree and 1 cup of the simple syrup in a quart-size container. Cover and refrigerate the sorbet base until fully cold, about 3 hours.

3. Pour the chilled sorbet base into an ice cream maker and freeze according to the manufacturer's instructions. Place the container in which you refrigerated the sorbet base in the freezer so you can use it to store the finished sorbet. Churn the sorbet until it resembles Italian ice. Transfer the sorbet to the chilled storage container and freeze until hardened to your desired consistency. The sorbet will keep, frozen, for up to 7 days.

LIME, GINGER, AND LEMONGRASS SORBET

At Selamat Pagi, our Balinese restaurant, lime, ginger, and lemongrass are mainstay ingredients, appearing in many dishes. We were thinking about making a sorbet that reflected some of these ingredients and wondered what would happen if we threw all of them together. Our initial taste transported us back to the lush green hills of Bali, after which we were all too disappointed to find ourselves standing in our test kitchen. Along with lemon sorbet, this might be our go-to refreshment when we desperately need to cool off.

MAKES ABOUT 1 QUART

2 thick lemongrass stalks, cut into 2-inch pieces

2 cups (400 grams) sugar, plus more as needed

½ cup fresh ginger juice (from about 160 grams peeled fresh ginger; see Ben's Note)

½ cup fresh lime juice (from about 8 limes)

1. In a blender, combine the lemongrass with 3 cups water and puree until mostly smooth. (Lemongrass is very fibrous, so you will not get to a completely uniform consistency; that's okay.) Transfer the puree to a saucepan and bring to a simmer over medium heat. Remove from the heat, cover, and let the liquid infuse for 15 to 20 minutes. Strain the syrup into a bowl, pressing on the solids; discard the solids in the strainer. You should wind up with about 2 cups of strained "lemongrass tea"; be sure to measure out your final yield.

2. In a medium saucepan, combine the "lemongrass tea" with the same amount (by volume) of sugar. So, if you wind up with 2 cups tea, you will add 2 cups (400 grams) sugar. Stir the mixture over medium-high heat until all the sugar has dissolved and the syrup comes to a simmer. Remove from the heat and let cool completely.

3. Transfer the cooled syrup to a quart-size container and stir in the ginger juice and lime juice. Cover and refrigerate the sorbet base until completely cold, at least 3 hours.

4. Pour the chilled sorbet base into an ice cream maker and freeze according to the manufacturer's instructions. Place the container in which you refrigerated the sorbet base in the freezer so you can use it to store the finished sorbet. Churn the sorbet until it resembles Italian ice. Transfer the sorbet to the chilled storage container and freeze until hardened to your desired consistency. The sorbet will keep, frozen, for up to 7 days.

ben's note To get ½ cup fresh ginger juice (or any amount that's small enough to avoid using a juicer), finely grate your ginger, wrap the resulting pulp in a tripled layer of cheesecloth, and squeeze the juice out manually.

RASPBERRY SORBET

If you love the idea of sorbet but find lemon (page 168) too tart and cantaloupe (page 164) not tart enough, we think you might find raspberry sorbet to be the perfect balance of the two. Besides its beautiful deep red color, it will offer just enough pucker to liven your palate but not so much that you might want to scrunch up your face. And if you're anything like me, you'll find the combination of Chocolate Ice Cream (page 17) and this sorbet incredible. It tastes like a super-decadent Creamsicle.

MAKES ABOUT 1 QUART

4 cups packed and mashed raspberries (from about 6 pints)

2 cups Concentrated Simple Syrup (see page 169)

1. In a blender, puree the raspberries until smooth. Strain the puree into a bowl, pressing on solids; discard the solids in the strainer. Stir in the simple syrup. Transfer the sorbet base to a quart-size container, cover, and refrigerate until fully cold, at least 3 hours.

2. Pour the chilled sorbet base into an ice cream maker and freeze according to the manufacturer's instructions. Place the container in which you refrigerated the sorbet base in the freezer so you can use it to store the finished sorbet. Churn the sorbet until it resembles Italian ice. Transfer the sorbet to the chilled storage container and freeze until hardened to your desired consistency. The sorbet will keep, frozen, for up to 7 days.

MANGO SORBET

Mangoes lend themselves very well to sorbet thanks to their creamy texture, which results in a full, luscious sorbet that is smooth, not granular—unlike, say, lemon sorbet. In general, we prefer Alphonso, Champagne, or Ataulfo mangoes to the Tommy Atkins variety, both for sorbets and for eating directly; we find the latter to be too fibrous and tough.

MAKES ABOUT 1 QUART

3 ripe medium mangoes (about 10 ounces each), preferably Ataulfo, Champagne, or Alphonso

½ cup Basic Simple Syrup (see page 168)

1 tablespoon fresh lime juice, plus more to taste

½ teaspoon ground cayenne pepper (optional)

1. Slice the mangoes around the pits and dice the flesh. Transfer the mango flesh to a blender and puree until smooth; you should wind up with about 2 cups mango puree. Add the simple syrup, lime juice, and cayenne (if using) and puree until combined. Transfer the sorbet base to a quart-size container, cover, and refrigerate until fully cold, about 3 hours.

2. Pour the chilled sorbet base into an ice cream maker and freeze according to the manufacturer's instructions. Place the container in which you refrigerated the sorbet base in the freezer so you can use it to store the finished sorbet. Churn the sorbet until it resembles Italian ice. Transfer the sorbet to the chilled storage container and freeze until hardened to your desired consistency. The sorbet will keep, frozen, for up to 7 days.

FROZEN YOGURT

A few years ago, as the frozen yogurt craze swept the country, shops opened on virtually every block in New York City. It was a great idea, but executed poorly: The yogurt was packed with so many additives and stabilizers that any health benefits were instantly negated. We prefer our frozen yogurt pretty basic: yogurt, sugar, a touch of lemon zest, and hint of vanilla extract. The result is a creamy, slightly tangy frozen treat that gives the manufactured stuff a run for its money.

MAKES ABOUT 1 QUART

3 cups full-fat plain yogurt (see Ben's Note)

¾ cup (150 grams) sugar

½ teaspoon finely grated lemon zest

¼ teaspoon pure vanilla extract

Pinch of kosher salt

1. In a large bowl, stir together the yogurt, sugar, lemon zest, vanilla, and salt until combined. Cover and refrigerate the yogurt base until completely cool, at least 2 hours.
2. Pour the chilled yogurt base into an ice cream maker and freeze according to the manufacturer's instructions. Place a quart-size container in the freezer, so you can use it to store the finished frozen yogurt. Churn the yogurt until the texture resembles "soft serve." Transfer the frozen yogurt to the chilled storage container and freeze until hardened to your desired consistency. The frozen yogurt will keep, frozen, for up to 7 days.

ben's note You can use any kind of plain full-fat yogurt, including Greek, for this recipe. We prefer non-Greek yogurt here, as it's a bit more tangy, but it all depends on what you like best. Also, stick to full-fat (not low-fat) yogurt—it delivers more creamy results.

WATERMELON GRANITA

As much as we love the soothing whirr of our ice cream machines, sometimes it's nice to make a low-tech frozen dessert, especially if we're guests in someone's house—someone who most likely doesn't own an ice cream maker. Most people we know own a blender, and it takes just a minute to puree the fruit with sugar and lime juice, pour it into a dish, and place the whole mess in the freezer. A few scrapes with a fork, and a couple of hours later, your granita is ready!

Ben and I discovered watermelon granita at this wonderful old-timey place, Pellegrini's Espresso Bar, in Melbourne, an Italian lunch counter with an old *nonna* dishing up amazing plates of pasta. Pellegrini's was also home to Melbourne's first espresso machine way back in the 1950s and to this day continues its tradition of expertly made coffee—and, clearly, other things too!

MAKES ABOUT 3 CUPS

4 cups cubed seedless watermelon

½ cup (100 grams) sugar

1½ tablespoons fresh lime juice

1. In a blender, combine the watermelon, sugar, and lime juice and puree until smooth. Transfer the pureed watermelon to a 9-inch square dish and freeze for 1 hour.
2. Using a fork, scrape the contents of the pan, mashing any frozen parts so the mixture stays slushy. Cover; freeze until firm, about 2 hours. Using a fork, scrape the granita vigorously to form icy flakes. The granita will keep, frozen, for up to 2 days.

ESPRESSO GRANITA

Whenever we visit Italy—which is not often enough!—one of our favorite things to eat is this granita topped with unsweetened whipped cream. You can make your own stovetop espresso in an inexpensive (and compact) moka pot, no fancy machine needed. How about replacing your morning coffee with this in the dog days of summer?

MAKES 2 CUPS

2 cups freshly brewed
    espresso
½ cup (100 grams) sugar
1 cup chilled heavy cream

1. In a medium bowl, stir together the espresso and sugar until the sugar has dissolved. Pour the mixture into a 9-inch square baking pan and freeze for 1 hour. Place a bowl in the freezer to chill.
2. Using a fork, scrape the contents of the pan, mashing any frozen parts so the mixture stays slushy. Cover; freeze until firm, about 2 hours. Using a fork, scrape the granita vigorously to form icy flakes.
3. Right before serving, whip the heavy cream in the chilled bowl until it holds stiff peaks. Divide the granita among demitasse cups and top with a dollop of the whipped cream. Keep in mind that espresso is more concentrated than coffee, so consume an appropriate portion for you (see Ben's Note). The granita will keep, frozen, for up to 7 days.

ben's note This makes less granita than our usual yields, because espresso granita is quite strong and we encourage you to exercise moderation—lest you get a strong caffeine jolt!

MINT ICE MILK

We made this icy frozen dessert for Taste Talks, a food symposium focused on artisans and innovators in the food community, a little while back, and loved how fresh and cooling it turned out to be—lighter than ice cream but fuller than sorbet. When this ice milk freezes, it'll be harder than ice cream, so you will need to give it a few minutes at room temperature before scooping.

MAKES ABOUT 1 QUART

2½ cups whole milk

¾ cup (150 grams) sugar

¼ teaspoon (1 gram) kosher salt

1½ cups (30 grams) fresh mint leaves

1. In a medium saucepan, combine the milk, sugar, and salt and heat over medium heat, stirring, until the sugar has dissolved. Remove from the heat, cover, and refrigerate until fully cold, at least 2 hours.

2. Transfer the chilled milk mixture to a blender, add the mint, and blend until smooth. Pour the ice milk base into an ice cream maker and freeze according to the manufacturer's instructions. Place a quart-size container in the freezer so you can use it to store the finished ice milk. Churn the ice milk until it resembles Italian ice. Transfer the ice milk to the chilled storage container and freeze until hardened to your desired consistency. The ice milk will keep, frozen, for up to 7 days.

ICE CREAM SANDWICH, PAGE 188

four

TOPPINGS, SIDES, AND ADD-INS

While our ice cream is mostly known for its simple flavors, and we love nothing more than a simple scoop, every once in a while we want a sundae replete with chocolate fudge sauce (page 183), nuts, whipped cream (page 184), and maybe a few other things.

While working on this book, we got to explore lots of different possibilities—some flavors went on to become seasonal specials in our stores. We played around with adding some brittle (page 188), swirling in some compote (page 198), tucking in some shortbread (page 192), or folding in marshmallow swirl (page 195). We've even topped our ice cream with granola (page 193) in hopes of trying to fool ourselves that we were making ice cream a bit more nutritious (it might be better

sprinkled over our morning yogurt). But what we realized is that sometimes our purist approach needs to be shaken up a bit.

Whether it's ice cream au naturel or with some toppings, add-ins, or sides, we've provided you with a few options to mix things up, so to speak. And the best part is that many of the recipes in this chapter, like cookies (pages 187, 192) or brownies (page 191), for instance, make plenty to have left over as a snack—a win-win!

CASHEW MILK

Less fussy to make than almond milk, cashew milk requires no cheesecloth for straining. To make our vegan ice cream, you need to follow our milk formula below, which is weight-specific. These proportions will give you a 12 percent fat cashew milk, which, when combined with regular (not light) coconut milk, will deliver really lush ice cream, the kind that will make you wonder whether it really is vegan. It will be noticeably thicker than the cashew milk you would make for drinking or for cereal. If you want to make cashew milk for drinking, just keep adding water until you get the consistency you like.

MAKES ABOUT 1 QUART

400 grams (about 3 cups) raw, unsalted cashews

Place the cashews in a large bowl and add water to cover by a couple of inches. Soak the cashews overnight. In the morning, drain the cashews; they take on 50 percent water weight, so you should wind up with 600 grams soaked cashews. Weigh them just to be sure, and for 600 grams soaked cashews, measure out 750 grams (about 3½ cups) water. (For the record: For every 100 grams raw unsalted soaked cashews, use 125 grams water—or just multiply the cashew weight you wind up with by 1.25 to get the amount of water you need.) Transfer the soaked cashews to a blender and add the appropriate amount of water. Starting the blender on low speed and gradually increasing to high, blend the cashews until smooth. If you use a Vitamix, there will be no need to strain—the milk will be perfectly smooth; for other blenders, check the consistency and, if necessary, strain the cashew milk through a fine-mesh strainer. Cashew milk will keep well, covered and refrigerated, for up to 4 days.

HOT FUDGE SAUCE

This is the hot fudge sauce we drizzle over sundaes at our shops, and dare we say it has a bit of a cult following. We adapted this recipe from Ben and Pete's mom, and spent a long time getting it just right; we got downright obsessive about it. We wanted a sauce that had a deep, pronounced chocolate flavor, with a smooth, luxurious sheen. Many batches later, we finally got to our magic formula. The trick, as we learned, was to use unsweetened 99% cacao chocolate and some unsweetened cocoa powder for a deep chocolate taste.

MAKES 1½ CUPS

½ cup (100 grams) sugar

4 tablespoons (56 grams) unsalted butter

1½ ounces (43 grams) unsweetened chocolate (99% cacao), preferably Michel Cluizel (see Sources, page 218)

5 tablespoons (35 grams) unsweetened natural cocoa powder, preferably Michel Cluizel (see Sources, page 218)

¼ teaspoon (1 gram) kosher salt

½ cup heavy cream

1. In a small saucepan, combine the sugar and the butter and heat over low heat until the butter has melted. Add the chocolate and let it melt, stirring from time to time. Stir in the cocoa powder and salt until fully incorporated.

2. Remove the sauce from the heat and slowly whisk in the heavy cream until fully incorporated—the chocolate sauce will be smooth and shiny. Use immediately or cover and refrigerate until needed. The sauce will keep, refrigerated, for up to 8 weeks. To rewarm, microwave the sauce a few seconds at time, or place in a saucepan over very low heat.

BITTER VEGAN CHOCOLATE SYRUP

Don't be turned off by the word *bitter*—this might become your go-to chocolate syrup for drizzling on all your ice cream. It's immensely delicious and rich tasting despite containing only chocolate, sugar, and salt (and maybe a pinch of chile powder).

MAKES ABOUT 1 CUP

3 ounces (85 grams) unsweetened chocolate (99% cacao), preferably Michel Cluizel (see Sources, page 218)

7 tablespoons (88 grams) sugar

½ teaspoon (2 grams) kosher salt

Pinch of chile powder

In a small saucepan, combine the chocolate, sugar, salt, chile powder, and 1½ cups water. Stir over low heat until the chocolate has melted and the sugar has dissolved. Cook, stirring occasionally, until the syrup is uniform and smooth. Use immediately or cover and refrigerate until needed. The syrup will keep, covered and refrigerated, for up to 2 weeks.

WHIPPED CREAM

When you're making whipped cream, the key word to keep in mind is "cold." Everything should be cold for the best possible results: the heavy cream, the bowl, and the whisk. It takes only a few extra minutes of your time, but whipped cream, especially if unsweetened, is superlative, far more delicious than anything that comes out of a can. If you're adding sugar to your whipped cream, use a light hand; it can go from rich to cloying very fast.

MAKES ABOUT 2 CUPS

1 cup heavy cream

1 tablespoon (12 grams) sugar (optional)

¼ teaspoon pure vanilla extract (optional)

1. Using an electric mixer or by hand, whip the cream in a chilled stainless-steel bowl until it begins to thicken and hold its shape. Whisk in the sugar and vanilla (if using). Continue to whip until the cream holds soft peaks.
2. Serve immediately or refrigerate until needed—if the whipped cream separates as it sits, whisk lightly to revive.

SALTED CARAMEL SAUCE

People are always telling us they are afraid to make caramel, but in reality it's one of the simplest things to make, provided you take some care and read the recipe closely a few times before trying it yourself. Once you make caramel a few times, you'll get the hang of it—and will navigate your way not only visually but by nose as well (which is a great way to test for doneness). We also recommend that you seek out the best-quality butter you can find—cultured butter will have a more nuanced taste, which will make a marked difference in this sauce. However, we still want you to be careful while making it. Caramel gets hot, and if you're not watching yourself, it could splash and sputter. You could wind up with a pretty nasty burn, so always pay attention!

MAKES ABOUT 1½ CUPS

1 cup (200 grams) sugar

½ cup plus 2 tablespoons heavy cream, at room temperature

1 teaspoon (3 grams) flaky sea salt, such as Maldon

1. Place the sugar in a deep, heavy saucepan set over medium heat. Stir continuously and break up any lumps of sugar—this will help the sugar caramelize evenly. Bring to a simmer over medium heat, stirring with a spatula to dissolve the sugar, then simmer, without stirring, until the caramel turns the color of an Irish setter, about 4 minutes. If, while the caramel cooks, any sugar crystallizes on the sides of the pan, brush the sides down with a clean, wet pastry brush (see Ben's Note).

2. Reduce the heat to low, and slowly add ½ cup of the heavy cream (the caramel will rise and bubble and might spit, so be careful). Stir until the heavy cream is well incorporated. Remove from the heat and stir in the salt. Should the caramel seize and harden, return the mixture to the heat and stir until it softens. Remove from the heat and use immediately, or cover and refrigerate until needed. The sauce will keep, covered and refrigerated, for up to 2 weeks.

ben's note Caramel, while simple, can be a finicky creature. In our kitchens, we keep a pastry brush just for caramel-making. This means the only ingredients the brush comes in contact with are sugar and water. Some people prefer silicone brushes for this purpose (they wash off all traces of grease really well and you can use one brush for various needs, including basting), but we much prefer the traditional bristle pastry brush for better control.

VEGAN CARAMEL SAUCE

People often ask us how we make a caramel sauce without any butter or cream, and still have it taste like a million bucks. We don't have any fancy tricks up our sleeves: just sugar, coconut milk, and coconut oil, which gives our vegan caramel sauce a beautiful sheen and a full, luxurious body. Most often, we make it as-is, but sometimes we get all fancy and throw some sea salt in for good measure.

MAKES ABOUT 1 PINT

1½ cups (300 grams) granulated sugar

1 cup coconut milk or cream

2 tablespoons (30 grams) extra-virgin coconut oil

1 teaspoon (3 grams) flaky sea salt, such as Maldon (optional)

1. Spread the sugar in an even layer over the bottom of a clean, dry, heavy-duty pan or a deep skillet; oil and grease are caramel's mortal enemies so make sure the skillet is clean! Heat the sugar over medium heat, keeping an eye on it. Sometimes it'll start burning in a spot beneath the surface, where you can't see it; this happens especially if the layer of sugar is pretty deep. You should see it start to liquefy at the edges first, with perhaps some random blobs in the middle. Once you spot browning at the edges, shift the sugar toward the center to prevent any burnt spots. If caramel looks grainy, don't worry; reduce the heat and keep stirring gently and infrequently; stirring can often cause your sugar to lump and cluster instead of evenly melting. (If this happens, don't worry; just continue to use gentle heat, stirring as little as possible, to let the caramel form and the sugar melt.) If any chunks remain, they will most likely dissolve on their own and any stubborn chunks refusing to melt can be strained after. Cook the caramel until it's a rich brown color—the color of an Irish setter.

2. Reduce the heat to low; in a slow stream add the coconut milk or cream, stirring. Be careful, as caramel can spit and sputter. Stir in the coconut oil until melted, and stir in the salt, if using, until dissolved. Use immediately or cover and refrigerate until needed. The sauce will keep, covered and refrigerated, for up to 2 weeks.

CHOCOLATE CHIP COOKIES

We figured that if you make our Chocolate Chip Cookie Dough Ice Cream (page 41), you'll probably have lots of leftover cookie dough, which you can use to make these cookies. We prefer to use chocolate disks over chips as they spread out throughout the cookie, creating a continuous thin layer of chocolate, so that with every bite you get a perfect balance of dough to chocolate. We finish off the cookies with a generous sprinkling of flaky sea salt, which makes these cookies instantly taste more sophisticated. But if you don't like salt with your dessert (clearly, we do!), you can most definitely omit it.

MAKES ABOUT 18 (5-INCH)
COOKIES

2 cups (250 grams)
    all-purpose flour

2 cups minus 2 tablespoons
    (240 grams) cake flour

1¼ teaspoons (9 grams)
    baking soda

1½ teaspoons (6 grams)
    baking powder

1½ teaspoons (6 grams)
    coarse salt

1¼ cups (2½ sticks/
    283 grams) unsalted
    butter

1¼ cups packed (284 grams)
    light brown sugar

1 cup plus 2 tablespoons
    (225 grams) granulated
    sugar

2 large eggs, at room
    temperature

2 teaspoons pure vanilla
    extract

12 ounces (340 grams)
    bittersweet chocolate
    discs or chips (at least
    60% cacao)

Flaky sea salt, such as
    Maldon

1. In a large bowl, whisk together both flours, the baking soda, baking powder, and coarse salt. Set aside.

2. In the bowl of a stand mixer fitted with the paddle attachment, cream together the butter and both sugars on medium-high speed until very light, about 5 minutes. Add the eggs, one at a time, stopping the mixer before each addition and making sure the first egg is incorporated before adding the next. Add the vanilla.

3. Reduce the mixer speed to low and add the dry ingredients in several additions, beating until just combined; do not overmix. Add the chocolate disks and incorporate. Cover the bowl with plastic wrap and refrigerate for at least 24 hours and up to 36 hours before baking.

4. When ready to bake, preheat the oven to 350°F; position a rack in the middle. Line a baking sheet with parchment paper.

5. Using a large cookie scoop, spoon balls of cookie dough 2 inches apart on the prepared baking sheet (they should be the size of golf balls). Lightly sprinkle the dough balls with flaky sea salt and transfer to the oven. Bake for 18 to 20 minutes, until golden brown (you may need to work in batches). Let cool on the baking sheet on a wire rack for 10 minutes, then transfer the cookies to the rack to cool completely.

ICE CREAM SANDWICH

When you're lucky to be in the possession of both excellent vanilla ice cream and decadent chocolate chip cookies, there's only one thing left to do: make ice cream sandwiches, of course. We've yet to meet a single soul who doesn't love a good ice cream sandwich, and we certainly think it makes any party better. Be sure to freeze your sandwiches before eating them—otherwise the ice cream oozes out at the edges when you bite into them.

MAKES 1 ICE CREAM SANDWICH

1 scoop Vanilla Ice Cream (page 37)

2 Chocolate Chip Cookies (page 187)

Place the ice cream between the flat sides of the cookies, press down to compress, and using a spoon or a knife, smooth out the edges. Place on a wax-paper-lined tray and freeze for 15 to 20 minutes or until completely firm.

ALMOND-COCOA NIB BRITTLE

While we developed this recipe specifically for ice cream (see page 29), we also think it makes for a perfect edible gift. Who wouldn't want to get a small cellophane bag with delicious crunchy brittle? Instead of traditional corn syrup, we go a less-processed route and use brown rice syrup instead.

MAKES ABOUT ¾ POUND

Very cold butter, for greasing

1 cup (200 grams) sugar

4 tablespoons (½ stick/ 56 grams) unsalted butter

3 tablespoons (60 grams) brown rice syrup

¼ teaspoon (2 grams) baking soda

¾ teaspoon (3 grams) kosher salt

¾ cup (75 grams) sliced almonds

6 tablespoons (30 grams) cocoa nibs

1 teaspoon freshly ground Sichuan peppercorns

1. Lightly butter the bottom of a 9 × 13-inch rimmed baking sheet. Line the baking sheet with parchment paper trimmed to fit and very lightly butter the paper as well.

2. In a medium, heavy-bottomed saucepan, combine the sugar, 4 tablespoons butter, and the brown rice syrup with ¼ cup water; stir everything together so all the sugar is wet. Cook the mixture over high heat until it turns dark amber, 8 to 10 minutes. Remove from the heat and add the baking soda, followed by the salt. The caramel will rise and bubble.

3. Using a wooden spoon, fold in the almonds, cocoa nibs, and pepper. Pour the mixture over the prepared baking sheet and use the back of the spoon to spread it to about ¼ inch thick. Let cool completely. The brittle will keep in an airtight container for several weeks.

COCOA BROWNIES

We've made lots of brownie recipes in our time, but this one, inspired by Alice Medrich, the queen of all things chocolate, might be our favorite. These brownies err on the more fudgy—rather than cakey—side, and are deeply, intensely chocolatey, perfect for snacking or mixing into Butterscotch and Brownies Ice Cream (page 123).

MAKES 64 (1-INCH) BROWNIES

10 tablespoons (1¼ sticks/ 141 grams) unsalted butter

1 cup (200 grams) granulated sugar

1 cup (110 grams) unsweetened cocoa powder

½ teaspoon (2 grams) kosher salt

½ teaspoon pure vanilla extract

2 large eggs, cold

½ cup plus 2 tablespoons (79 grams) all-purpose flour

1. Preheat the oven to 325°F; position a rack in the lower third of the oven. Line the bottom and sides of an 8-inch square baking pan with parchment paper, leaving a generous overhang on two opposite sides.

2. In a medium heatproof bowl, combine the butter, sugar, cocoa, and salt, and set the bowl over a saucepan of gently simmering water (the bottom of the bowl should not touch the water). Stir from time to time until the butter has melted and the mixture is smooth. Dip your finger in the mixture; it should be hot enough that you will want to remove it rather quickly. Transfer the bowl to the counter and set it on a kitchen towel to prevent shifting; let the mixture cool to warm.

3. Using a sturdy spatula or a large wooden spoon, stir in the vanilla and the eggs, one at a time. When the batter is thick, shiny, and emulsified, add the flour and stir until incorporated; then beat vigorously for 35 to 40 strokes (we suggest keeping count!). Spread the batter evenly in the prepared pan.

4. Bake for 30 to 35 minutes, until a toothpick inserted into the center emerges slightly moist with batter. Let the brownies cool completely in the pan on a wire rack.

5. Using the parchment overhang, lift the brownies out of the pan and place them on a cutting board. Cut into squares of your desired size—we like the 1-inch bite-size squares.

PISTACHIO SHORTBREAD

Shortbread is one of our favorite cookies to make—it's easy, it gets better with time, and you can store it for up to a month, not that it's ever lasted that long around us. We've found shortbread perfect for feeding large crowds, transporting to picnics, and including in care packages (it travels remarkably well). You can make shortbread plain or with a number of flavorings. We share one of our favorites here with you, which we don't just greedily snack on—we also cut it into tiny bits and tuck it into our Orange Blossom Water Ice Cream with Pistachio Shortbread (page 117).

MAKES 81 (1-INCH) SQUARES

½ cup (64 grams) pistachios

2 cups (250 grams) all-purpose flour

⅔ cup (133 grams) granulated sugar

½ teaspoon (2 grams) kosher salt

1 cup (2 sticks/226 grams) unsalted butter, cut into ½-inch cubes

1 large egg yolk

1 teaspoon orange blossom water

1. Preheat the oven to 300°F; position a rack in the middle. Spread the pistachios on a rimmed baking sheet and toast in the oven for 7 to 10 minutes, or until fragrant. Transfer the nuts to a plate and let cool completely; roughly chop and set aside.

2. Raise the oven temperature to 325°F. Line a 9-inch square baking pan with overlapping, perpendicular pieces of parchment paper trimmed to fit the pan with about a 2- to 3-inch overhang (so that you can easily pull the shortbread out when you are ready to cut it).

3. In a food processor, pulse together the flour, sugar, and salt until combined. Add the butter, egg yolk, toasted pistachios, and orange blossom water and pulse until a scraggly, loose dough comes together. Dump out the dough, loose bits and all, onto the counter and knead until combined. Press the dough into the baking pan and score it all over with a fork.

4. Bake for 40 to 45 minutes, or until the shortbread is golden and firm. Transfer the pan to a wire rack and let cool completely. Using the overhanging parchment paper, lift the shortbread out of the pan and cut into pieces (we like 1-inch squares) on a cutting board. Transfer the shortbread to a cookie tin. The shortbread will keep in a sealed container at room temperature for about 1 month.

PUMPKIN SEED-COCONUT GRANOLA

A granola recipe in an ice cream book might seem random, but we actually love to snack on granola while we're playing around with new ice cream flavors. Sometimes, we'll even sprinkle it over ice cream and call it a nutritious snack. This recipe came from our coauthor, Olga, who came in one day bearing little cellophane bags of her signature granola. We loved its crunch and texture as well as its restrained sweetness, and were totally sold when we realized that the granola was completely vegan.

Olga's trick is to bake the granola at a low temperature, which ensures even crisping throughout and is less likely to result in burnt bits and pieces. Olga favors maple syrup over sugar, and extra-virgin coconut oil over vegetable and on-trend olive oils. Moreover, she uses far less sugar and oil than any other recipe we've seen, and the best part is you can't even tell—the granola still tastes amazing.

MAKES ABOUT 7 CUPS

3 cups old-fashioned rolled oats

1½ cups raw pecans, coarsely chopped

1 cup unsweetened flaked coconut

1 cup raw pumpkin seeds, sometimes called pepitas

⅓ cup extra-virgin coconut oil

⅓ cup pure maple syrup

1 tablespoon raw white sesame seeds

1 teaspoon (4 grams) kosher salt

¼ teaspoon freshly grated nutmeg

¼ teaspoon ground cinnamon

1 cup dried tart cherries

1. Preheat the oven to 300°F; position a rack in the middle.
2. In a large bowl, stir together all of the ingredients except the cherries and spread the mixture evenly on an 18 x 13-inch rimmed baking sheet. Bake for 40 to 45 minutes, stirring every 10 minutes, or until golden brown and toasted. Let completely cool on the baking sheet on a wire rack.
3. Place the cooled granola in a large bowl and stir in the dried cherries. Transfer to a jar and seal. The granola will keep, well sealed, at room temperature for about 3 weeks.

HONEY GRAHAM CRACKERS

Once you make S'Mores (page 197) with these, you'll have a hard time going back to graham crackers from a box. The dough can be a little fussy and sticky, but if you roll it between sheets of plastic wrap or parchment, it is far more cooperative than if you were to do it right on a countertop. We love making it just for snacking, and of course for using in our homemade s'mores.

MAKES ABOUT 36 CRACKERS

2 cups (250 grams) all-purpose flour, plus more for rolling

½ cup (63 grams) whole wheat flour

½ teaspoon baking soda

½ teaspoon ground cinnamon

Pinch of freshly grated nutmeg

¾ teaspoon (3 grams) kosher salt

1 cup (2 sticks/226 grams) unsalted butter, cut into small pieces, at room temperature

¼ cup (55 grams) packed dark brown sugar

¼ cup (50 grams) granulated sugar

¼ cup (85 grams) mild honey

1. In a medium bowl, sift together both flours, the baking soda, cinnamon, and nutmeg. Stir in the salt. Set aside.

2. In the bowl of a stand mixer fitted with the paddle attachment, combine the butter, both sugars, and the honey and beat on medium speed until combined, about 1 minute. Add the dry ingredients in two portions, letting the first be fully incorporated before adding the second.

3. Place a piece of plastic wrap over your counter and dump the dough out onto it. Cover the dough with another piece of plastic wrap and shape the dough into a rectangle. Remove the top piece of plastic and wrap the dough using the bottom piece; use the top piece to double-wrap the dough. Refrigerate until well chilled, about 30 minutes or up to 2 days. (The dough can also be frozen, tightly wrapped, for up to 1 month. Let it to come to a "workable" temperature" by placing in the refrigerator overnight before rolling.)

4. Preheat the oven to 350°F; position a rack in the middle. Line two baking sheets with parchment paper.

5. Unwrap the chilled dough and, on a lightly floured surface, or better yet, between two pieces of plastic wrap or parchment paper, roll it out into a rectangle about ⅛ inch thick. Using a ruler and a pastry cutter, a sharp knife, or a fluted pastry wheel, cut the dough into 1½ × 3-inch rectangles. Use an offset spatula to gently transfer the cut crackers to the baking sheets as you go. Gather the scraps of dough, chill, and re-roll to make more crackers. Using a fork, pierce each rectangle with 2 rows of 4 to 6 marks. Refrigerate the crackers on the baking sheets for 15 to 20 minutes, until firm.

6. Bake the crackers for 15 to 20 minutes, until golden brown, rotating the baking sheets halfway for even baking. Transfer the sheets to a wire rack and let the crackers cool completely. The graham crackers will keep in an airtight container at room temperature for up to 1 week.

HOMEMADE MARSHMALLOWS

Homemade marshmallows are a total game changer—they taste nothing like the stuff that comes out of a plastic bag, and a single bite of one may alter your marshmallow-eating course forever. Despite the page-long instructions for this recipe, it's a pretty straightforward process. Just be sure to exercise a bit of caution while pouring scalding-hot syrup down the side of the mixer bowl. That requires just a bit of concentration but, after you do it once, you'll have the hang of it going forward.

MAKES ABOUT 8 CUPS
MARSHMALLOW CREAM OR
ABOUT 54 (2-INCH) SQUARE
MARSHMALLOWS

SPECIAL EQUIPMENT
Candy thermometer, stand mixer

¾ cup (150 grams) granulated sugar

½ cup (180 grams) Lyle's Golden Syrup (see Sources, page 218)

¼ teaspoon (1 gram) kosher salt

2 large egg whites, at room temperature

¼ teaspoon cream of tartar

1½ teaspoons pure vanilla extract

½ cup (80 grams) cornstarch, plus more as needed (optional, if spreading on a baking sheet)

½ cup (60 grams) confectioners' sugar, plus more as needed (optional, if spreading on a baking sheet)

1. In a medium, heavy-bottomed saucepan, stir together the sugar, golden syrup, salt, and ¼ cup water until combined. Clip a candy thermometer to the pan and bring the mixture to a boil over high heat, stirring occasionally, until it reaches 240°F on the candy thermometer.

2. Meanwhile, place the egg whites and cream of tartar in the bowl of a stand mixer fitted with the whisk attachment. Starting with the mixer on low and gradually increasing to medium-high speed, whip the egg whites until they hold soft peaks. (Be sure to have those whipped before the syrup is done.)

3. Once the syrup has reached 240°F, remove it from the heat. With the mixer on low speed, slowly add 2 tablespoons of the syrup to the egg whites to temper them. Raise the mixer speed to medium and carefully drizzle in the remaining syrup, making sure that the syrup flows along and down the inside of the bowl (this will help cool the syrup before it reaches the egg whites). Raise the mixer speed to high and whip until the marshmallow cream is stiff and glossy, 4 to 5 minutes. Add the vanilla and whip for a minute more.

4. If making individual marshmallows, combine the cornstarch with confectioners' sugar in a bowl, then sprinkle a generous layer of the mixture over a rimmed baking sheet. Using an offset spatula, spread the marshmallow cream evenly over the baking sheet, smoothing the sides, edges, and top. Sprinkle the remaining cornstarch-sugar mixture over the top and let the marshmallow dry overnight at room temperature before cutting into 2-inch squares. You may need more cornstarch-sugar mixture to coat the individual pieces once they've been cut. Use immediately in S'Mores (page 197) or cover and refrigerate for up to 2 weeks.

ben's note For cutting marshmallows into individual pieces, kitchen shears dipped in a cornstarch–confectioners' sugar mixture work best.

S'MORES

Making and eating s'mores reminds us of beach cooking on the Oregon coast where Ben and Pete have been vacationing with family forever. I was lucky to get to know this special spot and fell for s'mores, a decidedly American treat, hook, line, and sinker the first time I tried them. In fact, we love s'mores so much that we insist on eating them year-round. When it gets too cold to make them outside, we simply fake our s'mores under the broiler. It beats having to wait until it's warm again, and the broiler, surprisingly, does the trick!

MAKES 1 S'MORE

1 2-inch square Homemade Marshmallow (page 195)

2 Honey Graham Crackers (page 194)

1 2-inch square milk chocolate, preferably Michel Cluizel (see Sources, page 218)

OPEN FLAME INSTRUCTIONS

Place a marshmallow on a skewer and hold it over an open flame until toasted. Place the toasted marshmallow on a graham cracker, top with the chocolate, and place the second graham cracker on top. Press lightly to flatten.

OVEN INSTRUCTIONS

Place the marshmallow on a graham cracker and cook under the broiler for 30 seconds to 1 minute, or until toasty. Place the chocolate square on top of the marshmallow and return the cracker to the broiler for 15 seconds more. Top with the remaining graham cracker and press lightly to flatten.

BLACKBERRY-RED CURRANT COMPOTE

For this recipe, our production manager, Jane Nguyen, uses equal parts frozen fruit and sugar by volume. For large-scale production we prefer to use frozen fruit because it allows us to make this compote year-round; guarantees us that we have fruit picked at the height of season; and ensures greater consistency than if we made various batches using fruit from different farms and seasons.

If you decide to use fresh berries, you may need to cook the compote for less time, since the berries, sans ice, will most likely have less moisture. If it looks like there's too much sugar in the recipe, bear in mind that sugar does double duty here, sweetening the compote and acting as a thickener. You can swirl this compote into ice cream (see Goat Cheese Ice Cream with Blackberry-Red Currant Compote, page 88) or use it as a sundae topping, or even spread it on your morning toast. We like to make a robust batch and keep it in our fridge for months; it makes ice cream making much simpler when you have one component out of the way.

MAKES ABOUT 4 CUPS

SPECIAL EQUIPMENT

Immersion blender or
    standing blender

3 cups frozen blackberries

2½ cups frozen red currants

4 cups (800 grams)
    granulated sugar

Pinch of kosher salt

In a medium saucepan, combine 1½ cups of the blackberries and 1¼ cups of the red currants with the sugar and the salt. Cook over medium to medium-low heat, stirring from time to time, for about 20 minutes. Remove from the heat, and using an immersion blender or in a standing blender, puree the compote until smooth. Strain the compote back into the saucepan, pressing on the solids—discard the seeds and skins left in the strainer. Return the saucepan to the stove and set over medium heat. Add the remaining 1½ cups blackberries and 1¼ cups currants and cook, stirring from time to time, until thickened, 10 to 15 minutes. Remove from the heat and refrigerate, uncovered, to prevent condensation. The compote will thicken overnight in the refrigerator. Once chilled, cover, and keep for up to 2 weeks.

CANDIED CITRUS PEELS

Candied citrus peels wears many hats: from moonlighting as sorbet topping (page 167), to playing a supporting role in Cassata Siciliana Ice Cream (page 97), to holding the spotlight as one of our favorite edible gifts. Because making candied citrus peels seems to have a few fussy steps (blanching three times isn't our idea of fun but is necessary to remove the bitterness from the pith), why not make a sizable batch and give some as gifts to friends and family? We've never seen anyone unhappy to receive them, and it's a great way to use every part of your citrus.

MAKES ABOUT 5 TO 6 CUPS OF CANDIED CITRUS PEEL

4 large oranges or medium grapefruit, or 6 large lemons, preferably unsprayed

4 cups (800 grams) sugar, plus more as needed

1. Slice the ends off the citrus and score the peels from one end to the other; remove the peels. Slice the peels into thick strips, trimming the edges.
2. Bring water to a boil in 2 medium saucepans. Place the peels in one saucepan; blanch the peels for 2 to 3 minutes. Drain the peels, rinse, and transfer to the second saucepan. Repeat the blanching, draining, and rinsing process. Fill the first saucepan with fresh water and bring to a boil. Repeat the blanching, draining, and rinsing process. Set aside.
3. In a large saucepan, combine 3 cups of the sugar with 3 cups water and bring to a simmer over medium heat, stirring until the sugar has dissolved completely. Add the blanched peels to the saucepan, reduce the heat to low, cover, and simmer for 1 hour, until the peels are soft and translucent.
4. Using a slotted spoon, transfer the peels to a wire rack set over a rimmed baking sheet and let them cool and drain. When the peels come to room temperature, transfer them to a large bowl and toss with the remaining 1 cup sugar until well coated. Spread the candied peels out on the wire rack and let dry at room temperature overnight or for up to 48 hours. The candied citrus peels will keep in an airtight container at room temperature for up to 8 weeks.

ROOT BEER FLOAT

While you can pair just about any ice cream with any soda, a root beer float is indisputably the king of all floats. This fizzy, creamy, sweet, and spicy concoction is a team favorite at Van Leeuwen—as well as a crowd pleaser with our patrons. A simple and impressive dessert for any summer dinner party.

MAKES 1 ROOT BEER FLOAT

1 scoop Vanilla Ice Cream
(page 35)
1 (12-ounce) bottle cold root
beer

Place the ice cream at the bottom of a chilled tall glass and gently pour the root beer over it. The combination of ice cream and root beer will create a lot of foam, so you'll probably have to add root beer as you drink your float.

AFFOGATO

I first discovered affogato when I was living in Rome in 2001. I was presented with a small scoop of vanilla gelato and was first shocked, and then quickly delighted, when the waiter poured a fresh shot of espresso on top. The direct translation of *affogato* is "drowned"; in this case, cold gelato or ice cream is drowned in hot, freshly brewed espresso—and the outcome is simply divine. We like to think of it as one of the most perfect desserts—and our customers agree. It's a best seller at our cafés.

MAKES 1 AFFOGATO

1 scoop Vanilla Ice Cream
(page 37) or gelato
1 shot freshly brewed
espresso

In a chilled glass, add a small scoop of vanilla ice cream. Pour a full shot of fresh, hot espresso over it—we like stovetop percolator espresso, but any method will do the trick—and eat immediately.

PAVLOVA, PAGE 204

five

SOME IDEAS
FOR EGG WHITES

When making ice cream at home, you'll be rewarded with egg whites. And if you make batches and batches of ice cream as we do, you will have lots and lots of leftover egg whites. There are many delicious things you can make with egg whites: from making soufflés to lightening waffle batters, to whipping up wonderful (and healthy) egg white omelets. Here we share with you some of our favorite desserts that will make good use of your leftover egg whites and leave you without any wasted resources—always a good thing. We've selected only a handful to get you started, but we hope you explore other possibilities.

PAVLOVA

Even when you think you don't have room for dessert, you always have room for pavlova. I grew up in Australia, where it's very popular. In fact, one of my favorite childhood memories is of my mum grating peppermint crisp (a mint chocolate bar) on top of a pavlova one birthday; it really served as the canvas for just about any topping.

Pavlova is a classic dessert created to honor the celebrated Russian ballerina, Anna Pavlova. It consists of airy meringue—slightly crispy and firm on the outside, soft and marshmallowy on the inside and is topped with fruit and whipped cream. While a pavlova takes just mere minutes to put together, you must be patient with it in the oven.

These days, I like to continue the pavlova tradition by baking them for our Van Leeuwen staff parties each summer—our team loves it! I stick to pretty traditional toppings: berries, kiwifruit, passion fruit, and of course, a generous heap of whipped cream. Most Americans are unfamiliar with fresh passion fruit and, while it's always a bit of a hunt to find them in New York, it's so worth the effort. Last time I needed passion fruit for a pavlova, I had my friend Skye, who lives in Topanga in California, mail me five pounds of passion fruit, which shows you the lengths I'm willing to go to for this remarkable dessert. I originally adapted the recipe from my year 9 home economics textbook, *Cookery the Australian Way*, and after many years of pavlova making, the recipe has evolved into something that has my own distinct imprint.

MAKES 1 (8-INCH) PAVLOVA

SPECIAL EQUIPMENT
Stand mixer

4 large egg whites

1 cup (200 grams) superfine sugar

1 tablespoon (10 grams) cornstarch

1 teaspoon pure vanilla extract

2 teaspoons distilled vinegar

1 cup heavy cream

1½ cups mixed berries (strawberries, blueberries, and raspberries)

1 mango, cubed

1 passion fruit, halved and flesh scooped out

1 kiwifruit, peeled and sliced

1. Preheat the oven to 250°F; position a rack in the middle. Line a baking sheet with parchment paper and draw an 8-inch circle on the paper. Flip the paper over—you should still see the circle through the paper.

2. In the bowl of a stand mixer fitted with the whisk attachment, starting on low speed and gradually increasing to medium-high, beat the egg whites until they hold soft peaks. Gradually add the sugar, raise the mixer speed to high, and beat until stiff peaks form. Mix in the cornstarch, vanilla, and vinegar.

3. Gently spread the meringue inside the circle drawn on the parchment paper, smoothing the edges and making sure the edges of the meringue are slightly higher than the center. Make a slight well in the center of the meringue for the whipped cream and fruit. Bake for about 1 hour and 15 minutes, until firm and dry on the outside but still white. If the meringue appears to be taking on color or beginning to crack too soon, reduce the oven temperature by 25°F, and rotate the pan. Once baked, turn the oven off, leave the door slightly ajar (use a wooden spoon to prop it open), and let the meringue cool completely in the oven. This is what you're looking for: The outside of the meringue should feel firm to the touch if gently pressed, but as it cools you should get a little cracking and you will see that the inside is soft and gooey like a marshmallow.

4. Right before serving, in a cold bowl, using a whisk or a mixer, beat the cream until stiff. Place the pavlova on a serving plate and spread half the whipped cream on top. Cover with the berries, mango, passion fruit, and kiwi. Top with the remaining whipped cream. Serve immediately.

SALZBURGER NOCKERL

If you haven't heard of *Salzburger nockerl*, don't worry. A little off the beaten path, it's one of Austria's dessert highlights, and one of the best ways to use up those leftover egg whites. *Salzburger nockerl*, named for its home city, Salzburg (which happens to be Mozart's birthplace), is traditionally served with three beautiful domes, one for each of the heights around Salzburg: Gaisberg, Mönchsberg, and Nonnberg. Traditionally served with some lingonberry or gooseberry jam, it will work with any tart berry of your choosing.

   To the best of our knowledge, the only place in New York where you can sample this magic is at Wallsé, one of Chef Kurt Gutenbrunner's Austrian restaurants. Our coauthor Olga waxed poetic about it for months, claiming to never miss an opportunity to order it when at the restaurant. We thought it would be a great idea. The soufflé is really easy to assemble, and not only looks stunning but also tastes like a dream.

SERVES 6

SPECIAL EQUIPMENT

Stand mixer

Butter, for the baking dish

2 large egg yolks

1 teaspoon pure vanilla extract

1 teaspoon finely grated lemon zest

1 tablespoon (8 grams) all-purpose flour

4 large egg whites

Pinch of kosher salt

2 tablespoons (25 grams) granulated sugar

Confectioners' sugar, for dusting

1. Preheat the oven to 350°F; position a rack in the middle. Generously butter an 8 × 10-inch oval baking dish attractive enough to serve from.

2. In a medium bowl, break up the egg yolks with a fork and stir in the vanilla and lemon zest. Sprinkle the flour all over the yolk mixture.

3. In the bowl of a stand mixer fitted with the whisk attachment, beat the egg whites with a pinch of salt until they cling to the beater. Add the granulated sugar and beat until the whites form stiff peaks. With a rubber spatula, stir a generous tablespoon of the whites into the yolk-flour mixture, then reverse the process and fold the yolk mixture into the egg whites.

4. Using your rubber spatula, make 3 mounds of the whipped egg white mixture in the prepared baking dish. Bake the *nockerl* for 10 to 12 minutes, or until it starts to lightly brown on the outside while remaining soft inside. Sprinkle with confectioners' sugar and serve immediately.

COCONUT PALM SUGAR MACAROONS

Macaroons are one of Ben's favorite cookies—I remember trying some of his mom's chocolate-dipped macaroons, lovingly sent in a care package, when I met him in London. Macaroons are easy to make and are incredibly addictive. Not to be confused with a French *macaron*, a macaroon is a loosely-held-together, chewy coconut cookie. These come together in a flash and are a definite crowd-pleaser. We make ours with palm sugar to give the macaroons a more Southeast Asian feel.

MAKES ABOUT
16 MACAROONS

4 large egg whites, at room
    temperature

3½ cups (263 grams)
    unsweetened dried
    coconut flakes

¾ cup (90 grams) unrefined
    palm sugar

1 teaspoon pure vanilla
    extract

½ teaspoon (2 grams)
    kosher salt

1. Place the egg whites, coconut, sugar, vanilla, and salt in a large heatproof bowl (a stainless-steel bowl, for instance) and set the bowl over a saucepan of gently simmering water (the bottom of the bowl should not touch the water). Stir the mixture with a wooden spoon, scraping the bottom to prevent burning, until the mixture is very hot to the touch and the egg whites stiffen, 5 to 7 minutes. Remove from the heat and set the mixture aside for about 30 minutes.

2. Preheat the oven to 350°F; position the racks in the upper and lower thirds of the oven. Line two baking sheets with parchment paper.

3. Using 2 tablespoons, place the coconut mixture in neat heaps on the cookie sheets, 2 inches apart from one another. Bake for 5 minutes, then rotate the baking sheets. Reduce the oven temperature to 325°F and bake for 10 to 15 minutes, until the macaroons start to get light brown. Transfer the baking sheets to a wire rack and let the cookies cool completely before peeling them away from the parchment paper. Macaroons are best on the day they are made, but will keep in a sealed container at room temperature for about 4 days.

HAZELNUT-BLUEBERRY FINANCIERS

For such a fancy-sounding cookie, financiers are so incredibly easy to make that they might become your go-to recipe for using up leftover egg whites. Here, we use hazelnut flour, but you can use almond, pistachio—whatever you prefer. Likewise, you can omit the blueberries or swap in a berry of your choice—almond-cherry has a nice ring to it, don't you think?

½ cup (1 stick/113 grams) unsalted butter, plus more for the pan

½ cup (100 grams) granulated sugar

½ cup packed (110 grams) light brown sugar

½ teaspoon (2 grams) kosher salt

4 large egg whites, at room temperature

½ cup (63 grams) all-purpose flour, plus more for the pan

½ cup plus 2 tablespoons (70 grams) finely ground hazelnuts

1 teaspoon baking powder

½ pint fresh or frozen blueberries

1. Prepare an ice bath in a large bowl; set aside.

2. In a small saucepan, melt the butter over low heat, letting it cook until the solids turn brown and the butter smells nutty, about 5 minutes. Strain the butter into a heatproof bowl and set the bowl over the prepared ice bath to cool. Stir for about 5 minutes, or until the butter is cool.

3. In a large bowl, combine the sugars, salt, and egg whites and whisk until smooth. Add the flour, ground hazelnuts, and baking powder and stir until combined. Add the browned butter and stir until smooth. Cover and refrigerate for 1 hour.

4. Preheat the oven to 350°F. Butter and flour 2 mini-muffin tins.

5. Pour about 2 teaspoons of the batter into each well of the prepared muffin tins; place a blueberry in the center of each financier. Set the muffin tins over a baking sheet and bake for 14 to 16 minutes, until golden brown. Let cool completely in the tins on wire racks before unmolding.

CITRUS-SCENTED ANGEL FOOD CAKE

When you're faced with lots and lots of egg whites (think a dozen), there's no better way to put them to good use than in an angel food cake, which is pretty much just some egg whites whipped with some sugar and a bit of flour folded in. The batter stays billowy, like a cloud, and the cake is lighter than air, with a delicate, moist crumb and a faint hint of citrus. We think ripe berries or juicy stone fruits are perfect complements to this citrus-scented cake.

MAKES 1 (9-INCH) CAKE

SPECIAL EQUIPMENT
9-inch tube pan, stand mixer

1 cup (130 grams) cake flour (not self-rising)

1½ cups (300 grams) sugar

¼ teaspoon (1 gram) kosher salt

1½ cups egg whites (from about 12 large eggs), at room temperature

1½ teaspoons cream of tartar

1 teaspoon finely grated lemon zest

2 teaspoons fresh lemon juice

½ teaspoon finely grated orange zest

½ teaspoon pure vanilla extract

¼ teaspoon almond extract

Fresh berries or sliced stone fruit, for serving

1. Preheat the oven to 350°F; position a rack in the middle. Have ready a 9-inch tube pan (not nonstick) with a removable bottom.
2. In a medium bowl, sift together the flour, ½ cup (100 grams) of the sugar, and the salt. Set aside.
3. In the bowl of a stand mixer fitted with the whisk attachment, whip the egg whites on medium-low speed. When they become foamy, raise the mixer speed to medium and add the cream of tartar, lemon zest, lemon juice, and orange zest.
4. Raise the mixer speed to high and continue to whip the egg whites until they just begin to form soft, droopy peaks and barely hold their shape. Add the remaining 1 cup (200 grams) sugar, ¼ cup at a time, streaming each ¼ cup into the bowl. Take care to not overwhip the mixture; you don't want dry, stiff egg whites, but fluffy ones. When almost done, mix in the vanilla and almond extracts.
5. Using a rubber spatula, gently fold the flour-sugar mixture into the whites, one-quarter of the mixture at a time.
6. Gently spoon the batter into the tube pan, smooth the top, and bake for 35 to 40 minutes, or until the top of the cake grows golden brown and springs back nicely when lightly pressed with your fingertip. Remove from the oven and immediately invert the tube pan over a wire rack to unmold. Cut the cake into pieces and top with berries or sliced fruit before serving.

ACKNOWLEDGMENTS

Thanks to everyone who has helped us along the way, we are eternally grateful that we have been able to grow this little idea into a career we love. Here's a brief list of family, friends, and team members who have helped make Van Leeuwen what it is today.

A bottomless thank-you to...

Susanne, Harvey, Robbie, Diana, and Sally O'Neill, for being OK with Laura living on the other side of the world! Your support and love is always felt.

Ellin, Louis, Jenny, John, Josh, Bruce, and Joy, the extended Van Leeuwen family, for your endless support, love, advice, fudge recipes, and shameless promotion of our ice cream!

Jane Nguyen. Thank you for putting your heart and soul into this little ice cream factory. We marvel at your drive and passion. Thank you also for assisting on the recipe development for this book.

Our ice cream production team, Robert Meldrum, Alvaro Flores, and Edison Gomez, who work tirelessly to keep our freezers full. You guys amaze us daily!

The Van Leeuwen managers, truckers, baristas, and scoopers, past and present. You're a motley crew and we love you guys!

Chef Vinh, Chef Jason, and the Selamat Pagi team, thanks for putting up with the ice cream stampede during brunch and for providing the best "shift-drink" bar in town.

Taylor Vaught, you gracefully wear so many hats. You are a delight, and we don't know what we'd do without you.

Kristin Vita, thanks for everything—everything! We miss you all the time!

Adrienne Winterhalter, for your friendship, number crunching, beautiful designs, and countless other things! (And for being the reigning champ of the three-cone-one-hand maneuver.)

Chelsea Wilkes, and the Van Leeuwen baking team of yesteryear, thanks for showing us what the best baked goods on earth taste like!

Sophia Loch, for all the many hats you wore and the delicious things you brought to us!

Matt McKenna, for tirelessly schlepping ice cream all over the city year-round and charming NYC's bodegas the way you've always charmed us!

Jon Okon, for your larger-than-life demeanor and southern phone charm. Thanks for keeping things running at HQ.

To Jim Derway, thank you for all your support and endless knowledge. We've learned so much from you.

The Suarez family, for your support in those early days. Thanks for giving the Eagle and Bobcat a home in Connecticut and for feeding us Bonnie's granola and other treats!

Mike Kagan, Ben Colombo, Sarah Colombo, Skye Byrne, Christian Brammar, Eddie Otoka, Tom Bouman, Amanda Hegarty, and Mike Cahil, for believing in this little idea right from the start. We couldn't have done it without you.

Our friends and lovers, for stepping in to taste ice cream, scoop ice cream, make ice cream, carry ice cream, draw ice cream, and mostly hear us talk about ice cream for the past eight years. You're the best.

Chris Rosi and the LA team, for pioneering our West Coast chapter.

Our beloved home of Greenpoint, Brooklyn. Thanks to the community for embracing us from day one. We love our neighborhood!

And, of course, thank you to the incredible team that got behind us and helped make this book . . .

Olga Massov, what an incredible delight and alignment of the stars it has been to work together. You've so beautifully brought our story to life and kept us on track through the roller-coaster ride of writing our first book. We are so very grateful to you and happy that little baby Freedman was grown on Van Leeuwen ice cream!

John McElwee, Anna Stein O'Sullivan, and Jenni Ferrari-Adler, for believing in this book and getting it into the right hands!

Dan Halpern, Gabriella Doob, Libby Edelson, Suet Chong, Sara Wood, Allison Saltzman, and the wonderful team at Ecco, we are so delighted to be a part of the family! Thank you for your meticulous attention to each and every word—and for having the vision to make such a beautiful book!

Sidney Bensimon, the world's greatest photographer, your talent, vision, and energy have made this process so memorable and special.

Thank you to Filippo Tarentini for all the magic light and amazing retouching.

To Chelsea Zimmerman, our wonderful food stylist, for creating such beautiful scoops and staying cool when the temps were soaring!

To Paola Andrea, for the gorgeous props styling.

To Jordan Colon, our dear friend, for allowing us to shoot at the beautiful EAT Greenpoint.

Special thanks to:
   Helen Levi
   Caitlin Mociun
   Virginia Sin
   Ren Yagolnitzer
   Greg Yagolnitzer
   Logan Polish

SOURCES

CEYLON CINNAMON
Penzeys (http://www.penzeys.com/)

HAZELNUT PASTE
Gourmet Sleuth (http://www.gourmetsleuth
.com/ingredients/detail/hazelnut-paste)

KAFFIR LIME LEAVES
Bangkok Center Grocery (http://www.bang
kokcentergrocery.com/)

LYLE'S GOLDEN SYRUP
Whole Foods and other fine stores; Amazon
(http://www.amazon.com/Lyles-Golden
-Syrup-16-0-Fluid/dp/B000WR22CA/ref=sr_1_
1?ie=UTF8&qid=1401039613&sr=8-1&keywords
=lyle%27s+golden+syrup)

MICHEL CLUIZEL CHOCOLATE
Whole Foods and other fine stores

PALM SUGAR
Big Tree Farms (http://bigtreefarms.com/)

PASSION FRUIT PUREE
http://www.perfectpuree.com/index.php
/Products/passion-fruit.html

PISTACHIO PASTE
Amazon (http://www.amazon.com/Fiddyment
-Farms-Gourmet-Pistachios-35008/dp
/B00D49G80K)

RED CURRANTS (FROZEN)
http://www.currantc.mybigcommerce.com
/farm-fresh-frozen-red-currants-5-99-lb
-packed-in-a-5lb-vacuum-sealed-bag-coming
-soon/

SICHUAN PEPPERCORNS
Penzeys (http://www.penzeys.com/)

TEA
Rishi (https://www.rishi-tea.com/)

INDEX

NOTE: Page references in *italics* refer to photos.

ABOUT THE AUTHORS

LAURA O'NEILL left behind her life in Melbourne, Australia, to move to Greenpoint, Brooklyn, in 2007, after meeting Ben on a trip to London. Among the many facets of running a small business, she handles the company's design and marketing. Laura shares her home with her musician and artist boyfriend, Greg, and a very talkative cat, Gypsy. Outside of focusing on ice cream and Indonesian food, Laura spends her time playing in a band and throwing a weekly dance jam in the dark called No Lights, No Lycra.

BEN VAN LEEUWEN, the mad genius of ice cream recipe testing and recipe development, is the point person for the day-to-day number crunching. He also oversees and guides the growth of the Van Leeuwen business. When not in the test kitchen or perfecting spreadsheets, Ben regularly practices yoga and meditation and spends as much time as he can surrounded by nature.

PETE VAN LEEUWEN wears many hats, from initiating the launch of new products to getting his hands dirty fixing ice cream trucks. Not only does he spread his skills across the many aspects of the ice cream business, but he spreads them from coast to coast, overseeing Van Leeuwen's California expansion. When he's not dreaming up future novelty items, he can be found playing in a puppet rock opera, exploring the planet, or cooking for his little family of two dogs and one girlfriend.

OLGA MASSOV is a cookbook editor and food writer. She has written cookbooks with chefs Marc Forgione and Marc Murphy as well as coauthored a book on kimchi. Her work has been featured in the *Wall Street Journal*, the Huffington Post, the Kitchn, Serious Eats, and the *New York Times*, among other publications and websites. She also keeps a food blog, sassyradish.com. Olga lives in Brooklyn with husband, baby, and their linebacker-sized cat.